# No Word for Welcome

# No Word for Welcome

## The Mexican Village Faces the Global Economy

Wendy Call

WENDY CALL

For my querida amiga Donna ~
Thank you so much for all you
have done, for this book, for our
writers' community, and for your
beautiful writing. Love to you!

University of Nebraska Press | Lincoln & London

Seattle · July 2011

Library of Congress Cataloging-in-Publication Data
Call, Wendy (Wendy Louise), 1968–
No word for welcome : the Mexican village faces the global economy / Wendy Call.
p. cm.
Includes bibliographical references and index.
ISBN 978-0-8032-3510-6 (cloth: alk. paper)
1. Economic development projects—Mexico—Tehuantepec, Isthmus of. 2. Indigenous peoples—Mexico—Tehuantepec, Isthmus of. 3. Protest movements—Mexico—Tehuantepec, Isthmus of. 4. Globalization—Mexico—Tehuantepec, Isthmus of. I. Title.
HC137.T44.C35 2011
972'.7084—dc22 2010046944

Set in Sabon by Bob Reitz.

For my parents,
Douglas William Call
and
Marilyn Kay Schust Call (1943–2007)

**Map 1.** Southern Mexico.

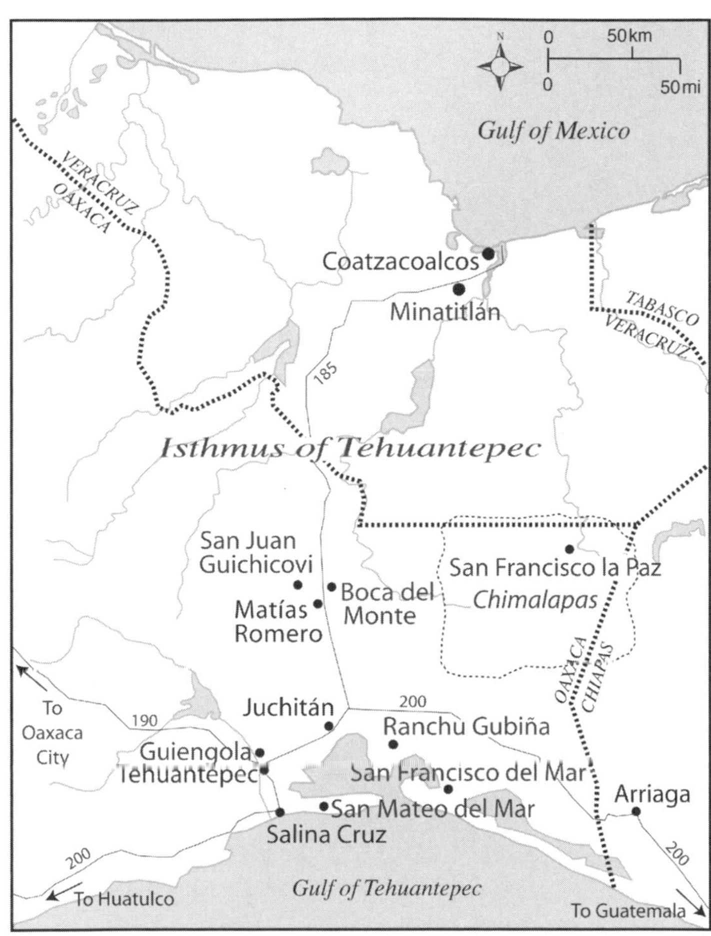


**Map 2.** The Isthmus of Tehuantepec.

MAP © 2008 BY ELLEN KOZAK, USED WITH PERMISSION.

# Contents

# Acknowledgments

One afternoon I sat on a park bench in a beach town not far from the Isthmus of Tehuantepec, reading a novel. The southern Mexican sun pummeled the back of my neck. A woman sat down next to me, close, resting two bags full of shoes on the ground. She told me her feet hurt and asked me if I wanted to buy a pair of sneakers. A few minutes into our conversation, Francisca Díaz asked me what I did for work. I told her that I lived on the Isthmus of Tehuantepec and wrote about the people, places, and events of the region.

"They pay you to do that?" she asked, in the calm way that Mexicans do, making even the rudest question completely acceptable.

"Well, in a sense, yes."

Francisca paused for a long moment. When she finally spoke, her tone was thoughtful and careful. "Well, I guess for people who can read, that would make sense."

Many thanks to the Institute for Current World Affairs, its board of trustees, and its former director, Peter Bird Martin, for funding the two years I lived full-time on the Isthmus of Tehuantepec (2000 to 2002). Many thanks, also, to the organizations that have supported my return visits, other research, and writing of this book: 4Culture, Artist Trust, Bread Loaf Writers' Conference, Oberlin College Alumni Association, Richard Hugo House, Seattle Mayor's Office of Arts & Cultural Affairs, Seattle University, and the Washington State Arts Commission. The Anderson Center for Interdisciplinary Studies, Blue Mountain Center, Centrum, Hedgebrook Retreat for Women Writers, New College of Florida, Helen Riaboff Whiteley Center, and my dear friend David Palmer in Oaxaca City all offered much-needed time and quiet space. The source notes include a long list of libraries, grassroots organizers, activists, scholars, elders, writers, and nonprofit organizations to whom I owe great debts.

I am ever grateful to the readers of large portions of this manuscript (including painfully early drafts): Sven Birkerts, Lucha Corpi, Alma García, Allison Green, Donna Miscolta, Phillip Lopate, George Scialabba, Bob Shacochis, Nirmala Singh-Brinkman, Chris Tilly, and Sasha Su-Ling Welland. I am thankful also for the wise words of Barbara Lazear Ascher, Garnette Cadogan, Ted Conover, Louise Dunlap, Adam Hochschild, Pam Kasey, Mark Kramer, Jina Moore, Dickey Nesenger, Christle Rawlins-Jackson, Maribel Sosa, and Lynne Weiss. My deep appreciation to Wendy J. Strothman, who believed in this book when it seemed no one would, and to Heather Lundine and the wonderful team at University of Nebraska Press, who brought it into the world. Muchas gracias to Bertha Rodríguez, Liliana Valenzuela, and María de Lourdes Victoria, for help with fine points of translation; to Ellen Kozak, for elegant maps; to Magda Lanuza and Victoria Campa Monreal, for transcription expertise; to the Macondo Workshop, for good company; and to Sandra Ruiz Harris, for courage. My everlasting gratitude to all of them, and most of all to Aram Falsafi, my first reader and best editor. He had the idea that has become this book and supported it even when the idea and its realization seemed to make very little sense at all. This book exists thanks to him, and thanks to the guidance and counsel of Lucía Antonio, Leonel Gómez Cruz, Maritza Ochoa Jarauta, and, most of all, Carlos Beas Torres. I swim in an ocean of gratitude to those four istmeños, to everyone else whose name appears in these pages, and to many others on the Isthmus of Tehuantepec who gave me—generously and without question—their time, wisdom, good food, comfortable hammocks, medicine from bottles and from plants, scarce fresh water, rides in canoes or motorboats or trucks, loans of cars and saddled horses, excellent advice, incisive political and philosophical analysis, and seemingly limitless patience.

# Introduction

## Drawing an Old Map

There is a word in Spanish that we don't have in English: *protagonismo*. It means unwarranted self-promotion, seeking the limelight, or, as the *Real Academia Española*—the Spanish version of the OED—puts it, "an eagerness to prove oneself to be the most qualified or important one for a given activity, independent of whether one deserves it." The word would translate literally as "adopting the role of the protagonist." In the Spanish-speaking communities described in this book, protagonismo verges on sin. At the very least it indicates poor character.

Most of the people whose names appear here were perplexed by my decision to focus on them, among the hundreds of isthmus residents whom I interviewed and followed around. Only one of them, Carlos Beas, understood my decision. During one of my first visits to the Isthmus of Tehuantepec, he explained to me how he'd come to recognize a fundamental difference, as he put it, between *estadounidenses* and *latinoamericanos*. He told me a story of attending a gathering of Native people from all over the Americas—northern Canada to southern Chile—held on a reservation in the Southwestern United States (or, as he liked to say, "in old Mexico"). One by one people told stories of communal insults suffered: land

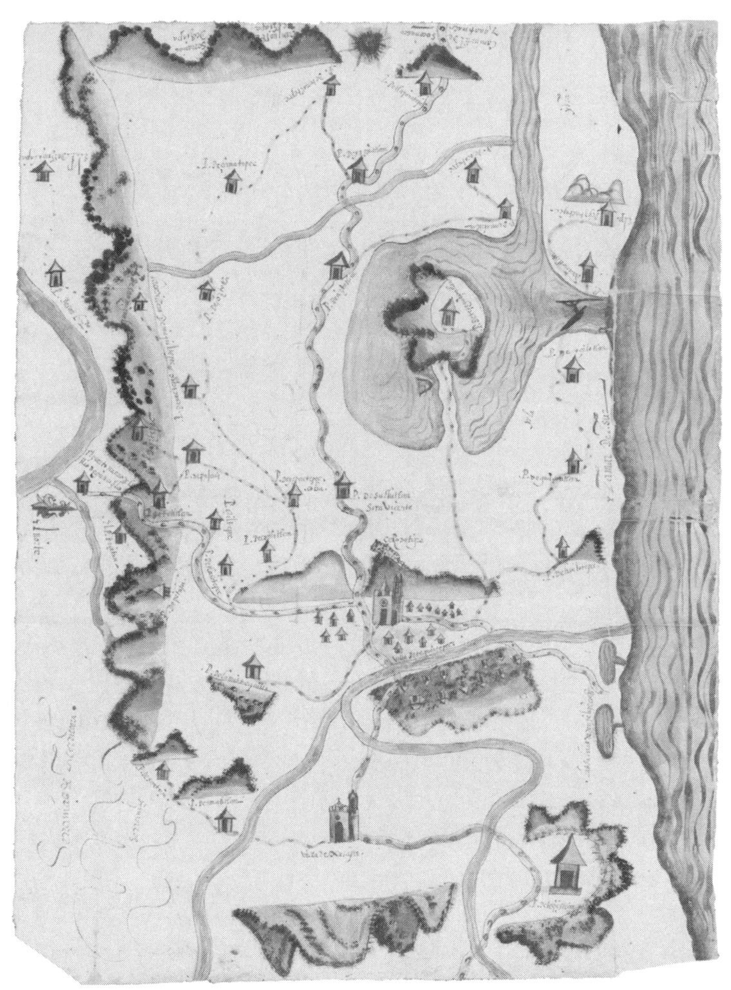

**1.** This map of the Isthmus of Tehuantepec from the 1580 *Relación Geográfica* was produced by an unknown indigenous cartographer.

COURTESY OF THE NETTIE LEE BENSON LATIN AMERICAN COLLECTION, UNIVERSITY OF TEXAS LIBRARIES, UNIVERSITY OF TEXAS AT AUSTIN.

stolen, villagers murdered by death squads, crops and forests poisoned by mining, babies dying of malnutrition, languages lost after decades of Spanish- or Portuguese- or English-only education. An elderly man from the United States stood and spoke about his personal struggle with cancer and the trauma of chemotherapy. Carlos Beas thought, *Who cares about this? It's just one man's story; it has no place here.* Then he noticed others from the United States drawing toward the old man, their faces grimacing with concern, their arms reaching out to touch him. That man's story of individual suffering affected them as the stories of collective suffering had not.

Recounting this experience to me years later, Carlos Beas said, with regret and a touch of wonder in his voice, "That's how I came to understand that your people are different. You focus on the individual tragedy, not the collective concern."

This book is my attempt to distill for my people some of what I learned about collective concerns on the Isthmus of Tehuantepec. The people whose stories appear here represent many people, countless stories. On these pages I have adhered to the facts as I understood them, but I am recounting only my interpretation of what I saw and heard. I am a translator of sorts, attempting to express for readers of English what I heard in Spanish or what was translated for me into Spanish from the Native isthmus languages of Huave, Mixe, Chinantec, Zapotec, or Zoque. I have tried to render what I learned of another place and several cultures that were unknown to me fifteen years ago.

This book is, of course, an interpretation by an outsider — a foreigner for whom Mexico has always been a close neighbor. When I was four years old my midwestern parents moved to a military base in California's Imperial Valley, 8 miles north of the U.S.–Mexico border. In a photograph from my second-grade school yearbook I lean against a playground slide, blue eyes squinting into desert heat, pixie haircut pale under the midday sun. It's 1976 and I'm wearing Seeley School's bicentennial t-shirt. Stars and stripes run down the sleeves; on the front an eagle stretches its wings to full span and clenches three arrows in its beak. The t-shirt was red, white, and blue, but my seven-year-old mind considered it a blending of U.S. and Mexican images. I wasn't yet clear on the history of our two nations, or just exactly what a "nation" was, but I did know that Mexico's flag featured a hunting eagle and ours did not. For me that shirt perfectly represented my school: nearly half of my classmates' parents spoke to them in Spanish. The town of El Centro, California, was the center of my childhood world, with deep-fried quesadillas at the Mount Signal Café a few yards north of the border, luminaria on Christmas Eve, carne asada and boiled kielbasa on the dinner table, and Stir 'n Frost cupcakes and deep-fried buñuelos at Seeley School birthday parties.

The border meant little to me. A trip in our '68 Chevy Malibu, easing over the rock-jumble, desert-bare mountains to San Diego, took me to a land more different than Mexicali just a short ride away. At seven I knew that "wetback" was the worst thing you could call a person, I could roll my Rs, and I liked to eat Mount Signal Café's hottest salsa. But I didn't learn much Spanish and I thought that all of urban Mexico looked like the Tijuana tourist strip. Still, northern Mexico was a real place for me, and the Upper Midwest, where my parents and grandparents had grown up, was not.

Two decades after that Seeley School yearbook photograph, I visited the Isthmus of Tehuantepec in southern Mexico for the first time. I knew nothing of the place, traveling there for a three-day conference to represent the nonprofit organization

I worked for in Boston. At that time I had devoted the better part of a decade to working for grassroots groups in Seattle and Boston, learning more Spanish than I'd ever learned living on the border. In May 2000, three years after my first visit to the Isthmus of Tehuantepec, I packed up my life in the United States and moved there for a two-year stay. That may sound rash, but it is only an indication of the power of the place. The isthmus had little in common with the places I knew and yet, little by little, I encountered familiar images woven into its landscapes.

Mexico's little waist, as the locals call it, connects the Yucatan Peninsula to the rest of the country over a narrow strip of subtropical land. Not far from there, six thousand years ago, early farmers domesticated corn, the staff of American life. Somewhere very close to the isthmus, writing was invented —the only time that happened in this hemisphere—three thousand years ago. Whispers of isthmus history float north. In the nineteenth century the U.S. government wished it part of the United States. Forget California; they wanted passage to Asia. In the late 1800s the *New York Times* had a regular front-section column called "Tehuantepec."

Though the name has long since faded from the front pages of our newspapers, even isthmus fashion looks familiar. Think of billowing skirts, ropes of gold necklaces, rings on many fingers, square-cropped tunics, and long braids woven with strips of fabric and twisted around the head. Frida Kahlo, of course. Yes, and she borrowed every detail of her famous fashion sense from the women of the Isthmus of Tehuantepec.

The isthmus is a small place, far less than 1 percent of Mexico's territory. Nonetheless, it looms large in the Mexican imagination. Frida Kahlo is the least of it. "The Isthmus of Tehuantepec," Mexicans will say, smiling and nodding, "where women control the economy, where gay men have been accepted since long before the conquest, and where locals have warded off imperialism for more than five centuries." Yes, that place.

I first recognized Frida's style on the cover of a book about the Mexican isthmus. I picked up *Mexico South: Isthmus of Tehuantepec* from a bookstore sale table, half a century after Miguel Covarrubias wrote it. The cover illustration had grabbed my attention: an isthmus woman with gold earrings and long necklaces heavy with medallions. Her square, sleeveless tunic and generous red skirt are threaded with black and golden flowers. A crisp pleated petticoat hangs below her skirt hem. *Frida,* I thought, as I studied the image, not yet knowing that Covarrubias had been the painter's contemporary.

I did not read *Mexico South* from beginning to end until after I moved to the isthmus. One evening, alone in the sherbet-cement row house that I rented for fifty dollars a month, I pulled Covarrubias's book from my shelf. The rattle of my neighbor's radio and the hyper-amplified sermon from the evangelical church across the street faded away as I entered Miguel Covarrubias's version of 1930s Isthmus of Tehuantepec. The decades between the author's experience and my own evaporated as I read. His words described the world around me: "jungles that seemed lifted from a Rousseau canvas," and women "dressed like tropical birds" going "to market in stately grace with enormous loads of fruit and flowers on their heads," where vendors sold grilled iguana and boiled sea-turtle eggs amid the buzz of "the heat and the ferocious insects."

Even as his descriptions pulled me in, I kept turning back to the first page of *Mexico South*: a fanciful map of North

America, all wavy-lined rivers and chevroned mountain ranges. On the map the U.S.-Mexico border is not marked, so the Sierra Nevada and Rocky Mountains flow uninterrupted into Mexico, not pausing until they reach the narrow lowland strip indicated by a fat, black arrow and labeled "Isthmus of Tehuantepec."

Visitors have always felt compelled to make maps of the isthmus—perhaps as part of their attempt (conscious or not) to control it. I have been compelled to gather their work: since my first visit to the Mexican isthmus in 1997 I have collected maps of the place. A large portfolio holds part of my collection. On a cocktail napkin an indigenous Zapotec politician drew a diagram of his ancestors' hometowns located on the isthmus, elsewhere in southern Mexico, and in Germany, showing the varied bloodlines that pulse in his *istmeño* veins. On a vegetation map an ecologist sketched the boundaries of the rainforest in the center of the isthmus, showing where it has been threatened by forest fires, by road building, and by cattle ranching. On a quotidian road map Carlos Beas marked, with ballpoint-blue squares, all the dozens of isthmus villages where his community organization has members. The neat squares scatter past the ends of dotted gravel roads onto the map's white blankness.

Most of the collection in my portfolio was gathered far from the isthmus, photocopied from library collections in Austin, Oaxaca City, Mexico City, Washington, and Seville. Those who make maps have always carried them far away.

The other half of my collection I carry in my memory. On a shimmering Pacific coast beach an indigenous Huave fisherman traces through the sand with a stick. In a shaky hand he draws the path of his people's maritime migration to the isthmus one thousand years earlier. In the shade of a thatched hut another fisherman swings his arms through the late evening's sapphire air, tracing the migration of the shrimp he will catch later that night. On a coastal map stretched across a wide mahogany desk a government official shows me potential sites for industrial shrimp farms. In front of a one-room adobe house an indigenous Mixe man holds up a full-color map of the isthmus and traces a line: where the government plans to slice a new highway through the village's farmland and forest.

In building my personal atlas of the Mexican isthmus, a map of one visitor's developing understanding, I have shuffled all the maps together, mentally stacking them one upon another. The Isthmus of Tehuantepec land bridge stretches east to west, with the Gulf of Mexico to the north, and the Pacific Ocean to the south. I visualize the layers of maps that have endeavored to represent this land: the deerhide and pounded bark from six hundred years ago, the sixteenth-century Spanish cotton rag, nineteenth-century onionskin, early twentieth-century blueprints, and late twentieth-century satellite photographs. I imagine all the sheets transparent, the lines of watercolor, India ink, cyan, clay, and indigo all visible at once. Poring over this composite map, the atlas of my imagination, I have learned that everything old is new again. A nineteenth-century railway across the isthmus traces the horse path that conquistador Hernán Cortés had dreamed of building almost four hundred years earlier. Both projects intended to connect the oceans. Plans for twenty-first-century highways connecting the isthmus to the rest of Mexico match pre-Columbian footpaths almost perfectly. Long-ago isthmus residents didn't need surveying equipment or satellites to tell them the best routes across their home terrain.

The continent stretches thin at the Isthmus of Tehuantepec, where only 120 miles of rich earth separate the Pacific from the Gulf. For this reason outsiders have dreamed and imagined and reimagined this thin link since the Spanish arrived in 1519. And for this reason, istmeños—the people of the isthmus—have told me over and over again: "Globalization is nothing new." For this reason I believe the istmeños when they insist that time is better represented by a spiral than a straight line.

When I finally opened Covarrubias's *Mexico South* and read it through, time folded over on itself. Reading his book I was simultaneously in the squawking, blaring isthmus of the early twenty-first century and in the singing, murmuring isthmus of the 1930s. Covarrubias renders those songs and whispers in my mother tongue, not in his own. Though he was Mexican, Miguel Covarrubias chose to write his book in English. Published in 1946 by New York's Knopf, *Mexico South* never appeared in Spanish. As I sat in my small istmeño house and read his words, that fact filled me with relief. Covarrubias calls the indigenous Huave—the residents of fishing villages where I have been hosted often, and elegantly—"the simplest, most timid and distrustful people." He reports that the Mixe—who welcomed me to their villages, in the green hills around the isthmus town where I lived—are "the most rabid isolationists." Covarrubias writes blithely, "The Mixe are primitive, shifting agriculturalists only a step forward from the digging-stick agricultural level," and "the daily life of the Huave is one of listless simplicity." Not really. The Mixe were (and are) sophisticated horticulturalists; the Huave are fishermen and healers by night, cattlemen and weavers and musicians by day. Covarrubias might not have visited the Mixes' villages at all, as he comments about them: "No one ever visits them except for rare Zapotec traders and stray missionaries."

As I sat in my humid living room and turned page after page, a kernel of self-righteous anger formed within me.

Eventually, though, an itch of uncomfortable recognition replaced it. I could not simply dismiss Covarrubias because I was, unknowingly, emulating him. My journey to the Isthmus of Tehuantepec repeated his almost exactly. He wrote of his experience: "I was driven to delve into ancient chronicles of the Isthmus, to read local histories, to argue with archaeologists, economists, politicians, labor leaders, peasants, land owners, market women, and traveling salesmen. I searched for reports and documents of the period when the isthmus was a paradise for American railroad promoters and oil magnates on the make; studied the Zapotec language; raced to newly discovered ruins or to the inauguration of roads, dams, schools; finally listened to the complaints and aspirations of schoolteachers, tribesmen, peasants, workers, and shopkeepers." Covarrubias's words described almost perfectly my time on the Isthmus of Tehuantepec. The differences were slight. He had studied Zapotec; I picked up scattered words and phrases in several local languages—Huave, Mixe, Zapotec, and Zoque. He had stayed nine months; I stayed three years in all.

In the end, it is not Covarrubias's words, nor even his famous illustrations, but his maps that have stayed with me. Most of all, it is the map on the first page of *Mexico South*, "Map of North America," with the city of San Francisco in the northwest corner, the nation of Colombia in the southeast corner, and Mexico City balanced in the center. Covarrubias has become one of many cartographers guiding me through the region, a group that includes a few istmeños but many more outsiders: ancient Aztecs, Spanish conquistadors, U.S. government officials, British engineers, foreign scholars, World Bank consultants. They map geography, hydrology, topography, and history, but even more, they map their own imaginations.

A Spanish map dating to the late eighteenth century renders

the Pacific Coast in great detail. It names only the inland towns that fall on the path between the coast and Oaxaca City. The isthmus existed only as blank landscape on the way to somewhere else. An equivalent map from the same era, of the isthmus's Gulf Coast, uses a scrolling letter "K" to mark a spot near the Coatzacoalcos River as "Land appropriate for establishing a small Fort, free from all domination, to defend the entrance to the river."

In 1870 a military cartographer drew a map for the U.S. Navy. Its style is reminiscent of an architectural blueprint, with fine lines mathematical in their precision. A path stretching across the isthmus like a double-line of Morse code represents an imagined canal connecting the oceans, fed by a feeder canal of rushing waters from the mountains at the isthmus's center. Along the map's left margin, an EKG-like graph indicates the altitude of the planned route from north to south. Few villages are labeled on this map: it is the physical geometry, not the human reality, of the place that is important. The map focuses on the lowlands, part of the search for the best place to dig a canal. It names landforms I never heard mentioned by locals—Plains of Xochiapa, Tarifa Plains—while many of the villages remain anonymous.

On another map, this one from the early 1900s, shortly before the Mexican Revolution, "National Real Estate Company" is written in English on a banner across the top. A railroad zigzags from the Pacific Ocean to the Gulf of Mexico; triangles and wedges and trapezoids apportion much of the isthmus land to various private landholders. Each shape carries a label: "S. Pearson and Son," "Being Colonized by Mexican American Land Company," "J. B. Henry and Sons Company," and several, simply "Hearst." Colonial geometry carved a gameboard from the tropical rainforest that fills the isthmus's central highlands.

Other isthmus maps in my collection show the best salt flats, the homes of ancient kings, where certain trees grew, the land Hernán Cortés thought he owned, and the intended paths of nineteenth-century roads for wagon and rail. These maps manifest the dreams of those who commissioned them and display how they strained to impose their visions on the contours of the landscape.

In 1998 I found a contemporary map of the imagination in a Mexico City newspaper, with an article describing the "Trans-Isthmus Megaproject." The map calls the isthmus by its nickname, "the little waist of Mexico," and dots the land with the iconography of a planned industrial future: smokestacks for petrochemical plants, wheeled carts for possible mining projects, triangular trees for paper-pulp plantations, tiny shirts for textile factories, a slim ribbon for a new trans-isthmus highway, and a curled prawn for industrial shrimp farms. These last two icons represent the focus of my own isthmus sojourn. I attended a three-day conference there in 1997, an event that called itself "The Isthmus Is Our Own." After that, I returned again and again, driven to know more about the place and why it has been desired for so long, by so many. For three years I traveled to the places marked by the prawns and the ribbon, as well as by the smokestacks and shirts and trees, all part of the industrial imagination that envisioned the "Trans-Isthmus Megaproject." Through those travels I slowly came to see the istmeños' own "map" of their land.

On a map painted in 1580 by an indigenous cartographer, words in calligraphic script tell the Spanish crown about its colonial lands: "La mar del Sur, El camino de Soconusco a Guatemala, y serramás, serramás" (the southern sea, the Soconusco trading route to Guatemala, and more mountains, more mountains). The Pacific Ocean undulates along the left margin of the map, and along the right the cartographer has painted a mountain range. In spite of all the words, the artist has used a pictogram to title the map: at the peak of a hill, towering over the spires of a Catholic church, a spotted jaguar crouches. The image means Tehuantepec, or "Hill of the Jaguar," the name given to the region by the Aztecs. Spanish nobles gazing at the map would not have recognized that symbol, placed squarely in the center. I smile at the inferred message from the local cartographer to the far-off Spanish government: "You might think you own this but you don't even know what it's called." On this map landforms flow from one to another, connected by watercolor rivers. Tiny footprints mark narrow paths; hoof prints mark wider wagon paths. There are no property lines, no borders, no fences: the only boundary is where land meets sea.

Andrés Henestrosa, one of Mexico's great twentieth-century writers and an indigenous Zapotec, came from a small isthmus town. He writes of his home place, "It's small, it fits in the palm of the hand, it doesn't weigh heavily on the shoulders, yet it overflows the heart."

Like Miguel Covarrubias, I have fashioned my map of the Isthmus of Tehuantepec in the form of a book. It is not an easy choice because text implies story, a narrative that stretches out on a straight, unbroken line from beginning to end. But like a map, this story is not linear; it is two-dimensional, extending in many directions at once. Just as every map is provisional, so is this story. It is a story of people pushing back against globalization even as they participate in it. It is a story of people refusing to accept spilled oil seeping into soil, pavement rolling where forest once stood, pollution draining into sparkling lagoons. The istmeños, who seine a livelihood from brackish waters, coax crops out of black earth, and dig roots from the forest floor, are staving off destruction with their words and their actions, by mere dint of their continued existence. They do this anonymously. Endlessly. The moment they stop the road will be built, the forest felled, the lagoon poisoned. The story will have reached its bitter end. And so this story stretches out like a road toward the horizon, beyond the covers of this book, disappearing into the mist of the future.

# No Word for Welcome

# 1

## Learning the Lay of the Land

On the porch of the general store fifty villagers sat on piles of wood or carefully stacked bags of cement mix, waiting. The murmur of their words, in the throaty tones of Mixe, mixed with the thrum of late September rain. The porch was large enough to accommodate the whole group without crowding, small enough to allow them to speak without raising their voices and still be heard. Beyond the porch, webs of barbed wire separated backyard gardens of banana, papaya, mango, and tangerine trees from velvet patches of low-slung forest. Past the gardens, buses and tractor-trailers grunted along a two-lane highway, slowed by axle-cracking speed bumps and potholes. Far beyond the highway, green-draped hills undulated toward blue mountains, the Sierra Sur of Oaxaca State.

Carlos Beas ducked his head under the rusted edge of the porch roof, striding into the meeting a bit late. He wore old blue jeans and a t-shirt; the villagers wore wide-brimmed hats and sun-bleached work clothes. People nodded and mumbled their hellos to Beas as he stepped onto the porch. "Buenas tardes. Ya llegaste." They welcomed him to their village with the normal greeting, "You have arrived." He bobbed his head in response. A smile skittered across his face but his light

**2.** Señor Vásquez attends a community meeting organized by UCIZONI, the Association of Indigenous Communities in the Northern Zone of the Isthmus (2000).
PHOTO BY THE AUTHOR.

brown eyes stayed serious. The villagers' huaraches scuffled the cement floor as they moved forward to shake his hand. Only a few—mostly the local leaders—looked up to meet his gaze directly. Beas towered over everyone, though he is not quite six feet tall. He was the only one who sweated as the rain's steam rose around them.

The meeting had been called a few days earlier, after villagers had seen several strangers poking around their farmland. Those strangers had said they were surveyors working for the government. They offered no further information before they finished whatever it was they were doing and drove away in their shiny trucks. News of the visiting surveyors spread from house to house, crossing dirt roads and lines of flapping laundry. People got to thinking. Was this somehow related to the rumor that had been floating around for the past couple of years? About the new highway? What were those strangers doing, tromping through their fields, looking through boxes attached to metal tripods, taking notes and measuring distances? Did all this interest in their land mean that the rumored highway would cut right through their village?

The two-lane highway, the one visible from the porch of the general store, had been built in the 1950s. It grazed the fringes of this village, called Boca del Monte, in the center of Mexico's Isthmus of Tehuantepec. The villagers still referred to the opening of the current trans-isthmus highway with the derision reserved for old insults that might be repeated: "Cuando viene un rico con su carretera" ("When a rich man comes with his highway"). Once a remote outpost several miles from the railroad tracks, Boca del Monte became a roadside pit stop when the highway opened. Travelers stopped to buy sodas and eat grilled chicken. Some did not stop, but tossed their trash out rolled-down windows. Villagers built roadside shops and organized a litter patrol. The western edge of the village became a front doorstep to the world, a short detour from the Pan-American Highway, which ran across the isthmus east to west.

The village's name, Boca del Monte, means gateway to the mountains, or to the wildlands. It marks the entryway to the Chimalapas rainforest that covers the hills of the central region of the Isthmus of Tehuantepec, where a road veered away from the trans-isthmus highway, through the village and many miles into the rainforest. Thanks to that side-route, much of the rainforest that it cut through had been turned into field and pasture. The people of Boca del Monte had seen decades' worth of chainsaws and bulldozers pass by their general store and into the rainforest, while truckloads of timber and cattle come back. As some of the villagers liked to joke, "Pretty soon, we'll be Boca de Nada—Gateway to Nothing." Still, they took the long view; their ancestors had lived on the isthmus for several thousand years.

One of the men standing on the general store's front porch—one of the few who looked Carlos Beas straight in the eye—asked him about the route of the rumored new superhighway. As Beas began to speak, everyone turned toward him, subtly shifting position until the circle closed around him. "Maybe it's going to pass right through the village, maybe it's going to pass to one side," he said, tilting his head in a gesture of *Who knows?* Either way, it would separate farmers from their fields. "I don't know how the farmers are going to cross it—flying or what?"

Amusement riffled through the group. Unlike farm towns of the American Midwest, where single houses sit in the middle of corn or soybean fields, rural Mexican villages tend to cluster their houses near the small buildings where residents pray, buy cooking oil and sugar, and make telephone calls. In Boca del Monte some villagers walked more than half an hour from their homes, machete in hand, to the far-flung fields where they grew corn, beans, yucca, malanga, hot peppers, and tamarind.

"We just asked the government for more information about the route, so for the moment, we're only guessing," Beas said. "Look, here are some documents about it." He held up a thick manila folder, then slid out a letter and waved it. He began to read: "'The Director General of Federal Highways has contracted the services of the COINSA company to do the necessary fieldwork for the highway project.' So, according to this, on May 24th they have already contracted out the highway project." Beas paused as the younger ones whispered to a few of the older ones, translating his words into Mixe, the local language. Beas slipped the sheet back into the dog-eared folder and pulled out a second letter. "And here, on August 25th, they tell you that's not true." He shuffled the papers again and held up a third letter: "And on September 22nd, they're telling you they're just at the research phase." His closed the folder and held it aloft. "What does all this mean, compañeros and compañeras?" He continued without a pause. "It means they're not taking you into account. I'm just here to tell you to prepare yourselves. This isn't like fifty years ago, when they paved the carretera. You can't walk across a superhighway; the cars go very fast. Those of you who have traveled to Mexico City know what a superhighway is."

Most of the people gathered on the porch had never made that trip of ten hours in the fastest, most expensive bus. From where they stood they could see the bus stop on the far side of the highway, where buses carried their young men north toward the U.S. border. Away. Vehicles on the current trans-isthmus highway passed Boca del Monte at residential speeds; children and old women sold bags of peeled oranges and baked *totopos* to drivers and passengers. The trans-isthmus road they saw from the edge of the porch felt no more like a superhighway than their general store felt like a Wal-Mart.

Beas continued: "If you don't pressure the government, I doubt they will build bridges for ox-carts and for people. Then how will you cross it? You can't fight this alone. If we don't watch out, the heavy machinery will be here at work before we know it."

Beas stepped out of the center of the circle. Several men rose slowly to speak. One mentioned that people had come from a nearby village, saying they had seen the surveyors, too. A second man stepped forward. "They have to get permission before they can come on our farmland. They can't just walk in here like cattle rustlers, screwing around." Another villager insisted it was important to confront those mysterious workers directly if they showed up again. If the villagers didn't complain, he said, the government would never know their concerns. Nods and ayes circled the porch. Until they knew more, the discussion was closed.

The group moved on to the final agenda item: an ongoing conflict between Boca del Monte and the national oil company, Petróleos de México, or PEMEX. The narrow PVC tubing of oil pipelines laced Boca del Monte's farmland. One line had ruptured the previous month, pouring PEMEX oil over cornfields and into the Sarabia River that wound through them. Black poison slicked their farmland and dead fish piled up on iridescent riverbanks.

The villagers had demanded retribution and PEMEX had offered a lump-sum payment of one thousand pesos per household, or nearly one hundred dollars, as much cash as a typical family earned in several months. It was one-time compensation for what could be a long-term problem. The soil would absorb the petroleum but would release some of it during each year's rainy season, bringing back the impacts of the oil spill—lower soil fertility, less oxygen for plant roots, and stunted plant growth—year after year.

"Perhaps the heavy rains have washed the oil away?" one man ventured.

"Yes," Beas replied. "Some of it has been washed away, but what about all the oil that had already seeped deep into the soil before the rains came?"

A middle-aged man stepped forward to speak in favor of PEMEX's proposal. Raindrops pummeled the porch roof more insistently. The circle loosened; people avoided one another's eyes. The man switched into Mixe, closing Carlos Beas out of the debate. He went on for a long time while Beas stared at the gray floor, concentrating so he might catch the general gist of the speech. The man finished, tipped his head in a slight bow, and stepped back to his pile of wood. The group seemed to soften a bit; the man was pulling them to his side.

Beas kicked at the floor and all eyes turned toward him. "What if, three years from now, your farmland doesn't produce?" A faint note of irritation tinged his words, his long hands cut the air sharply. "That money will be gone and you still won't have a way to feed your families."

A third man, the leader of the village assembly, spoke up to agree with Beas. With his words the tenor of the gathering shifted once again. The group murmured its assent as the rain faded away. Beas walked around the circle and shook hands with each person. He thanked them and said he would return as soon as there was more news. He turned and stepped off the porch into the last moments of daylight.

Throughout the meeting I had stayed at the porch's edge, shaking hands and introducing myself only to the few who were brave and curious enough to approach me—as much a stranger as the surveyors who had prompted the gathering. I explained to those who asked that I, too, had come because of the rumored highway. I worked with a community organization in the United States that was concerned about the same things that concerned them. I wanted to learn from their experience, from the way they organized meetings like this one. I wanted to know what the highway would mean for Boca del Monte and the rest of the isthmus residents, the istmeños. They nodded and thanked me for coming and for my interest in their community. Their labored Spanish carried Mixe's deep rumble.

I attended that meeting in September 1999 as part of a month-long visit to the Isthmus of Tehuantepec. It was my third visit to the isthmus since first learning about the rumored highway in the summer of 1997. I'd planned my 1999 trip after receiving a letter from Carlos Beas in July. His note to me had begun, "Ya nos cayó el chahuixtle." He continued: "El chahuixtle in Mexico is a disease of corn plants. When people say that it has come, it means something bad has happened. Very close to Matías Romero, work has begun for the Highway." Even writing in Spanish he had to translate for me; indigenous words like *chahuixtle* didn't appear in most dictionaries. And his use of a capital "H" on highway, a dramatic flourish typical of him, carried great weight in Spanish, which capitalizes far fewer words than English does. He concluded his letter: "We've asked for information about its route and we'll organize a demonstration soon. We're still fighting with PEMEX about the oil spill, and there's not been much progress. I think we'll block the carretera. Warm greetings from all of us."

It had been nearly three years since the news of a planned highway had trickled south from Mexico City to the Isthmus of Tehuantepec. The rumor went like this: The new *supercarretera* would be four lanes wide, if not six; it would carry tractor-trailers at blistering speeds; it would cut obliviously through fields, forests, and villages; and it would return the Isthmus of Tehuantepec to the global prominence it had enjoyed in the years before the Panama Canal had been completed. The highway would run almost directly north-south, connecting the Gulf of Mexico to the Pacific Ocean. It would bisect the isthmus, which stretches east to west.

On July 22, 1996, a front-page headline in a Mexico City newspaper had announced, "Isthmus to Be Opened to Foreign Capital." The article was casually optimistic about the speed with which the highway would be built, claiming that half of the funds would come from "the royal families of the United Arab Emirates." The newspaper was wrong about that. Five days later it reported the istmeños' response to the news: "Three thousand campesinos, indigenous people, and residents of the Isthmus of Tehuantepec will begin a march to Mexico City next Monday, to demand . . . a national referendum on the Trans-Isthmus Megaproject that the government is promoting." In spite of the immediate response from thousands of istmeños, who asked for the opportunity to comment on the grandly named Trans-Isthmus Megaproject, news was slow to filter into the region's smallest towns and villages. For the most part the only thing that people heard about was the highway, but that was enough for people to identify it as chahuixtle, as Beas explained in his letter to me: *una desgracia*, a misfortune.

The "we" of Beas's letter referred to UCIZONI, the organization he had cofounded in the early 1980s. The Spanish acronym, pronounced "oo-see-SO-nee," stood for Association of Indigenous Communities in the Northern Zone of the Isthmus. It was a loose association, not a formal union, and required no particular political, ethnic, or religious affiliation—in this sense it was unusual among istmeño civic groups, which tended to draw membership from people of a single ethnicity, political party, or church. UCIZONI's members lived in indigenous communities—rural villages or, more rarely, urban neighborhoods. The large majority of the members were Mixe. Some belonged to one of the other ethnic groups of the isthmus: Zapotec or Mixtec or Chinantec or Huave. A few members weren't indigenous at all, but *mestizo*, like Carlos Beas. Nearly all UCIZONI members lived in the "northern zone" of the Oaxacan isthmus, which is to say, the central isthmus, because the northern isthmus belonged to the state of Veracruz.

When it came to troubles like the highway rumor, central-isthmus residents turned to UCIZONI, the organization could get responses even from government agencies that ignored everyone else. UCIZONI staffers had written letters and made phone calls, asking state and federal government officials for more information about the new highway's path. The fat manila folder that Beas had brought to the meeting in Boca del Monte was the result of that work. The letters in that folder provided the sort of answers they often received from the Mexican government: confusion and contradiction. The plan for a new four-lane superhighway across their land might have been an outrage, but as far as UCIZONI members were concerned, it was no surprise.

Having said our good-byes to the Boca del Monte village assembly, Beas and I got back into UCIZONI's company car, a sixties-style Volkswagen Beetle. It was a half hour drive to Matías Romero, where Beas had lived for fifteen years, starting in UCIZONI's earliest days. As he drove he was uncharacteristically quiet, staring hard at the carretera that ribboned before us. Carretera can translate as either "road" or "highway," but this trans-isthmus road wouldn't count as a highway anywhere north of the Rio Grande, or maybe even north of Mexico City. The tires drummed across speed bumps and pitched in and out of potholes.

I ventured into the silence. "Difficult meeting." His expression softened, as if he agreed, but then he said firmly, "No, I've seen pistols at meetings. That was not difficult."

We arrived in Matías Romero long after dark, just about time for dinner. We passed UCIZONI's office on the town's main street, Calle de Hombres Ilustres ("Street of Illustrious Men")—or, as the women of UCIZONI liked to call it, "Street of Illustrious Women and Men." Brightly painted banners draped the office's chipped cement façade: "No to the Megaproject!" "505 Years of Resistance!" A few moments later Beas angled the Volkswagen Beetle to the high curb; we'd arrived at his home. Because Matías Romero only had the sort of hotels where you could rent rooms by the hour, I was Beas's houseguest.

He dug through the contents of his wheezing refrigerator. On the fridge door magnets from Aruba, Panama, and New York—all places he had visited—held a poster of the most famous Zapatista, Subcomandante Marcos. In the poster, Marcos raises his middle finger to the camera and puffs on his pipe through a hole in his balaclava. In the neighboring state of Chiapas, the Zapatistas had raised arms against the globalized, free-trade economy five years earlier. All over Mexico, organizations like UCIZONI had taken great inspiration from the Zapatistas' declaration of independence from economic globalization. Beas had served as an advisor to the Zapatistas during their negotiations with the federal government, while UCIZONI members had visited Zapatista villages, and vice versa.

Beas assembled one-quarter of an onion, a few shriveled cloves of garlic, and a half-dozen pockmarked tomatoes and tomatillos on the kitchen table. I chopped the vegetables into half-moons as he laid a dented pan on the stove and twisted on the gas full blast. Blue flames curled up and around the skillet as he poured in cooking oil. He towered over the small stove but he was very much at home in the kitchen. He snapped week-old tortillas into pieces and dropped them into the roiling pool.

A mold-mottled Frida Kahlo print hung above the stove. In the self-portrait, one of her most famous images, a headdress blooms out around the artist's face with floral white lace filling the space around her grim stare, over the viewer's left shoulder. It is a portrait of Frida as a *tehuana*, a woman from Tehuantepec. Kahlo adopted almost every element of the region's dress: the cropped tunics and long skirt, the twisted braids, and heavy gold jewelry.

As the tortillas fried, I thought about Frida's obsession with istmeño symbols. I inhaled the breeze that drifted in the window, redolent of gardenias and propane, banana blossoms and ripe mangos. The neighbor's parrots screeched, a broom rasped across wet pavement, the last of the afternoon rain plinked from the roof.

When I had first visited the Isthmus of Tehuantepec, Mexican friends had said, "Ah, the isthmus, the place the Spanish never truly conquered, the place women command economic power, the place where globalization is embraced and rejected with equal force." These comments were oversimplified yet all too true. As such, the isthmus has always held a central place in Mexico's cultural imagination. By the time I prepared that dinner with Carlos Beas, two years after my first visit to the isthmus, I had become obsessed with the story of the isthmus. Would the highway be built? Would industrialized towns completely replace villages of farmers and fishermen? If not, how would organizations like UCIZONI prevent it? It seemed an impossible task, yet the istmeños had accomplished the impossible before. How? Why was community organizing more successful here than it was in the United States?

Beas tipped the cutting board over the blender and whined the vegetables into salsa. He drained the oil from the frying pan and poured in the gritty puree. I poured water from the five-gallon jug into tall, slim glasses with worn images of the Virgin of Guadalupe. Beas slid the greenish stew onto two plates.

I tasted all of the isthmus as my mouth closed around a forkful of *chilaquiles*: earth, corn, grease, hot chile, and sour tang.

"This is a perfect meal," I said to Beas.

He laughed. "This is the food of the very poor."

Though his full name is Juan Carlos Beas Torres, most people called him Licenciado or simply Lic. Unlike most of the people he worked with at UCIZONI, he had a college degree. Those who addressed him by name, mostly good friends and younger people, called him Beas. A Spanish homophone for "You may see," it was an unusual and most appropriate surname: Beas was an excellent teacher and a compelling public speaker but he could be insistent to the edge of bullying.

Born into a middle-class mestizo family in the northern city of Guadalajara, he'd left home at fifteen, landing in Mexico City just as the sixties turned to the seventies. Eventually he finished college, but before that he—like many others of his generation—marched through city streets, got arrested, went to jail, and was tortured there. Beas came to the Isthmus of Tehuantepec for the first time when he was twenty-three years old. Just out of college, he landed a job teaching anthropology to young villagers, to the children of families called *indios*, the ones who had long been the subject of outsiders' anthropological research. His job was to turn traditional anthropology on its head, to transform those who had been studied into the researchers. His students would no longer simply answer long lists of questions, but devise the questions themselves. The same government whose jailers had tortured Beas handed him the job. This was not an unusual turn of events, but an example of the long Mexican tradition—stretching back to the conquistadors—of officials trying to co-opt opposition. A couple of years after young Beas moved to the isthmus, the government canceled funding for the anthropology program. As Beas explained, "The program got out of their control." He gave up only that last detail easily. He would stack up details about his background like children's blocks, then knock them down and rebuild them in a different pattern.

Watching the meeting at Boca del Monte's general store, I had wondered whether people had truly agreed with the decision made about PEMEX, or had felt pressure to meet Beas's fervor with acquiescence. By the time of that assembly I had attended perhaps twenty community meetings with Beas. He had been the first person I'd met in the Isthmus of Tehuantepec and had become my guide. I admired his long experience and easy skill at the sort of work I'd done, not always successfully, through the 1990s: grassroots organizing. I had nudged together small groups of people in Idaho or Massachusetts or New York or South Carolina or Washington, cajoling action from concern. I organized people who opposed the North American Free Trade Agreement, or nuclear weapons; or U.S. military aid to Central America. The hardest part of the work wasn't grappling with complex, interconnected issues, it was inspiring people to overcome the lure of short-term, short-sighted decisions—the equivalent of accepting PEMEX's one-time payment for long-term damage.

During the decade that I had worked as a grassroots organizer, it seemed to me that our collective efforts had become less effective, our strategies narrower in both vision and results. Four months out of college, during my first week as a grassroots organizer in a cramped office in Oakland above a hardcore porn shop, the trainer had told us, "Burnout is the long despair of doing nothing well." A decade later I turned this statement over in my mind. I was burned out, but was this because our organizing was so effective at doing *nothing* or because we were not doing anything *well*? I decided that stepping outside my own country, culture, and context was the best way to gain the perspective I needed. I wanted to learn how grassroots organizing worked in a community very different from my own. I didn't know of a place more different than the Isthmus of Tehuantepec.

During the Isthmus Is Our Own forum that I'd attended in 1997, hundreds had gathered in the mud-and-cement courtyard of a municipal community center not far from Boca del Monte. I was there representing a nonprofit organization in Boston, where I worked at the time. At the isthmus forum, I squeezed into a narrow space on a wood-plank bench. A handful of languages settled around me as Beas, whom I had just met, called the meeting to order. The peasants, fishermen, teachers, environmental activists, village leaders, and university professors who crowded the space had only recently learned about the plans for the Trans-Isthmus Megaproject, and they came to the forum to debate their options. Some wanted to hold a second forum, inviting federal government officials to come and explain to them what the Megaproject plans entailed. Others dismissed that possibility because, as one person put it, "the government does whatever it wants with the peasants."

The group constructed a list titled "We Don't Want the Megaproject Because":

> The government must not accept foreign or private investment without first consulting directly with our communities.
>
> The municipal presidents are our *only* appointed negotiators.
>
> We know it's going to hurt our communities and not benefit us.
>
> It doesn't respect the earth, and where will our children live?
>
> The superhighway is going to displace people who live near it.
>
> We have the right to an opinion because it's *our* land.
>
> It divides those who have land from those who don't.
>
> The government hasn't kept its promises to us.
>
> It will bring vices to our communities, like drug addiction, prostitution, and more cantinas.
>
> It will bring environmental degradation.

The forum concluded with a public statement that asserted, "With the development of an industrial corridor, we see glimmers of the 'proletarianization' of the farmers and the indigenous people. We will lose our dignity. Without land, we will become factory boys, simple workers with miserable wages and inferior jobs."

On the last day of the gathering, one of the founding members of UCIZONI, Delfino Juárez Toledo, stood up before the group to insist that maintaining their identity as indigenous istmeños was crucial to any campaign to stop the Megaproject. "If we deny that we are Huaves, Zoques,

Nahua-Popolucs, Chontals, Chinantecs, or Zapotecs, then we're already screwed." Later Delfino would tell me that there were two things about the 1997 forum that had made it one of the most important he had ever attended. One was a change in the participants: the academics and "the people who barely spoke Spanish" began to realize "they weren't part of separate worlds." The other was a change in the world beyond the gathering: the grassroots groups that had organized The Isthmus Is Our Own were taken more seriously by the media and by the government.

It was the conversations between the university professors and the peasants that interested me most. In a decade of grassroots organizing I had never seen such a wide range of people sit down together and debate their options.

The week I received the letter from Beas telling me of the chahuixtle, I quit my all-consuming grassroots campaign job and planned a month-long trip to the isthmus. I dreamed of moving there altogether; I simply had to know how the story of the highway would end. Would it be built? Would istmeños like those in Boca del Monte have a say in the plans? If the highway were built, what would it bring with it?

The chahuixtle wasn't just a superhighway, but a large spiderweb of industrial-development projects known collectively as the Trans-Isthmus Megaproject. Many istmeños referred to it as El plan de Ochoa. Felipe Ochoa's name appeared regularly in Mexico City newspapers, as did details from the plan he had authored. The phrase repeated by Boca del Monte villagers, "When a rich man comes with his highway," wasn't just a figure of speech. I was able to interview Mr. Ochoa twice, once via phone and once at his office.

The first time I spoke to him, in November 1997, he greeted me in perfect English, listened to my introduction, and offered a quick mental map of his plan for the Isthmus of Tehuantepec. The Trans-Isthmus Megaproject included one hundred and fifty proposed projects, including twenty-four petrochemical facilities, a dozen industrial shrimp farms, two oil refineries, several industrial parks for maquiladora assembly facilities, a quarter-million acres of tree plantations, and a new network of highways and railroads to carry the products of all this industrialization away, to international markets.

As he rattled off the long list I tried to picture his imagined landscape of a future Isthmus of Tehuantepec, with square-edged cement highway dividers, shiny metal factories, and ruler-straight blocks of shrimp farm tanks. This map contrasted sharply with the isthmus I had visited: pale adobe or sherbet-hued cement buildings, weed-filled pavement, and everywhere vegetation in twisting, anarchic profusion.

Felipe Ochoa began our conversation by telling me the central question that drove his work. It was, interestingly, precisely the same as UCIZONI's central question: How can the development of the Isthmus of Tehuantepec be achieved? It was not just the answer to that question, but the definition of the word "development" that created the wide gulf between UCIZONI and Ochoa y Asociados. As one UCIZONI member described that gulf: "We want green development, not one made of concrete."

Felipe Ochoa explained that several U.S. timber companies had already begun investing in southern Mexico. "They looked at the rest of the continent after the problem with the spotted owl up there." I asked him about the opposition—both local and international—to replacing forests and cropland with eucalyptus tree farms.

"You have heard about that?" He paused. "Ecologically, they have a point. No one would agree to covering the isthmus with eucalyptus plantations." Another pause. "Maybe limited plantations."

And what about the national conferences that had been organized by isthmus residents opposed to the Megaproject? "There *are* social groups that feel they will not benefit," he said.

"Why are they opposing the project?"

"They haven't been briefed appropriately. The social groups there are very far behind the rest of the country socially and economically."

There was a grain of truth in his last word at least. Some of the villages on the Isthmus of Tehuantepec ranked among the country's poorest. Still, the isthmus had a strong regional economy—if a very different one than Felipe Ochoa imagined for the region, from the vantage point of his eighth-floor glass-and-brick office building in a leafy neighborhood on the southern fringe of Mexico City. I visited him there a year before the Boca del Monte assembly meeting about the highway.

As I stepped out of the elevator, OCHOA Y ASOCIADOS glittered in gold tone. "Buenos días, good morning," the secretary said, sliding from one language to the other so fluidly that I couldn't tell which was her native one.

She led me to a conference room and I sank into a puffy leather chair, taking in the gleam of the long table and the skyline view out the generous windows. The large room had only two decorations: a pair of handmade clay pots from Oaxaca and a large map of the entire country. As I waited for Felipe Ochoa, I gazed at the map, thinking about the great distance between Mexico City and the U.S. border and the much shorter distance between Mexico City and the Isthmus of Tehuantepec.

Felipe Ochoa settled himself at the head of the conference table and smoothed his yellow tie against his ample belly. "So, you're from Boston. I lived in Boston for five years—or, as I say, I spent five *winters* in Boston. I was on the faculty at

MIT. My wife is from Seattle." His tone was casual but his words were careful, as he made sure I appreciated his U.S. connections, and that I understood the distance from his eighth-floor office to the long corridors of the Massachusetts Institute of Technology was not so great.

My conversations with Ochoa were among the only interviews I conducted in English through nearly a decade talking to people about the Trans-Isthmus Megaproject. Carlos Beas liked to say about people like Felipe Ochoa, "They think in English." I liked to remind Beas that I, too, thought in English. He would nod and say, as if making a special allowance, "Well, you can't help that."

Felipe Ochoa and I talked first about the "global chaos" reported in that morning's newspapers. It worried him. "With all these things that are happening worldwide, we don't know what the hell is going to happen." He raised his palms to emphasize the point.

Still, he was in it for the long haul. For twenty years, he told me, he had dreamed of building a transit corridor across the Isthmus of Tehuantepec. His entire career, from Mexico City to Boston and back, had been leading directly toward El plan de Ochoa: more than five hundred pages of charts, maps, project lists, and proposals, all collected at the federal government's request. Ochoa referred to the document over and over again, as he had when we'd talked on the phone.

I asked him if I might get a copy of the plan.

He waved his hand and gave a helpless look. Ochoa y Asociados had done that work at the pleasure of the federal government, he replied. I would have to get permission from the secretary of communications and transport.

He stepped into the hall and asked his secretary to bring me the cabinet minister's name and phone number, then returned to his overview of El plan. At its center was a new, four-lane supercarretera—the equivalent of a U.S. interstate—and a high-speed railroad that would connect two deep-water ports (one on the Pacific Ocean and one on the Gulf of Mexico), plus all manner of industrial development. It was supposed to be a "two-track" development, so to speak, based on both railroad and highway, but Ochoa felt the plan hinged on privatizing the trans-isthmus railroad. That was important because, as he explained, publicly held railway systems made corporate customers nervous. Most of Mexico's railroad had already been privatized.

He unrolled a map of the Isthmus of Tehuantepec on the table between us and patiently pointed out town after town, explaining where a shrimp farm, or a railroad depot, or an expanded port would be built. His voice was upbeat and full of pride as he spoke of the progress he envisioned for the isthmus.

"So, given all this opportunity, why are so many istmeños opposed to the Megaproject?" I asked.

He shrugged. "The experts haven't been able to portray or communicate properly what the idea is." His voice rose with excitement as he changed the subject. "Did you see the news from yesterday?"

I nodded. He waved the news article, wanting me to share his enthusiasm. It announced a steel mill to be built on the isthmus, a two-billion-dollar project. The mill was planned for Santa María Zaniza where, as I would learn later, the average adult's annual cash income was under two hundred dollars. "The whole thing is going to fly because of that!" Ochoa said. "It's a hell of an investment and a hell of a boost for the region. Once you make an announcement that you are going to have three thousand employees, the opposition is going to be there to see how they can get a piece of the action. If you are talking about three thousand jobs in one little spot, you are feeding fifteen thousand mouths, at least."

I nodded. "There have been announcements like this for several years but nothing seems to come of them."

He smiled. "In Mexico, nothing happens until it happens. And when it happens, *everything* happens."

I knew what he meant. I had seen this phenomenon in activities ranging from fiestas to car accidents. Plans would be delayed until the last possible moment, then come off flawlessly. In other cases, seemingly hopeless attempts would be made to solve big problems, then suddenly the band would start playing or the jack-knifed truck would be spirited off the road, and life would continue as usual.

I had asked Ochoa on the phone about the Megaproject timeline and he had said, "We are ready to go. But I have been saying for the past twenty years, 'We are ready to go.'"

After about an hour in the conference room, I stood to leave. I thanked Mr. Ochoa for his time and told him I would call the secretary of communications and transport about getting a copy of El plan de Ochoa. He nodded and asked about the rest of my stay in Mexico.

I told him I would be spending most of my time in the isthmus region.

"The isthmus?" Surprise, then puzzlement, crossed his face. "Why are you going there?"

"Well, that's where the Megaproject is happening." I said.

He shrugged. "Yes, but there is no information about it there."

On that point, he was precisely right. But that did not mean there was no information to be found. In the days that followed I called the office of the secretary of communications and transport at least a dozen times. In spite of multiple polite conversations with the receptionist, I was never able to speak with Secretary Aaron Dychter nor formally request a copy of the Ochoa plan. It was one of the only times I ever had an interview request declined in Mexico.

Nonetheless, a week after my meeting with Felipe Ochoa, I met a staff person from a Mexican environmental organization at an indoor shopping mall not far from Ochoa's office. He and I sat near a noisy fountain, where we wouldn't be overheard, as women clipped by in high heels, swinging fat shopping bags. He pulled a thick manila envelope from his shoulder bag and handed it to me. El plan de Ochoa was almost completely intact, if in a somewhat haphazard order. A cousin of his worked in Secretary Aaron Dychter's office and had made a copy for him. He didn't think this was unethical, he told me, because people had a right to this information. I made several photocopies, too, and sent them to UCIZONI and to other community organizations on the Isthmus of Tehuantepec.

Just as "nothing happens until it happens, and when it happens, everything happens," this, too, is how things work in Mexico. Formal information channels are blocked, clogged, or simply nonexistent, so information and resources flow through informal passageways, dug in the dark, by hand.

# 2

## Time Travel

"Matías Muy Feo" ("very ugly Matías") is the nickname Mexican urbanites gave Matías Romero. The town's architecture was, to be generous, plain but functional. Its main street had originally been lined with wooden, Swiss chalet–style buildings. Slowly, perhaps because of the relentless tropical termites, or perhaps because of changing tastes, those buildings were replaced by one homely cement block after another. Matías Romero was a new isthmus town, which is to say it had existed for just over a century. Before that, there had been a small village called Rincón Antonio, "Antonio's Corner." As the nineteenth century turned to the twentieth, British engineers arrived to build a railroad joining the Atlantic and Pacific Oceans across the Isthmus of Tehuantepec, bringing their own plans, tools, even bricks to build English-style apartments and offices.

Matías Romero was founded as engineering headquarters. The town was named for a Mexican ambassador to the United States originally from Oaxaca, who in the 1880s and 1890s pressed U.S. officials to invest in a trans-isthmus train. Matías Romero is both geographic center and cultural margin of the isthmus. Indigenous villages fill the humid hills that stretch away from the town. In those places, people will

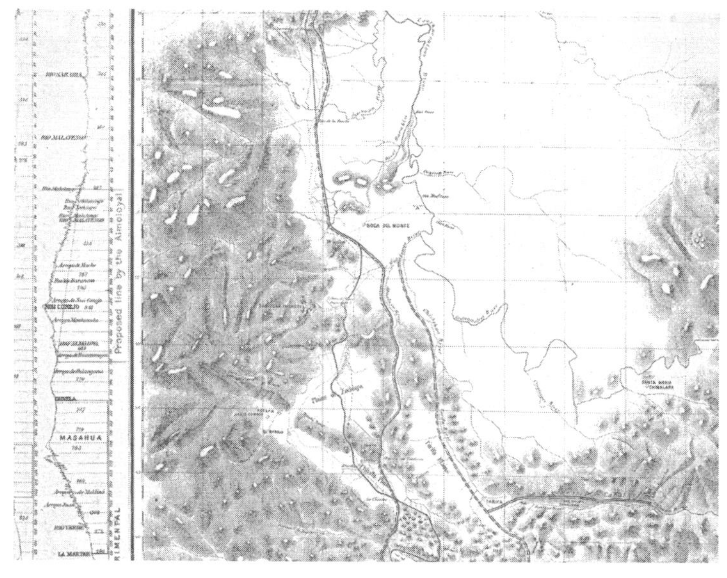


**3.** J. J. Williams and Col. Eduardo Garay produced this map for the U.S. Navy in 1870, at a time when the landforms of the low-lying Isthmus of Tehuantepec were of crucial interest to the U.S. government. COURTESY OF THE LIBRARY OF CONGRESS, MAP AND GEOGRAPHY DIVISION.

offer you stacks of baked corn totopos and cups of cool, sweet *horchata* as they speak to one another in the local languages of Mixe, Zapotec, or Chinantec. In Matías Romero you can buy hotdogs from a roadside stand or even that most gringo of foods, peanut butter, at the grocery store, and you will hear Spanish almost exclusively. Matías Romero is a mestizo town in an indigenous region.

In 1924 a *National Geographic* writer noted that his spirits dropped when he arrived in Matías Romero:

> This had once been a well-built village of burned brick, where were the headquarters of the railroad officials, away from the steamy heats of the two oceans. Once there had been railroad shops. . . . Decrepit, rusting and unkempt cars and engines were scattered through the almost empty yards.

That was, more or less, the way most Mexicans described Matías Romero to me eighty years after that *National Geographic* article was published. Because it sat close to the Pan-American Highway on the route from Mexico City to Chiapas, the Yucatan Peninsula, and Guatemala, many had passed through it. Few stopped.

I, to the amazement of almost everyone who knew the town, decided to move there. Ten months after the assembly meeting at the Boca del Monte store porch—nearly three years after I first learned of the Trans-Isthmus Megaproject—I made the leap, packing up my life in the United States and settling into a cement-block *casita* in Matías Romero just three blocks from the UCIZONI office.

The central market town for a broad swath of villages, Matías Romero has stores and market stalls for nearly everything. On the short walk from my casita to the bus stop I passed only a few of the town's shops, but in those four short blocks I could buy plumbing pipe, mangoes, tortillas, a gas oven, Mickey Mouse printed fabric, black-and-white film, a tank of cooking gas, sheets of roofing metal, apples (an exotic treat), a polyester negligee, a used blender, a backpack, large quantities of pesticides, a case of live twittering chicks, or a case of cold beer. Several times each week I set out from home for the bus stop. I would pull the metal door closed behind me, shutting out the coolness of the green yard and stepping onto the searing street. As I walked, the road underfoot shifted from heaving cement to clumps of grass to brown hardpan to a metal grate over a fuming, fluorescent sewer, and back to cement. Under a glowing sign that read "Elektra" in large letters and "Western Union" underneath it in small letters, I waited for the bus. Some of the buses had reluctant brakes and a few had aggressive cockroaches, but nowhere I had lived in the U.S. had as comprehensive a public transit system as the Isthmus of Tehuantepec. With a little money and a lot of patience I could reach any town or city, or many of the smallest villages, in the region, or the state or national capital. The office of Estafeta, Mexico's FedEx, marked the halfway point between house and bus stop. At Estafeta, I could send an express letter to the United States for two hundred pesos, about eighteen dollars. The letter would arrive five days later, with everything inside the cardboard mailer slit open and unfolded but more or less intact. Estafeta letters mailed from Mexico City arrived untouched; customs officials paid more attention to mail from areas known for drug trafficking, like the Isthmus of Tehuantepec. The region had always been a transit zone—for items both legal and illicit.

Waiting for the bus during the day, I would sit on a cement ledge with my back to Elektra's plate-glass window, pulling myself into the bus stop's only strip of shade. Usually only men and children sat on the shady ledge. Women were more likely to stand, no matter how long the wait or how brutal the sun. In the cooler hours after sunset, everyone stood in the middle of the sidewalk, watching Elektra's display televisions through the window's maze of cracks and duct tape. Though I rarely watched television, I would stand with everyone else, staring at the radiant squares, tiny to huge, monochrome or green-tinged to full rainbow color. The televisions beamed their silent messages all night long in a town where electric bills sometimes ran higher than the rent.

One evening I watched a woman—or, rather, twenty of her, each ranging from four inches tall to thirty inches tall, sallow-skinned to pinkish—driving around in a pickup truck, searching for Australian roadkill. The man standing next to me looked back and forth from the woman on the screen to me. I had noticed how much she resembled me: short, blue eyes, light brown wavy hair, and a big Germanic nose. During my first few months in Matías Romero people variously confused me with a dark-haired Greek woman six inches taller, a light-skinned woman from Mexico City, and a series of gringa missionaries who had passed through town years earlier. The istmeño standing by me surely thought the Australian woman and I were sisters—or maybe it was, somehow, a documentary about this woman standing next to him on the street.

The wall of televisions cut to the next scene: dozens of baby joeys bounding around an orphan kangaroo farm.

"Rats that jump?" the man asked me.

I wasn't sure I had the correct vocabulary to explain the biology of marsupials without sounding crass. "They're animals that live in Australia," I began, then stopped. It was no explanation but it was the best I could do. Each new topic I encountered in Spanish was a steep hill on a never-ending hike. Just when my pace picked up and I became sure-footed—gaining all the vocabulary necessary to talk about fishing or trade agreements or railroad construction—the path curved sharply upward and something new slowed me down. That night it was kangaroos.

Not long before the marsupial conversation, I had visited Elektra to buy the smallest refrigerator and firmest mattress in the store. Elektra was, even more than the bus system, a place that connected Matías Romero to the world. Each day villagers streamed in to collect remittances. They walked past metal shelves stacked twenty feet high with shiny stereos, televisions, video players, and microwaves, each with a red tag advertising the amount of the monthly installments for twelve-, twenty-four-, or thirty-six-month payment plans. The shoppers' sons, husbands, brothers, mothers, daughters, or grandchildren wired dollars from El Norte via the Western Union window at the back of the store. Western Union paid out the relatives' precious dollars in pesos after skimming a healthy percentage. Many of the people who walked in didn't walk out with cash: on some previous visit they had purchased a television or refrigerator or gas range on an installment plan. They would go in regularly for a year or two or three to make high-interest payments using the wired money.

When I asked the price of a four-foot-tall refrigerator, the teenaged clerk pointed to the red tag. "No, sorry, I don't want to pay monthly," I said. "I want to pay the whole thing right now."

The clerk blinked a few times; my question made no sense. He consulted several co-workers. He came back with another clerk, who explained that I just needed to multiply the top price by twelve.

I shook my head and smiled. "I'm sorry, but no. I shouldn't have to pay any interest. I want to pay the full price today."

The first clerk went to find the manager, who directed him to a dusty three-ring binder. He hefted it open and flipped several sheets back and forth, then quoted me a price. I handed over twenty crisp two-hundred-peso notes, paying a bit more than the mattress and fridge would have cost in the United States, and left them gaping after me. Because I could afford to hand over all at once the amount a family member in El Norte might send in over the course of six months, I had received, by local standards, an amazing bargain.

Most Thursdays an express bus passed by the Elektra store. It traveled all the way to the Texas border, a one-way service. In the main bus station of the region—40 miles away, in the city of Juchitán—the express route appeared as a thick white line painted across the brown map of Mexico. The white line ended at the border, where it bumped into the red-and-blue-striped land of El Norte. The passengers on that express bus arrived at the border more quickly than the letters sent via Estafeta. People left Matías Romero, but often only their money, pieces of paper at Elektra's Western Union window, returned.

The istmeños' relationship with the two-lane highway that cut across the isthmus—part of that white line that headed toward the red-and-blue-striped land of El Norte—was complicated. The carretera made it possible to get farm products to market, and for children to attend school, and for the sick to reach the hospital. Yet it lures their young people away. Still, the rumor of a new highway—one that couldn't be crossed on foot, one whose buses wouldn't stop anywhere along the roadside—loomed large but amorphous, fearsome but unconfirmed. Shortly after I moved to Matías Romero in June 2000, I went to visit Oaxaca state's SCT headquarters, the federal government's Communications and Transport

Department, to interview the regional director, Reynaldo Guajardo Villarreal. Arriving at his office, I told the receptionist I was there to learn about the SCT's plans for the Trans-Isthmus Megaproject.

"The supercarretera?" she replied. At least in this office there was no question that the Trans-Isthmus Megaproject included a new high-speed highway.

Reynaldo Guajardo told me immediately that the highway across the isthmus was not the highest priority of the project; it was still in the planning stages. The goal was to finish construction by 2004, more than four years in the future. "It's part of the modernization program—a four-lane highway from Salina Cruz to Coatzacoalcos," he said, naming the Pacific and Gulf ports of the isthmus. Ochoa's Trans-Isthmus Megaproject had many nicknames, including "the modernization program." Guajardo went on to tell me that part of the highway would be a toll road, while the rest would remain free. By saying this, he confirmed UCIZONI's worst fear: even the few istmeños rich enough to own cars or trucks could never afford to pay highway tolls. A typical toll to travel 30 miles equaled more than a typical day's wages.

"I'm very curious about the route of this new highway," I said to Director Guajardo. "Might you have a map of it?"

He didn't have a map available right then, but he told me that if I returned the following afternoon, a Saturday, he would have one ready for me. As implausible as this sounded, it turned out to be true. The next day I returned to his office and his receptionist handed me a huge map of the state of Oaxaca. A thick, black marker line traced the path from the state capital southeast to Salina Cruz, on the Pacific Ocean, then north across the isthmus to the Gulf of Mexico. Just like that, an unknown gringa received information that had been denied the istmeños for more than two years.

On the days I spent at home in Matías Romero, perhaps one out of every three, my mornings started with a cold shower or a sponge bath from a pot of water heated on the stove, then a few hours in front of my computer. Four households shared the walled front yard. Each morning, all the men went to work and all the women stayed home to do the same. One neighbor scrubbed dishes at the outdoor sink while another laced the yard with lines of freshly washed clothes. A four-year-old boy stalked the square of cement and grass in front of my living-room window—the only part of the yard not filled with his mother's dripping handiwork. He looked for things to shoot with his plastic machine gun, stopping frequently to make faces at me and stare at the glowing L-shaped piece of plastic before me. I would stay at my desk until the early afternoon and then make my daily trip downtown. Most of the year my mid-afternoon shopping trips forced me into the street at the time of day when nearly everyone else stayed inside. I faced the day's hottest hour because my laptop computer didn't function when the temperature in my living room went over 91 degrees—an event that usually occurred around noon. More important, visiting the newsstand in the early afternoon was the only way to get a newspaper. Four or five days a week, at around 2:30 p.m., twenty copies of *La Jornada* arrived from Mexico City. Most days they sold out in less than an hour. The Oaxaca state newspaper, *Las Noticias*, arrived a little earlier and sold out more slowly but usually wasn't worth the special trip.

During the worst of the rainy season, July to October, I wasn't the only one on the street in the steamy early afternoon. At that time of day the rain usually abated. It didn't quite stop but came down with far less fury. Though it rained most of the year in the isthmus humid zone, the "rainy season" was marked by days that seemed consumed by wetness.

Mornings remained so dark that when my alarm pulled me awake, I sometimes thought it was still night. My neighbor's elaborately woven laundry lines stayed in our yard for days and days, awaiting moments of sun. When the rain paused, the streets filled with people doing whatever they needed to do before the storms resumed in the late afternoon.

On September 5, 2000, one of those colorless days under a milkglass sky, I unfolded *Las Noticias* and was greeted by the new president's foot. The front page included a half-page photo of Mexico's then president-elect, Vicente Fox. He stood with one cowboy boot—embroidered with "Fox 2000"—perched on a conference table, inches from a water glass. Teeth bared and eyes squeezed shut, he seemed to be laughing at his own joke. To the left of Fox's shiny boot and wide grin the headline read, "Fox Presents Plan for Southern Development." The article announced that President Fox would travel to Central America to "lobby for an ambitious regional development proposal." The article gave only one real hint about what it might contain: it was related to the proposed free trade agreement for the Americas—a sort of NAFTA for the hemisphere. I took the newspaper to the UCIZONI office, where the news sparked a long discussion. Was this related to the Trans-Isthmus Megaproject? If so, what did that mean for the highway?

A week later the istmeños received the first hint of an answer to those questions. The newspapers reported that Fox had visited Guatemala City to meet with the Guatemalan president. Fox dubbed his new proposal the "Plan Puebla Panama." That title gave me another map to add to my growing collection. Puebla was the state north of Oaxaca, the richest state in southern Mexico. The PPP, as everyone came to call it, pressed all of southern Mexico and Central America onto a crowded single map, then criss-crossed it with planned new highways, ports, and airports. Fox's original list of projects also included new and improved universities and technical education centers, but as the program unfolded those items weren't mentioned again. Most of the talk focused on transportation—moving goods across and out of the region. The basic idea was the same as the Trans-Isthmus Megaproject but the geographic area the PPP involved was vastly larger.

By September 2000 the only stretch of railroad in all of Mexico still owned and operated by the government was the trans-isthmus line. To the disappointment of Felipe Ochoa, the government had decided not to sell the line. UCIZONI, the railroad workers' union, and many other community organizations had called for a national referendum on whether to privatize the trans-isthmus railroad. The government responded by scrapping the idea of privatization altogether. I thought it a stunning victory: the government actually responded to the organizations' demands. Carlos Beas thought it pitiful. He shrugged his shoulders and said with regret, "It was the only thing we received." By that he meant that the Trans-Isthmus Megaproject was otherwise moving ahead. Even worse, it was now part of the enormous Plan Puebla Panama. Still, for Felipe Ochoa and other Megaproject promoters, the decision not to privatize the rail line presented a bit of a problem.

It was to be a two-track development plan with investment in both railroads and highways. But could it happen? The rail line would remain in government hands and, as Ochoa pointed out, investors tend to shy away from government control. The trans-isthmus north-south railroad was supposed to be a linchpin of the Plan Puebla Panama, but I'd not met anyone who had used the train recently. Three weeks after the dreary September day when I learned of Vicente Fox's industrial dream for southern Mexico and Central America, I went looking for the train.

The sun had just lifted over the horizon when Mirna Godínez and I boarded a bus, leaving Matías Romero to travel southeast to Arriaga, Chiapas. It was the first time I had taken a road trip in Mexico with a woman; I was usually the lone female in the traveling party. Most istmeña women had too much work, too little money, too many small children needing care, or too little autonomy from a husband who didn't want them away from home. But Mirna was Carlos Beas's *compañera*, and our trip had been his idea. He waved goodbye from the roadside as she and I settled into our seats.

We took the bus out of Matías Romero so we could then take the passenger train back. That might seem odd, but finding a passenger train in southern Mexico required creative planning. Passenger train service on the trans-isthmus line had been suspended the previous year—around the time the Boca del Monte villagers noticed the surveyors wandering their lands—after years of the service growing less frequent and less efficient. Passenger service was no longer profitable, and so it was eliminated. With that change an important piece of Mirna's life passed into memory. Her family's life had been so intertwined with the trans-isthmus railroad that they once moved from house to house by loading all their belongings into a boxcar and riding the rails from one stop to the next.

Mirna's father had worked for Ferrocarriles Nacionales de México, the national rail company, for forty-three years. Two of Mirna's brothers were still rail workers. For years Mirna, her sisters, and her mother had gone to the railroad station in the evenings. They would set up a small grill, fill it with coals, and cook *tlayudas*, corn tortillas filled with string cheese, sausage, spiced pork, hot peppers, shredded cabbage, tomatoes, refried black beans, and a generous smear of pork fat. Mirna and the other Godínez women served the grilled tacos, big as pizzas, to passengers who reached their arms from the windows of slow-moving trains. From what I'd heard, Mirna had been the most successful *tlayudera*. She was a gifted cook, but all the train passengers would have seen was her dark, smooth complexion, wavy hair, intent stare, straight-toothed smile, and tall, perfectly curved body.

For ninety-two years the trans-isthmus train had sustained local trade even as it served international commerce. Istmeños shuffled on and off train cars, carrying their fresh sea-turtle eggs, baked corn totopos, salted shrimp, chortling turkeys, clay pots, panting iguanas, and chile paste—products that had been traded across the isthmus since long before the Spanish conquest. The baskets and bags and bundles of the traveling saleswomen filled every available space on the passenger cars, transforming the train into a rolling market. Alongside the tracks, villages grew into towns and towns grew into cities, while far from the route they withered. The end of passenger rail service halted trade for many local vendors. By August 2000 new, privately managed trains were running on government-owned tracks. The rail company—which was neither public nor private, but something in-between—announced it would renew passenger service. The hopes of forlorn isthmus towns lifted slightly.

Unlike the passenger trains of years gone by, this new service didn't traverse the entire isthmus from the Gulf of Mexico to the Pacific Ocean. Southbound trains from the gulf port stopped 25 miles shy of the Pacific Ocean, turning southeast and passing through the city of Arriaga, Chiapas, on the way to the Guatemalan border. After studying the timetable—which Mirna had been able to secure only because of her family connections—we decided to test out the new passenger service by traveling from Arriaga back to Matías Romero.

Our bus pulled into the Arriaga station at the edge of town and Mirna and I caught a twenty-peso taxi to the train station in the town center, arriving there shortly after noon. Two security guards blocked the station entrance. One, middle-aged, squatted on an overturned milk crate; the other, much younger, sat on a torn cushion balanced on a chunk of plywood. Their rifles lay across their laps.

"Buenas tardes," Mirna and I greeted them. They nodded and mumbled the same. We looked past them into the station's waiting room. Our shift in gaze put them on alert.

"How can we help you?" The two men leaned together to close the space between them.

"We'd like to take the train to Matías Romero," Mirna said.

"The one that leaves this station at 4:40 this afternoon," I said.

"Do you think it will be on time?" Mirna asked.

The men didn't know exactly when the passenger train would arrive. Maybe 7:30 or 8:30 that evening, they guessed. Mirna and I looked at each other.

"We'll wait," Mirna told the men. I nodded, letting Mirna take the lead. The daughter of a Zapotec woman, she had a bit of what Beas called *sangre pesada* ("thick blood"), meaning if people got in her way, they didn't stay there for long.

Twin expressions of surprise, then confusion, passed over the guards' faces. They shuffled their makeshift chairs apart, reluctantly, giving us just enough space to squeeze past, into the waiting room. Wasps' nests pocked the high, once-white ceiling. In the fluorescent light fixtures, birds nested; their droppings grayed the long benches. The ticket windows gaped like toothless mouths at the far wall. A wooden sign listed four daily trains but the arrival and departure times had been painted out.

Mirna and I found a relatively clean spot and settled in for the wait. With the contents of our bags spread around us—water bottles, fruit, umbrellas, magazines, and notebooks—the scene we made reminded me of old photographs I'd seen of traveling market women half a century earlier. They would squat on the railway platforms or in the dust by the tracks, their wide skirts like moats around the tiny castles of their cropped *huipil* tunics. Their bundles and baskets, encircling their skirts, held everything they needed for several days away from home. Istmeño writer Manuel Matus wrote of the *vendedoras*:

> "The women in their long skirts and huipils with bundles and boxes, they were the railcar women. They watched the train's arrival with joy, and aboard it, created the culture of commerce, traveling all over. Little by little, they witnessed the waning of the train. It didn't even last a century, though made of iron; the grandfathers and the grandmothers lasted longer, made of flesh and bone."

Mirna and I chatted about the train station's overwhelming grime, her daughters' underwhelming school grades, and the fact that we seemed to be the only passengers waiting. A train passed shortly after one o'clock, another an hour later, and then a third. None stopped; each was cargo-only. After the third train wheezed and whistled by us, shortly before three in the afternoon, we asked the guards again: There *would* be a passenger train today, right? What time might it arrive?

This time they said they had no idea. Their reply annoyed Mirna, but she didn't let them know it. The trains hadn't been run this way when her father had worked the rails. "What about the schedule?" she asked. "If you don't know when the trains will arrive, how can you offer passenger service?"

Their reply seemed almost plausible: the dispatcher radioed the previous station to say whether there were passengers waiting to board the train and to find out when the train would arrive. Encouraged by their explanation, we walked to the back of the station to talk to the dispatcher. The door to his office was clearly labeled but locked tight. Aside from the two guards, the station seemed deserted.

We returned to the waiting room. We waited. I opened a bag of mandarin oranges I'd washed and cut up before dawn that morning. Mirna and I sucked the sour-sweet juice from the quarter-spheres, savoring the coolness still held in the center of each fruit, letting drops fall to the dingy floor. We passed the hours chatting with Agustín, the younger guard, who left his chunk of plywood and joined us inside.

"What sorts of people take the train?" Mirna asked.

"Well, there are market women who carry their dried shrimp and fish from the port," he said, his voice doubtful. That was how people had used the train in years gone by, when the service was slow but regular and cheap. These days all the market women took the bus or hitched rides in pickup trucks.

"Yes, *before*, but what about now?" Mirna said.

He looked confused and said nothing. I imagined his mental question: *What passengers?* I thought of how hard it had been even to get a copy of the timetable, and wondered if we were the only passengers Agustín had ever seen.

Shortly after 4:00, half an hour before the passenger train's scheduled arrival, Agustín told us that the (still invisible) dispatcher had announced our train would arrive from the city of Tonalá at 11:30 p.m.

"Do you think it's really going to arrive?" I asked.

"Maybe, or maybe not," he said. "Sometimes it stays in Tonalá for five or six days."

I pictured the theoretical vendedoras stranded and staving off hunger by eating all the dried shrimp they had brought to sell. This new, privately run isthmus-to-Guatemala route was intended for big companies exporting cement and cornmeal to Central America, not village women with big baskets of shrimp and fish to sell and small bags of money.

"The next one comes Tuesday," Agustín said, his tone reassuring. "So, there will be one Tuesday."

It was Saturday. I wasn't going to stay in Arriaga for three days, but I would have waited all night just to see what would happen. I'd been hearing about the great tradition of passenger trains in Mexico for years; that 11:30 p.m. train might have been my one chance, albeit slim, to experience it. But Mirna's patience had run out. Her daughters were waiting for her at home. The following morning, Sunday, she needed to visit the cemetery to place flowers at her mother's grave.

We left the train station to catch the bus back to Matías Romero. In this way, traveling in southern Mexico with women rather than men was different. In Mexico solitude is uncommon and undesired. I might have asked a man to take the bus home on his own, but a woman, never.

At 5:00 that afternoon Mirna and I climbed onto a bus that would have us back in Matías Romero before nine that evening. If the train *did* show up in Arriaga, it would follow almost the same route but would take twice as long.

The traveling istmeña saleswomen who had relied on the train followed a route that has been used for eons. Three thousand years ago obsidian, seashells, iron ore, and pottery moved between what is now Mexico City and what we call Central America—roughly the region covered by Fox's Plan Puebla Panama—through the villages and cities of the Mexican isthmus. Istmeños fashioned blades, darts, scrapers, and ornaments from Honduran obsidian. Still, isthmus residents traded more with one another than with outsiders. From the dry flatlands of the southern isthmus to the lush swamplands of the north, they traded across differences of language and culture, across the low hills that surround Matías Romero.

Six hundred years ago the Aztecs assiduously guarded trade routes that followed the Pacific coast of the isthmus through Chiapas to Guatemala. Porters, called *tlameme* (from the words for "something to carry") relayed goods along trade routes up to 1,000 miles long. Most were Aztecs; others were local people coerced into service. The people of ancient Mexico had domesticated only dogs and turkeys—no beasts of burden—so the tlameme carried every pound of stone, shells, pottery, textiles, fresh fish, ground flour, salt, and cacao on their backs. They began training for the job when as young as five years old, eventually learning to heft baskets or animal hide frame packs filled with 50-pound loads. They trekked up to 17 miles a day across rivers, over high mountains, through swamps. Istmeño fishermen living along the coast allowed Aztec porters to cross their land and ply their waters in dugout canoes. The path that Mirna and I traveled by bus, between Matías Romero and Arriaga, mirrored the Aztec cacao route and also a horse path that the Spaniards had built by 1550. In the eighteenth century the Spanish moved brass-cannon ordnance across istmeño lands.

When the U.S.-Mexico War ended in 1848, the Treaty of Guadalupe Hidalgo redrew the map of Mexico. All of northwestern Mexico became what we know as the U.S. Southwest: California and Texas, most of Arizona and New Mexico, and parts of Colorado, Nevada, and Utah. In the years that followed, debate about what other lands the United States might carve from Mexican maps filled the pages of our newspapers: the peninsula of Baja California? the northern states of Sinaloa and Sonora? or Tehuantepec? On April Fool's Day 1857, a two-sentence front-page *New York Times* article announced that the U.S. government planned to purchase the Isthmus of Tehuantepec for fifteen million dollars. It was no joke, but why buy Tehuantepec?

U.S. builders had just completed a packed-earth stagecoach path that linked the Pacific and Atlantic coasts: the Tehuantepec Turnpike. *Turnpike*, or toll road, comes from *turn pick*, Middle English words meaning "spiked barrier." When the gringos showed up in steamboats with scythes and rifles to cleave a dirt road into the fields and forests of the isthmus, the word's original meaning might have seemed particularly appropriate to the istmeños.

The building of the turnpike marked a turning point. The year after its inauguration, a *New York Times* editorial declared, "[L]et a stable government be established and the tide of American progress will set resistlessly toward the Isthmus of Tehuantepec." The next step was to transform the dirt road into a state-of-the-art planked roadway. The *Times* reported huge crates of wood arriving from Pensacola, Florida, and "white workmen" coming from New York with four months' provisions. Skilled carpenters willing to move to the isthmus could earn $2.50 to $3.50 a day—earning as much one hundred and fifty years ago as some istmeño farmers earn today. A few years after the turnpike was completed, a French visitor to the isthmus noted that the region's forest was "overly frequented by the North Americans, and had already lost a large part of its virgin beauty."

Before the turnpike opened, two routes for mail and news delivery existed between New York and San Francisco: the Pony Express across the U.S. plains or the more than 6,000-mile route by ship via the Panama railroad. Eleven years would pass between the Tehuantepec Turnpike's inauguration and the driving of the final, golden spike in Promontory, Utah, completing the U.S. transcontinental railroad. The first bundles of "California mails" traveled from San Francisco via the Mexican isthmus to New Orleans in November 1858. The packages arrived in New York in eighteen days—a full week earlier than those shipped via the Panamanian isthmus. "The mails have arrived from Tehuantepec," Eastern newspapers announced, reporting on life in the Oregon and Washington territories and the new state of California.

The isthmus is only 120 miles wide, as the quetzal flies. These days a bus covers the distance—slowing for countless potholes, sharp curves, and speed bumps—in about seven hours; a car can do it in five. In the nineteenth century the journey between the oceans stretched several weeks. Shortly after the Tehuantepec Turnpike opened, a young lawyer from San Francisco, John Ketattas Hackett, made the trip. I imagine him in a finely cut suit like the one he wears in the one photograph I've seen, leaving behind his attorney's office in San Francisco and boarding the *Golden Age* steamer on February 19, 1858. Six days later he and fifteen other passengers arrived in Acapulco and boarded the steamer *Oregon*, bound for the Mexican isthmus.

Hackett writes that the trip turned harrowing when the *Oregon* reached the unsheltered bay west of what is now the port city of Salina Cruz. The bay's name, La Ventosa, "the windy place," took on ominous import when the group arrived in the middle of the night and fierce winds tore at the boat until daybreak. As the sun rose on the first of March, two metal boats arrived shipside to carry the travelers and their baggage ashore. Huge waves pummeled the *Oregon*, threatening to smash the small boats against its hull. After the passengers flung first their steamer trunks, then their own bodies from ship to rowboat, seven istmeños strained against the oars, rowing the boats toward shore. Still 20 yards from shore, the boats bottomed out in the sand. To Hackett's amazement, the local longshoremen jumped into the water and hauled both passengers and luggage, on their shoulders, to dry beach.

The group cleared customs in a thatched-roof hut, then slogged three-fourths of a mile on foot across the beach. The stagecoach ride to the city of Tehuantepec, 15 miles away, took three hours. After the "tolerably smooth road" to Tehuantepec, the rest of the ride, Hackett reported, was "jolting to such an extent as to pound one almost to the consistency of a jelly." At times the road was so rough they had to abandon the coach and ride horseback. The group finally reached Suchil, where the Tehuantepec Turnpike ended at the Coatzacoalcos River. The name Suchil would have been familiar to *New York Times* readers; it was the dateline that often appeared on the articles titled "Tehuantepec." Hackett, who would have read many of those articles, was surprised to find that Suchil was nothing more than "an imposing city of three staked wig-wams and one wooden house." Hackett retired for the night on a cot, suffering mosquitoes, tarantulas, a "hard-backed, long-legged animal" that bit his throat as he slept, and "the largest, strongest, most able-bodied cockroach that ever shocked my gaze." Apparently not realizing it was the dry season, Hackett "earnestly hoped that the morrow would bring the steamer *Suchil*, to bear me away from so unenviable a place." But the Coatzacoalcos River ran too low for the steamship to pass. Hackett bragged that his traveling partners ended up rowing themselves in a mahogany canoe for a day and a half to the next port city, "with nothing to eat or drink save the river water."

Finally reaching New Orleans twenty days after leaving

San Francisco, Hackett wrote to the *New York Times* editors immediately, narrating his dramatic journey. He noted, "I have detailed without the slightest exaggeration my actual experience across the Isthmus of Tehuantepec, and regret that these embarrassments to the perfect success of the route exist."

In spite of the lawyer's grim report, *Times* articles datelined Minatitlán or Coatzacoalcos conjured images of a prosperous Wild West outpost. September 21, 1858: "We stand in need here of a newspaper, and a cabinet-makers' shop." "Most people upon their arrival have a slight attack of the calentura, but with care, and a low diet, it soon passes off. It is generally brought on by mixing fruit and liquor, and strangers can rarely be induced to believe the mixture injurious until they have felt the effects of indulgence." August 5, 1859: "Quite a number of wealthy Mexicans from the City of Mexico are now on the isthmus locating lands and taking up territory, which they feel satisfied must soon come under the United States."

The hopeful times didn't last even two years. By September 1859, newspaper headlines hinted at boom towns busting: "Isthmus of Tehuantepec: Rainy and Sickly Season—Desperation and Hard Swearing among the Employees." While temperatures topped 120 degrees and most of the foreigners sweated out severe fevers, armed robbers attacked the incoming ships from the United States, robbing passengers and pilfering the mail. Gringos who had moved to the isthmus in search of jobs languished, unable to afford return passage home.

Within a decade of its inauguration, the Tehuantepec Turnpike collapsed in economic ruin. A U.S.-Mexico treaty giving the North Americans permanent transit rights across the isthmus was signed in February 1860, but the U.S. Civil

War loomed. Yankees in the U.S. Senate likely feared the idea of bustling ports along the Gulf of Mexico—too much economic muscle for the U.S. South. The senate never ratified the treaty. In spite of the U.S. government's waning interest in the Mexican isthmus, North Americans living there would hang on for another decade, with occasional backup from the U.S. Marines. After the 1871 Mexican presidential elections, violence percolated through the isthmus. Death threats appeared mysteriously on the front doors of gringos' homes. The settlers abandoned their cotton plantations and mahogany sawmills and sent letters to the United States, saying they were "flying for their lives." One wrote: "We must abandon the Isthmus to God and the Mexicans."

The North Americans left the isthmus to the istmeños, but they left the trans-isthmus route to the British. A quarter-century later the Brits managed to link the Atlantic and Pacific via a trans-isthmus railroad. In 1894 railcars briefly ran on a badly constructed and stunningly expensive track. The first train to run along the track made the trip in ten hours and twenty minutes—besting the Tehuantepec Turnpike by many days. By the turn of the twentieth century the railroad offered nothing to international commerce, its tracks unable to support the weight of loaded boxcars and the ports at either end far too small for seagoing ships. Meanwhile, U.S. government attention had shifted south, to digging a canal across newly independent Panama, where both land and government were more compliant.

The British tried again in the early twentieth century to join the oceans at the Isthmus of Tehuantepec. Thousands of immigrants from the Bahamas, China, Korea, Jamaica, and Japan came to the isthmus to move earth, split wood, work steel, and hammer spikes. Those workers rebuilt 845 bridges, replacing wood with steel and laid railroad ties carved from both isthmus rainforest and California redwood stands. The entire town of Salina Cruz was moved and rebuilt from scratch, as port construction put the original town underwater. The trans-isthmus route was part of a national railroad network—a powerful symbol of Mexican economic progress and independence.

On January 23, 1907, President Porfirio Díaz inaugurated the new trans-isthmus railway. By that time the Mexican government had paid something close to thirty-five million dollars—the equivalent of more than seven hundred million dollars today—for its trans-isthmus dream. President Díaz stepped down from the railcar that had carried him from Mexico City to Salina Cruz. Wearing a dark suit, bow tie, and felt bowler hat, despite the heat, he untied the striped ribbons that held shut the gates to the port. He greeted an audience that included diplomats from Belgium, Cuba, El Salvador, Germany, Guatemala, Russia, Japan, Spain, and, of course, Britain and the United States. He spoke with nostalgia about the inauguration of the dirt road, the Tehuantepec Turnpike, which he had attended half a century earlier when he'd been military commander of the isthmus. After Díaz spoke, a military band played, the crowd shouted ¡Viva!, military rifle shots rang out, and at the appointed moment the president touched a button and an electric crane lifted fifteen sacks of Hawaiian sugar from the USS *Arizona* to a boxcar festooned with Mexican flags.

The Mexican president boarded a luxury railcar and the train departed Salina Cruz. In the city of Tehuantepec, Díaz's old friend (and, many claim, lover) Juana Catarina Romero, the isthmus's wealthiest woman, threw an all-out *pachanga* for the delegation of diplomats in attendance. As every good isthmus fiesta does, the party lasted until dawn. After bidding good-bye to Tehuantepec, President Díaz and his entourage headed north. Flowers and palm fronds, music and

Mexican flags greeted them at every rail depot. Díaz rode one of Mexico's first petroleum-powered trains, relying on Texas oil to power his car through tunnels, over bridges, and around hairpin turns, finally arriving in Coatzacoalcos. Mission accomplished, Díaz supervised transfer of the Hawaiian sugar onto automated conveyors to the *Louis Luckenbach*, which sailed north.

With the trans-isthmus train running regularly, Salina Cruz became a major international port. By 1910 Germany, Great Britain, Italy, Norway, Spain, and the United States all maintained consulates in the wind-whipped, sun-bleached city. North Americans returned and filled the isthmus foothills with coffee plantations and the lowlands with rubber plantations, while investors ranging from Texaco to William Randolph Hearst bought up isthmus lands. But just seven years after Porfirio Díaz's railroad opened, the first ship passed through the Panama Canal, carrying away the Isthmus of Tehuantepec's golden era. With the interoceanic route secured at the southern end of the Central American isthmus, Tehuantepec faded from the minds of North Americans.

When I lived in Matías Romero, eighty-five years after the Panama Canal had stolen its glory, it felt like a forgotten town. Once, while I walked around town with Beas, he gestured toward crumbling buildings across the street from the train tracks. Brick facades peeled away, exposing adobe bricks turning to dust; doors rotted away from their hinges; weeds grew through cracked tile floors. "This is a town en decadencia," he said, his voice matter-of-fact. I realized that, in Spanish, the word did not mean excess, but decay. Matías Romero's many cantinas and pay-per-hour motels still hosted plenty of low-budget decadence.

"Did you ever see it when it wasn't?" I asked. Beas had

been living in Matías Romero for more than twenty years but the city looked as if it had been crumbling for much longer than that.

"Go visit the railroad workers' clinic. I remember when it was open and I remember when it closed down." He shook his head. "The looting was incredible."

The medical clinic was several blocks east of the train tracks, far enough from my house and the Calle de Hombres Ilustres that I'd never happened to pass by it. When I went looking for it, I discovered another level of desolation in the town's retreat from prosperity. I had imagined a single storefront but found a complex of buildings the size of a large high school. The tiled walls and stone stairway looked as if they had been intended for a hospital in a much larger, wealthier city. When the clinic had shut down in the mid-1980s it fell victim to its own relative opulence. People stole everything from the beds to the wall tile to the bathroom fixtures. Now, palm trees towered overhead, dropping coconuts into empty, roofless rooms. I picked my way over the debris in the hallways, rousing sleeping dogs and sending tarantulas scattering among piles of bricks, rusting rebar, and dry leaves.

The words chiseled in the stone walls—*consulta externa, servicio dental*—conjured just a hint of the old Matías Romero when railroad workers filled the union hall, their families received excellent medical care, and train whistles pierced the air at all hours. By the time I walked through the clinic's carcass, nearly everyone at the union hall was a retiree and the lonely whistle cut the humid air only a half-dozen times each day. The trains passing through hardly ever stopped.

The morning after Mirna and I returned from Arriaga and our failed attempt to find a passenger train, I tried to catch up with the train from Tonalá at the Matías Romero train station. The two guards stationed there looked no busier than the pair we had met in Arriaga. A sign hung over the exit to the train platform: "Buy your ticket in the station to avoid a 25 percent surcharge on board." That seemed more encouraging than the sign in the Arriaga station, on which all the arrival and departure times had been blacked out.

"How can we help you?" one of the guards asked.

"I'd like to take the passenger train to Coatzacoalcos."

That startled them a bit. Rather than reply, one of them made a phone call. After putting down the receiver, he explained that there would be no train that day.

"But I was at the station in Arriaga yesterday afternoon," I replied, "and the guards said the train would arrive there around 11:30 p.m. That means the train should arrive in Matías Romero around 8:30 a.m., right?"

That prompted more confused looks and another phone call.

"There's a passenger here," the guard said to the person on the other end of the line. "She says that the train is coming from Arriaga; that's what they told her there." He listened. "Okay, very good." He hung up the phone and told me that the train had indeed arrived in Arriaga and come as far north as Ixtepec, 20 miles south of Matías Romero, and then turned back.

Why?

Well, he explained, during the rainy season they don't run the trains across the isthmus. The rail is in poor condition and it's dangerous.

I wondered why he hadn't told me that five minutes earlier. "So, in March, when the dry season starts, I can come back and take the passenger train to Coatzacoalcos?"

They assured me that I could.

Every couple of months I would stop by the Matías Romero

station and ask about the passenger train. Each time I would be given a different reason why there wouldn't be a train that day, as well as some hopeful hint about some future date when I might be able to take it. Eventually I stopped asking, but the istmeños never stopped talking about their lost train.

In years gone by they had accommodated the train and found a way to make the ever slower and less reliable passenger service continue to serve them. Today's rumor of a new highway seemed more baffling. What was the point of a highway they couldn't afford to use?

# 3

## Ocean's Mouth Empties

In the Pacific-coast villages of the Isthmus of Tehuantepec, south of Matías Romero, rumors of other sorts of chahuixtle floated through town. At the same time that istmeños began to hear about highway plans and people started talking about El plan de Ochoa, a story about another dreadful thing began to drift through the fishing villages: foreign investors were coming to replace the fishermen's hand-pulled nets and small motorboats with vast industrial pools. In these pools shrimp would swim so thick that the water would look like boiling soup, but away from the pools fishing nets would come up empty.

This rumor worried many—even villagers who had never heard about the new highway or new railroad plans. Those who had heard of both the shrimp farms and the highway knew the plans were connected. Why would the rich men come and build a big highway if not to take things away?

One of the people asking himself this question was Leonel Gómez, a fourth-grade teacher from the seaside village of San Francisco del Mar, or "Saint Francis of the Sea." Fishing wasn't Leonel's profession but it was his people's identity. He was one of twenty-five thousand indigenous Huave people, also known as *mareños* ("people of the sea"). He was the

**4.** Leonel Gómez Cruz visits a "rustic enclosure" for shrimp near his hometown in the Huave region of the Isthmus of Tehuantepec (2000). PHOTO BY THE AUTHOR.

grandson, son, and nephew of fishermen. The same week as the meeting held on the general store porch in Boca del Monte, in September 1999, Leonel had gone to UCIZONI to ask Carlos Beas about these rumors he'd been hearing. What was a shrimp farm? What would happen if one were built in his village? What could he do about it?

Beas told me about the conversation and we started to connect the dots. In El plan de Ochoa, the original 1996 Megaproject proposal, project number 25 of the seventy in "Phase One" was "non-intensive shrimp cultivation" in the southern part of San Francisco del Mar. Even before we could show that document to Leonel, the cloud of foreign-investor rumors had settled thickly in his village. People worried that the "non-intensive" shrimp farms they had heard about would be the stepping stones to huge, industrial-scale operations. The Huave didn't need to know about project number 25 to know that the Trans-Isthmus Megaproject was not for them. In August 1997 the Huave villages had issued a public statement that said, "All of us must unite in rejecting this Megaproject because it affects us, or sometime soon we will have neither fish nor jobs."

In the webs of global commerce, lines of cause and effect can confound. In the case of shrimp farms, however, they are startlingly simple. In the United States we eat more shrimp than any other seafood or fish. Something that was once a luxury product has become more popular than canned tuna because of a drastic price drop, made possible by intensive shrimp farming. Mother Nature offers no true bargains, however: the price has dropped for us, but others are making up the difference. Intensive aquaculture farms corral the shrimp into a much smaller space, but those artificial ponds still require the resources of a large expanse of wild mangrove. A mangrove forest provides the nutrients that the shrimp need and processes the waste they create, regardless of whether the shrimp are wild or farmed. If they are farmed, the wild population is starved. Tons of cheap shrimp in our supermarket freezer cases mean fewer tons in the nets of fisherfolk living near industrial shrimp farms. The Huaves' public statement had it precisely right: as a Natural Resources Defense Council policy expert bluntly explained it to the *New York Times*, "It's a case of some of the poorest people in the Hemisphere subsidizing the richest consumers in the world."

Wild mangrove forests make it possible to sate our taste for shrimp. On one of my early visits to San Francisco del Mar, a fisherman insisted that I visit the mangrove forest, far from where the shrimpers worked, the place that made their livelihood possible. As our canoe slid over the water, a double-breasted cormorant glided past the red mangrove trees and skimmed down to the water's surface, pulling a fish from the water. A dozen ducks flew overhead, calling their own name, *pixixi*—with the X of the Zapotec language that's pronounced *shh*. Red mangrove roots jutted from even the trees' high branches, splitting into multiple fingers that plunged down into the water. Mangrove hands held the ecosystem in place. Three different species of mangrove, black, red, and button, all grew together in San Francisco del Mar's swamp. Mesquite and wild plum grew there, too. Terrestrial and aquatic species tangled together in a wild place not quite earth and not quite sea.

Many types of mangrove trees nurse their young—some of the only trees in the world to do so. Young mangroves sprout still attached to the parent tree, already photosynthesizing and beginning to produce their own sustenance. When a new seedling reaches the size of a cigar, it drops into the water and floats for days, weeks, perhaps even a year before its embryonic root reaches into the mud and permanently anchors. There the sapling lives out the miracle that is life as a mangrove tree: pores on its aerial roots allow it to take in oxygen even though it lives in anaerobic mud. Before dropping its leaves each year it reabsorbs the nitrogen from them so it can survive in a low-nutrient environment. When the water becomes too salty it stores the excess salt in its leaves, or excretes it through special glands.

Our canoe passed below the mangrove overstory, a tangle of branches, leaves, and roots, and we wound through a path cut by fishermen. The noise of birds calling and fish leaping from the water dropped away, leaving only a fresh, clean-smelling quiet. The temperature dropped as we entered the place where shrimp spend their babyhood. No one knows how long they stay, nor the age of the trees that shelter them, because most mangroves don't have regular growth rings. Nor do we know the precise relationship between the trees and the animals, though it's clear that mangrove debris feeds the young shrimp and protects them from danger. The mangrove tangle of aerial roots—radiating out from the trees in undulating waves or half-moon humps or vertical spikes—creates a maze that confuses predatory fish hunting juvenile shrimp.

Lagoons, sandbars, and mangroves fragment the Huave people's lands. The shoreline curls around the lagoons in a shape resembling a cursive capital E lying nose-down. San Francisco del Mar is at the east end of the E. Two other Huave communities, San Mateo del Mar and Santa María del Mar, are at the west end. It takes only about an hour in a fast motorboat to travel from one end of the E to the other, but that path burns so much fuel that most locals take the terrestrial route: a six-hour trip on four different buses. In the centuries before the Spanish arrived the Huave traveled so infrequently between San Francisco del Mar and San Mateo del Mar that the two communities' languages, which were once a single tongue, are no longer mutually intelligible.

Shortly after I moved to Matías Romero, in June 2000, Leonel Gómez finished teaching for the school year, sent his fourth graders home for vacation, and decided to visit all the Huave villages. He wanted to find out how far the rumors of chahuixtle had spread and whether those rumors had any substance. Knowing of my interest in the shrimp farms and all things Megaproject, he invited me to join him on the tour. Leonel was so excited about the tour that he had t-shirts made for us to wear and to give to the people we met along the way. The front had a drawing of a traditional Huave dancer, feet and arms crossed as his body turned in a spin. On the back was this slogan, in Spanish: "When the last tree has died, when the last fish has been caught, then we will understand that we can't eat money."

Although Leonel had spent extensive amounts of time in the urban centers of the isthmus, as well as in Oaxaca City and Mexico City, like most Huave people he had only rarely visited the Huave villages far from his own. He barely knew the first two villages we visited together, San Mateo del Mar and Santa María del Mar. Because of this, he asked a friend from San Mateo del Mar, Maritza Ochoa, to host us and make introductions.

We arrived at her house late one morning, long after breakfast but far too early for lunch. Maritza greeted us elaborately, welcoming us into her home then seating us at a table and hurrying away. Leonel and I glanced at each other doubtfully, worried we had arrived at an inconvenient time. A few minutes later Maritza returned, carrying an enormous flat basket covered with handwoven textiles. I ran my hand over the fine geometric patterns of the cloth, perfect lines of corn plants and fish and donkeys and cows, along with names and dates commemorating baptisms and weddings. Leonel turned back a corner of textile, explaining with pride that they had been made right there in San Mateo del Mar. Maritza smiled and nodded, then asked us to eat and stepped away from the table. A plume of steam, redolent of corncakes and grilled mullet, rose from the baskets. We pulled the cakes into crunchy morsels and tore strips of salty fish from sharp bones. Once we'd eaten enough to last the day, Maritza, her father Gerardo, Leonel, and I all climbed into Leonel's car, for a tour of San Mateo's fishing grounds.

During the rainy season, fresh water flows down from the doughy green mountains at the center of the Isthmus of Tehuantepec. The water that flows south fills the Huave lagoons with brackish water, as the mountain springs blend with the brine of the Pacific Ocean. The day of our visit, in early July, the rains hadn't yet begun. The seasonal lagoon was still dry mud, checkerboarded with deep crevices. A double-layered fence of wood and wire mesh closed off the small lagoon's outlet to the much larger Laguna Superior, which connected to *el mar bravo*—the rough, wild sea. After the rains began and the lagoon filled with water, the fishermen would seine shrimp larvae, delicate as mosquitoes, from Laguna Superior, placing them inside the enclosure. With predators unable to reach them, the shrimp would grow to full size undisturbed, to be harvested late in the season.

"Rustic enclosures" like this one were a state government project. Groups of fishermen in all seven of the Huave villages had built them as a low-tech method for improving shrimp catches. Cement or wooden frames with removable screens controlled the entrance to the open water, keeping shrimp in, fish and other predators out, and water and micronutrients flowing back and forth as usual. The shrimp were raised to maturity in these enclosures and then netted by hand. The rustic enclosures were small projects, involving a small percentage of the fishermen in each village. Most preferred to wild-catch their shrimp in the churning waters where lagoon meets sea.

The basic concept of an industrial shrimp farm is the same: raise shrimp in an enclosure. The similarities end there. The rustic enclosure in Leonel's village covered nearly 1,200 acres, and the annual harvest was about 60 metric tons of shrimp. In contrast, a typical large-scale industrial shrimp farm's annual harvest is 24 to 39 tons per acre of tank. To put it in more straightforward terms: the productivity of a rustic enclosure is about one one-hundredth that of a similar-sized shrimp farm. A rustic enclosure is to a big shrimp farm as a horse-drawn cart is to an eighteen-wheel tractor-trailer.

Maritza's father, Gerardo, described how the fishing cooperative members had built the enclosure. He thought that the project had been a good idea, but aside from that he wanted to stick with traditional fishing methods. Sitting in a shadeless spot near San Mateo del Mar's enclosure, the brim of Gerardo's straw hat cast a pattern of tiny dots across his lean face. As he spoke his eyes passed slowly over the dry mud and across the blanched sky, while Leonel, Maritza, and I listened. The rustic enclosures probably didn't damage the *madre tierra*, Gerardo figured, but with a shrimp farm, who knew how mother earth would be affected? For that reason he didn't like the idea of the farms. If they didn't know the ecological cost, he was unwilling to agree to them.

I asked Gerardo what the local fishermen's cooperative, whose members had built the rustic enclosure, thought about the results of their project. Would they do it again? Gerardo wasn't sure; he wasn't a member of the cooperative. He didn't like other people telling him where and when he could fish.

Maritza set her mouth in a firm line and tugged on the visor of her baseball cap. She stayed quiet as her father narrated his long complaints about the cooperative, explaining his desire to work only for himself. Finally she spoke. Her thick black ponytail bobbed as she shook her head in disagreement with her father's decision to go it alone as a fisherman.

"The struggle is important," she said. "We have to be united and work together, or nothing will change."

Gerardo smiled and shrugged; the father-daughter conflict seemed familiar to both of them.

"The struggle," *la lucha*, is a general-purpose term. Organizing cooperatives, opposing new highways, and fighting industrial shrimp farms are all part of it. In poor communities like San Mateo del Mar, keeping a family fed and healthy is part of la lucha, too. Resisting the pressure to move to the city for work—and break up the family in the process—required constant vigilance. "The struggle" involved looking both inward and outward. At times la lucha seemed to represent almost opposite impulses, a sort of rowing in both directions: people want to keep cultural tradition alive *and* watch television; they want the familiarity of fishing or farming *and* the money of city jobs. Istmeños managed to do all these things, to somehow choose *all of the above*. Leonel exemplified this quality. Fiercely committed to his village, he founded a youth group in San Francisco del Mar to resurrect the songs and dances that had been performed in his village since long before the conquest. At the same time, he was perhaps the first person in his village to have an Internet Hotmail account, and against the wishes of his in-laws he had named his toddler son after Mahatma Gandhi, one of his heroes. The melding of the provincial and the cosmopolitan was what had first attracted me to the Isthmus of Tehuantepec. Still, in villages like San Mateo and San Francisco del Mar, pressure came from all directions, which meant people had to push back in all directions.

We left San Mateo's rustic enclosure to make the half-hour trip to Santa María del Mar, another Huave village, that also had a rustic enclosure. The process of visiting that site, because we weren't from Santa María, was complex. Around 3:00 in the afternoon, lunchtime, Leonel, Maritza, Gerardo, and I sat at a rough-hewn picnic table at the home of one of Maritza's friends, Rosalía. She served us *huevos ahogados* ("drowned eggs") scrambled and drenched in a mild tomato sauce. The warmth of Maritza's breakfast still filled our bellies, but sharing this second meal was the first step in seeking approval to visit the enclosure and Santa María's fishing grounds.

After we scooped up the last of the tomato sauce with the last of the tortillas, Rosalia passed around a tin bucket filled with small, hard apples—a rare and expensive gift. This extravagant gesture of welcome hinted that Maritza and Rosalía had planned our visit long in advance. Rosalia tucked the bucket under her arm, keeping it away from the puppy that nipped at her heels. She sat down at the head of the table to talk to us about Candelilla, her village's fishing grounds, named for the catkins that grow there.

The Candelilla lagoon lay north of the village, toward the small islands where the traditional Huave gods and goddesses lived. "It's a sacred place, you know," she said, swatting gently at the puppy. That was all she said, but we knew what she meant: We would have to ask permission from the fishermen's cooperative before we could visit. At this news, Gerardo lost interest and wandered off to the neighborhood bar. Leonel excused himself to find the leaders of the cooperative, called Fuerza del Pueblo. Names like "People Power Cooperative" aren't quaint or anachronistic, but simply an expression of how things work in villages like Santa María. An hour later, Leonel returned with a fisherman who had volunteered to take us to Candelilla.

Once we reached the water's edge, we realized there was one more step in the permission process: talking to the soldiers stationed in a hut on Santa María's beach. No one liked the irony of approaching the young men wearing green fatigues: Maritza, Leonel, and the Santa María fisherman had to ask representatives of the Mexican federal government for permission to visit fishing grounds that had belonged to the Huave people since long before that government had existed. In theory the soldiers were stationed at the beachfront to watch for Central American migrants. Their desperate efforts to reach the United States occasionally ended with their small boats shipwrecked on Huave beaches. Many Huaves thought the soldiers also watched the local residents a little too closely. And they felt empathy for the migrants who were, like they themselves, just poor people trying to provide for their families.

The soldiers approved our trip with silent nods, not even looking up from their card game. We piled into one of the cooperative's weathered boats, Maritza and I sharing a fiberglass bench.

"Open your hand," she said, reaching over and dropping several wave-polished auger shells into my palm. "We use these shells a lot in school, to teach the children how to count," she said. "And Rosalía makes them into curtains."

I nodded at Maritza, finally understanding she was not only a fisherman's daughter—the role she'd played that day—but also a schoolteacher. Maritza explained that she had worked her first three years at a preschool in San Francisco del Mar, Leonel's village; that was how they had met. A wailing motor pushed us over clear water toward a film of white land, drowning out our conversation. The distant strip of beach took shape as we approached.

The four of us splashed from boat to shore and headed for the Candelilla lagoon. During the rainy season the three-year-old rustic enclosure encompassed more than 150 acres of water. It shrank to a small pool in the dry season. There was one difference between this enclosure and all the others Leonel and I would see on our seven-day tour of the Huave region: solid wood sluice gates, rather than mesh, separated the small lagoon from the open water. The gates cut the pool off from the tide. A few tiny fish darted through the stagnant pond, and clouds of insects hung above. Shiny white wooden knobs, dead mangrove roots, protruded from the mud; dry branches leaned at awkward angles. The sun, softening toward sunset, illuminated a near-sterile expanse. The mangrove forest was dead. Away from the enclosure, blue-green thickets of healthy mangrove still trembled with life, the murmur and whir of birds, bees, butterflies, and beetles filling the branches.

I wandered through the labyrinth of bleached wood, crouching to trail my fingers though the water. It was far too warm. What had happened here? Leonel's and Maritza's faces mirrored my shock and confusion. We turned back toward the boat as dusk's quiet settled over the beach. I fell into step with Maritza but we didn't speak. In our sad silence I noticed the sound underfoot for the first time. It wasn't the swish of sand, but a faint squeaking and crunching: the entire beach was composed not of sand or pebbles, but tiny shells, called *tej* by people in San Mateo. I knelt down and picked up handfuls of them, peach, tan, and white cones, some no larger than pencil tips, and fingernail-sized saucers of blue and pink. How many millions of tej did it take to create an entire beach? Maritza knelt beside me, the sadness gone from her eyes. I thought of the fecundity of this place—so rich that the beaches were made of intact shells. Rosalía was right: it was a sacred place, but it was also wounded.

None of the other rustic enclosures Leonel and I visited showed the damage that Candelilla did. Every chance I had, I asked about it. *Why was Candelilla's mangrove dying?* Each person I talked to—several government officials, a consultant to the local fishermen's cooperatives, a biologist, and a few local fishermen—had a different answer: it was a normal die-off for that particular species of mangrove; there had been too much rain the last couple of years; there had been too little rain; local people had cut too much mangrove for firewood.

None of the answers seemed quite right; no one I asked seemed particularly concerned. The fisherman who had taken us to Candelilla had the only answer that made sense: the rustic enclosure itself had killed the mangroves because the solid wooden gates halted the water's flow. The other people I asked, the ones considered the experts, denied this was possible, but none of them had actually visited Candelilla recently.

In some ways mangroves are breathtakingly hardy, thriving in the improbable habitat of variably salty, wave-battered, oxygen-deprived mud. Mangrove forests survive hurricanes, raw sewage dumping, and all manner of ecological insults. Yet they are exceedingly fragile: a change in the size of the mud particles, or in the gases dissolved in the water that inundates their roots, or in the tides, salt concentration, or amount of freshwater runoff can be deadly. Mangroves are miracle trees, often surviving at the very edge of their ecological tolerances, which means that a slight change can kill them.

A few days after our visit to Candelilla, the image of dead mangroves appeared again, this time on a television screen.

The sterile white knobs that were once flourishing trees, appeared in a documentary called *Shrimp Fever*. Leonel had organized a showing of the video in Pueblo Viejo, San Francisco del Mar's "old town." He chose as a screening venue the only public space in the village: a combination bar–*tortillería*–video room. Only in the smallest villages are tortillas made, beer sold, and videos shown all in the same place. Though more than six thousand people live in San Francisco del Mar, only about five hundred of them live in what was once the town center, Pueblo Viejo. In the early 1970s, shifting sand dunes and erosion buried much of the village. Most of the residents moved inland, founding Pueblo Nuevo. In the new town some of the streets are paved and many of the houses have cement walls and floors. In Pueblo Viejo most houses are built of wood and palm fronds, while the floors and roads are sand.

Pueblo Viejo and Pueblo Nuevo were separated by a ribbon of water and connected by a rope. For a twenty-peso fare, one of the fishing boats would load the people, bananas, tamales, and whatever else needed to get to Pueblo Viejo. A fisherman would then lift the rope, rotting and hung with seaweed, and pull, hand over hand, tugging the boat across the shallow channel between the old and new towns. The short distance could have been easily spanned by a bridge, had there been the money and equipment to build one. Once across the channel, it was a half-hour walk around a small mountain to Pueblo Viejo.

The shrimp farm mentioned in El plan de Ochoa, project number 25 out of 170, was slated for the lagoon where Pueblo Viejo's fishermen threw their nets. In the days between our visit to Candelilla and our visit to Pueblo Viejo, the wet season had blown in with the furious *ncherrec*, the winds from the south. Rain barraged the corrugated metal roof of the bar–tortillería–video room. With no chance of seeing the fishing grounds during such a downpour, I stayed to watch the video. Leonel and I had arrived hours before the planned showing so that he could do the advance work. Several times that morning, the proprietor of the bar read a short script that Leonel had carefully lettered on a scrap of paper: "A video about shrimp, of interest to fishermen, will be shown at noon." The words boomed out to the village from a megaphone on the roof.

Leonel fiddled with his keys, an empty cup, the videocassette case, his high cowlick. His uncalloused hands worked endlessly, trying to avoid lighting up another cigarette. His eyes skipped around the room's dim jumble. What if no one showed up? What would people say about him: a young man who wasn't even a fisherman, an upstart from Pueblo Nuevo who had come with a gringo video, and a gringa visitor, to challenge what the government was telling them to do? Leonel's grandfather had founded the first fishing cooperative in Pueblo Viejo, but that had been a very long time ago. The hour hand on my watch ticked past the twelve, then inched toward one in the afternoon. Leonel and I didn't discuss it, but I could see his anxiety growing with each minute.

The previous night, Leonel had spent several hours with two of his brothers and two cousins, trying to connect two VCRs so he could make a copy of the video to leave in Pueblo Viejo. I watched the five young men braid and unbraid several long cables, hooking and unhooking, debating and testing. "How many Huave men does it take . . ." I said, laughing.

One of Leonel's cousins, Ismael, interrupted me, shaking his finger. "Excuse me, but no, that's racist." He turned away from the electronic commotion to face me, smiling, hands on his hips. "I have a joke for you. How many gringos does it take to change a light bulb?"

I had no idea.

"Ten. One to screw in the light bulb, and nine to watch everything he does and write it all down."

Four heads swiveled in my direction, the technical troubles momentarily forgotten. I burst out laughing; the joke was perfect. Through all the days that Leonel and I had toured the Huave villages, I had been following them around, watching and taking notes, doing nothing useful. Like almost everything Leonel attempted, no matter how ambitious or implausible, the video duplication eventually worked.

The Pueblo Viejo fishermen began to gather in the bar just after 1:00 in the afternoon. They arrived precisely on time, just not by my watch. In the mid-1990s, as part of the northward-looking trend that accompanied NAFTA, Mexico adopted Daylight Savings Time. At least the cities did. Villages tended not to spring forward and fall back, preferring instead to talk about *hora de Dios*—God's time—and *hora de Zedillo*—the Daylight Savings Time that had been decreed by President Zedillo.

Eight men took their seats while Leonel relaxed and fed the cassette into the machine. A few minutes into the video, a landscape of dead mangroves, much like Candelilla, flashed on the screen. This time the devastation was in Ecuador, where the hemisphere's tallest mangroves had once grown. The video panned across the view of white wood and leafless branches while the narrator explained an industrial shrimp farm's life cycle.

First, the palm trees, mangroves, and mesquite are chopped, plowed, or burned away. Many fishermen lose their jobs, replaced by a much smaller number of specially trained workers. Large pumps siphon fresh water from rivers and brackish water from lagoons, pouring it into artificial ponds near shore. Workers seed the tanks with larval shrimp from hatcheries, then add artificial nutrients, fertilizers to encourage the growth of phytoplankton, and antibiotics to suppress diseases. Pipes carry a stream of these ingredients, mixed with shrimp excrement, away from the tanks and into the lagoons. The shrimp are raised to maturity in the tanks, and then harvested with nets or by draining the ponds. Trucks arrive on freshly paved roads and carry away the harvest for export.

The documentary narration continued: "The production of a shrimp farm falls over time. Eventually, the farms are abandoned." The abandoned operation becomes the coastal equivalent of a desert: treeless shoreline, salinated wetlands, polluted water. The video went on to describe how mangrove forests act as the oceans' nurseries, with each acre of mangrove producing more than 30 tons of seafood each year. Since 1980 one-fifth of all the mangroves in the world have been destroyed. An estimated 8.8 million acres of mangrove forests have been bulldozed, burned, chopped down, or poisoned by pollution.

Leonel clicked off the television as the credits rolled. "I'm not saying *don't do this*," he told the fishermen gathered in the room. "I'm saying, *this is what a shrimp farm is*." He passed around a few copies of material that I'd found on a Oaxaca state-government website. The information explained that changes to the Mexican Constitution (which were required for Mexico to sign the North American Free Trade Agreement) made it much easier for foreigners to make "private co-investments" with local communities and own up to 100 percent of shrimp farm operations.

Some of the men read the sheets of paper that circulated around the room; others just glanced at them politely. Literacy was still something of a specialized skill among the Pueblo Viejo fishermen. After Leonel finished explaining the information from the website, there was a long pause as everyone turned over the details in their minds. One of the fishermen broke the silence to say that movie had reminded him of something that had happened a while back. A businessman from Ecuador had come to visit Pueblo Viejo. He'd promised them bridges and roads in exchange for permission to build a shrimp farm. It was a compelling prospect for the fishermen: the trip to Pueblo Nuevo would no longer take hours. But they wondered: What would the cost be to them? To their lagoon?

At the mention of their lagoon, the oldest man in the room stood up slowly. "It's a damn good place for a hatchery." His words opened up the conversation, though it was unclear from his tone whether he thought the shrimp farm was a good idea or if he were merely stating a fact. Someone purchased two large bottles of beer and passed them around. Each fisherman sipped politely; Leonel and I declined. A young man said, "Right now, what we have isn't affecting our resources. It's natural." A golden pendant, in the shape of a shrimp, glinted at his throat. "But if we put in chemicals, who knows?"

Leonel told a story about San Blas, a town in northern Mexico where foreign investors had built an industrial chemical-intensive shrimp farm. "They used to have 2,000 hectares of mangroves there, but 1,500 of them have been destroyed." Leonel had seen it himself while on a trip paid for by the Greenpeace office in Mexico City.

The man wearing the golden shrimp was worried that the government scientists who came to help them might already be putting chemicals in their rustic enclosure. Though his worry was almost surely unfounded, it brought up an important point: How would they know? Still, it could be worse. "The important thing is that foreigners don't come and take our natural resources."

After we left Pueblo Viejo, I asked Leonel what he envisioned instead of a shrimp-farm future for the Huave region. He said quickly, "I think the way we are living is good." Leonel's family *was* living quite well, better than most in his village. His parents bought shrimp from many local fishermen and then paid people by the hour to shell, boil, and bag the catch. They trucked it all to Juchitán, the market capital of the isthmus, or sometimes even to Mexico City. Thanks in part to the family business, Leonel had graduated from college and one of his brothers was a college student. None of the six siblings in Leonel's family was a fisherman.

Leonel and I talked about the future of fishing villages all over the world, about the worldwide loss of coastal mangrove forests. The tropical buffer between land and sea had been slashed into shreds. "That affects the lives of millions of people," I said.

Leonel shook his head dismissively; it couldn't possibly be that many. His village didn't even have ten thousand people; all of the Isthmus of Tehuantepec—most of them living far from the coast—held only two million.

"Leonel, do you know how many people there are in the world?"

He shrugged his shoulders; he had no idea. When I told him, he stared at me.

"No, Wendy, that can't be. Are you sure you mean *billions*? Not hundreds of millions?"

I nodded. The disbelief in his eyes darkened into fear.

"All those people . . ." he said, his voice fading. He paused and looked away, then turned back to meet my eyes, telegraphing his fear. "How can the planet ever support all of them?"

A few days after the video showing, I visited Boca Barra, the most important fishing grounds of the entire Huave region and the ecological engine of an economy that supported twenty-five thousand people. The Boca Barra's name translates, unmusically, as "barrier mouth." It is the sand spit dividing the Huave lagoons from the Pacific Ocean. Román Cruz, Leonel's uncle, was my host.

Leonel said of Román, "My uncle has been a fisherman, a tractor farmer, a mechanic, a businessman, and a carpenter. In a way, he's still all those things." His uncle had carved and hung all the interior doors in Leonel's house. The doors had impressed me, not just for the beautifully worked hardwood but for their very existence. Usually, bedsheets or woven textiles flapped between rooms. Leonel's was the first isthmus house I visited with interior doors.

Early one afternoon Román and I jostled down a dirt road toward the boat launch. Román told me he'd become a fisherman just a decade earlier. "Eight of those years, it was just enough to feed my family. For two years it's been enough to do more, like buy this truck." His right hand shifted grumbling gears. I watched gravel and rock speed by a foot below, through a large hole around the gearbox.

We arrived at the beach and loaded Román's motorboat, *Lila*, with coolers, plastic tubs of dry food, an anchor, and a dozen watermelons to sell. Román, his twelve-year-old daughter, Liliana, and I pushed off with Román guiding *Lila* through the shallow inlet toward the main lagoon. Tiny waves slapped the boat's scuffed sides; the afternoon heat melted into a gentle rush of spray.

The *Lila* entered the lagoon and the waves grew, curling over the gunwales. I turned away from the oncoming swells as the water hit me, buckets of pebbles tossed at my back. The skin over my knuckles turned translucent as I clamped the edge of the bench; the water's force nearly pushed me off the fiberglass seat. Román stood, bracing himself against the gleaming outboard motor facing the oncoming wind and waves. After each layer of salty water soaked him, he cleared his eyes with a jerk of his neck. The thin pink shirt knotted around his waist and cut-off pants clung to his lightly muscled frame. He smiled broadly as we sped away from the blistering land toward the Boca Barra, the sand spit that creased the horizon.

More than an hour after leaving the village center we reached Román's fishing *ranchito*, a home away from home. Three fishermen who worked with Román had already arrived. The hut was a perfect response to its environment: a high peaked roof of woven palm fronds reduced the heat while the frame of smoothed tree trunks guarded against the wind. A sack of several hundred totopos and a circle of netting holding tomatoes, onions, and chiles hung from the ceiling. The ropes that suspended the sack and netting ran through inverted plastic bottles, baffles to deter the mice. Only the cooking pit, a cardboard box for the nesting hens, a few coolers, a plastic table, and two folding chairs touched the ground.

As afternoon dissolved into evening Román stood in his improvised kitchen: a rusting refrigerator carcass turned on its side in front of the hut. He gutted fish and dropped them into a cast-iron pan encrusted with years of fish dinners. Román's large hands scaled and filleted as his eyes scanned the lagoon. He felt the wind and temperature of a good night's catch, while I felt only a hint of cooling and a welcome breeze. He handed the heaping pan to Liliana. "You're the woman here, so you have to cook," he told her.

I never had to cook. On visits to villages I often was seated at a table with only men while the other women waited in the kitchen. Was this because I was a guest? Or because I was more foreigner than female? Whenever I left my home in Matías Romero, I was unfailingly attended to, cared for, and honored far beyond what anyone had good reason to think I merited. I often wondered about my istmeño hosts' and neighbors' unvarnished opinions of me. I could not catch a fish, plant a cornfield, or even make an edible tortilla. I tripped often on uneven ground, turned bright red after just moments in the sun, sweated copiously, and couldn't squat without wobbling. I needed translation whenever the conversation wasn't in Spanish and asked the most dumbfoundingly ignorant questions. My most useful skills were driving (something few women could do) and taking photos of everyone's children with my huge camera (something few could afford). But cook? Never.

Liliana heaved the pan over the firepit coals and poked at the frying fish. The three men who worked with Román prepared for the night; Román settled into a chair and motioned for me to do the same. "My job as a fisherman is better than an office job," he told me. "I usually only sleep about six hours a night, but I sleep when I want."

"And you pee when you want," one of the men said. Everyone laughed. "That's important!" he insisted.

Román told only half the truth about his schedule. He could fish or not, as he chose, but he didn't set his own hours. The starting time and length of the Huave fishermen's workday (or, more accurately, night) changed with the season and phase of the moon. Those things controlled the shrimp's migration and that migration controlled Román's work schedule.

The men talked about what else they might do for work if they stopped fishing. This was not an idle consideration; like fisheries worldwide, the Huave lagoons were in danger. The conversation turned to human migration, as it often did. "It's better to drown here than to die in the desert up there," Román said.

His words reminded me of something he had said on the day I'd met him nine months earlier. By happenstance, I had arrived in San Francisco del Mar only a few days after the bodies of seventeen drowning victims had washed ashore there. The group of Salvadorans and Guatemalans had died on their secret journey to the United States, their tiny boat capsizing just offshore. As soon as I arrived, people asked if I had come to write about the Central Americans. I replied, not yet knowing about the tragedy, that I had come to write about shrimp farms. On hearing that, Román had thrown me a piercing look and said, "If they are going to put a shrimp farm here, they might as well kill us. That would be better than starving to death slowly."

While Román kept up the conversation, one of the men smoothed a hatchet blade over a sharpening stone. Another poured kerosene from a plastic soda bottle into lanterns made from tin cans and twisted wire. A third mended a fishing net suspended from one of the roof beams. He pulled fishing line from a long bobbin and wrapped it around a large wooden needle. Each knot he tightened added a penny-sized piece of netting. The net, imported from Brazil, had a nine-foot radius. Most Huave fishermen no longer wove their own nets; it was cheaper to buy them ready-made and repair them as they aged.

The much larger rectangular nets used at the Boca Barra were once handmade, too. Weaving one, which would last about six years, required a year of a fisherman's spare time. The machine-made version, imported from Japan, cost only about a thousand pesos, or a little over one hundred dollars. "Imagine!" Román said, as his eyes followed the flat, wide needle pulling loops into the mesh. Amazement and disgust mingled in his voice. "One thousand pesos for a whole year of your life!" How absurd that so much work could be replaced with so little money.

Román understood the strange and increasingly improbable economy of Boca Barra fishing—an activity that held little allure for many of his village's younger generation. "Several times family members have gone out fishing with me," Román said, referring to his nieces and nephews, including Leonel. "They all got professional jobs afterward." A "professional job" included anything that didn't involve putting one's hands into soil or water. Elementary school teacher, office worker, taxi driver, and mechanic all counted. Román and Leonel came from one of San Francisco del Mar's most prosperous families. While the younger members of more affluent families had abandoned fishing, many poorer people in the region had taken it up, desperate to find a way to feed their families.

Those poorer fisherfolk didn't have motorboats or fishing huts or outboard motors like Román's, but they did have one thousand years of Huave tradition. They stand thigh-deep in protected coves with a large wicker basket tied to the waist. Their fishing looks like a series of whirling circles. The fisherman turns his body to one side and then twists back quickly, releasing his circular net as a magician releases a spell. The net extends with a shimmer of droplets and then settles, full circle, in the water. He waits a few seconds and then gathers soft pleats of net, winding it around a clenched fist. The net quivers with the final struggle of the small fish inside it. He pushes his hand into each pleat to release the catch into the round mouth of the waiting basket.

It was not a livelihood that everyone in San Francisco del Mar aspired to secure. Probably one in four village teens left home in search of work. Teenaged boys with hardly anything to invest in a profession could either buy a net and start fishing or buy a bus ticket to a city in which a relative lived. The entry cost for either career path was about the same. If you fished by hand you would never get ahead. If you bought the bus ticket you might be able to earn and save enough money to buy that outboard motor. Román had done the latter. For ten years he worked in a restaurant in a petroleum boomtown on the Veracruz side of the isthmus. He returned to San Francisco del Mar in 1985, at the age of twenty-eight, married to a *veracruzana*, to farm his family's land. But then melon fever destroyed the town's primary cash crop. For three seasons in a row all the melons rotted on the vine. After that, like many other San Franciscan farmers, Román turned to the traditional Huave industry.

No one knows exactly how long the Huave have pulled shrimp, fish, and crabs from the Pacific waters of the Isthmus of Tehuantepec. We know only that they came here from elsewhere, probably somewhere in South America, by navigating the ocean waters by canoe. The Mixe were already here when the Huave arrived; the Zapotecs arrived much later, a little over six hundred years ago. The Zapotecs, currently the largest ethnic group of the isthmus, founded their cities—Juchitán and Tehuantepec—on what had been Huave land.

The Huave had been fishing the Pacific lagoons for more than a millennium—perhaps far longer—but it was not clear how much longer that way of life could continue. The possibility of a shrimp farm was not the only concern. Because of concerns about overfishing, the state government had outlawed the long rectangular nets that Román and the other fishermen used. Placed at the lagoon's mouth, the nets prevented young shrimp and other marine species from reaching the mangroves, where they reproduced. Román believed this practice was the only way for them to catch enough to make a living. The practice worried state fishing authorities. How much longer could that sort of fishing continue before the shrimp population collapsed? I talked to several government officials about this worrisome question. The one who seemed the most credible and serious about his job (he was fired a few months after I met him) told me that three things threatened the Huave shrimpers' livelihood: global climate change, the use of illegal nets, and big fishing boats coming from northern Mexico. Román shrugged off the illegality of his nets with a sneer and a guffaw. He figured that the Huave had been harvesting isthmus waters since long before the Spaniards arrived on Mexico's shores. Why should he pay attention to some mestizo government's regulation? Anyway, if the officials were worried about overfishing, the small-scale fishing methods used by Boca Barra fishermen hadn't created that problem. Why should it be their responsibility to resolve it? Could you really trust a government that wanted to solve problems by creating even bigger problems: industrial shrimp farms? Román finished his speech about government intervention and leaned toward me, looking at my notebook. He nodded toward it. "You aren't going to betray us, are you? You aren't going to say that everything here is perfect, are you?"

An hour before dusk, Román Cruz and another fisherman loaded their shrimping nets into the *Lila*. The black mesh nets, each seven feet high and perhaps a dozen yards long, nearly filled the boat's belly. I climbed into the boat and squatted on the soft netting. We motored to the churning channel where the Laguna Inferior and Pacific Ocean meet, between the Boca Barra's twin sandbars. Two other fishermen stood in the shallow water at the ocean's mouth. One of them had made a point of telling me that he, like many fishermen, could not swim. I thought of his words as the men struggled against the relentless current: "I can just float on my back a little." One of the men wore only shorts; the other, a t-shirt and underwear. The less they wore, the less energy they exerted and the lower the risk of being dragged out to sea. They wrestled with the nets' wooden poles, forcing them into the shifting sand. Despite the brute force required for this work, the image of the single fisherman casting a whirling net into the water persists in the local vocabulary. Even fishing with the large nets that are anchored in the sand for hours is referred to as *tirando*, or "throwing."

Standing in the boat, Román bellowed a stream of friendly instructions at the two men. The sky faded from pale salmon to blue-gray. Darkness settled as the *Lila* hummed through a thicket of nets, back to Román's hut. Wooden poles, which held the nets in place, periscoped above the ink of the nighttime water. Strings of brown pelicans and snowy egrets glided above, joining the fishermen in the catch. Tin-can kerosene lamps winked from poles and boats. The bobbing lanterns momentarily lit faces grimacing, arms dropping nets into water, shoulders pushing poles into place, fingers pointing, backs straining. The water glowed yellow where the nets, poles, and oars cut the surface. Overhead the stars hung close, as if mirroring the sea of lanterns.

After returning to the ranchito, Román and the others ate a quick dinner of pan-fried fish, baked corn totopos, and Coca-Cola, then returned to the open water to pull in the catch and throw their nets once again. The moon rose, two-thirds of a pink-tinged orb. Far-off lightning flashed across the clouded sky. Shortly before midnight the men returned to the hut. They tumbled into hammocks to sleep as their nets filled again; they had four hours until the next time they needed to attend to them.

As they worked, I slept, suspended by the hammock's mesh, on a lick of sand only a few dozen yards wide. Only an occasional crowing rooster or sputtering outboard motor cut the deep silence, rousing me slightly. Surrounded by air and water, I had never felt safer. It was hard to imagine that anything threatened the peace of this place; it all seemed too far away to matter. Román's pointed questions suddenly rose to mind. He had known that this would be my reaction to the Boca Barra: it would make me forget all the worries moored just offshore.

Later, pinpricks of lanterns and flashlights pierced the chalky dawn: the first boats returning with the catch. I left my hammock and slid down the sandy incline to the shore. The sky shone palest blue, the water a few shades deeper and cut with foamless deep-green waves. The fishermen, some wearing yellow rain slickers against the morning chill, pulled ropes and nets from their boats. Chickens ran along the shore, pecking at the seaweed swaying from the ropes. Glossy shrimp in shades of blue and coral filled every boat's belly.

I climbed aboard the *Lila* and Román motored us back to the beach, where the road from San Francisco del Mar ended. Each boat held 75 to 90 pounds of shrimp: four men's labor for the night. They scooped the catch into crates, then lugged the crates to the scales. A small portion of a regular night's catch was the prized giant tropical shrimp, each one selling for 50 cents. Román remembered that just a few years earlier those shrimp had been much bigger. Before overfishing had become such a problem, they sometimes weighed three-quarters of a pound each. Buyers came from Juchitán or from Chiapas, paying about $2.50 per pound for the catch. Within two years of that visit to the Boca Barra, the price had fallen by two-thirds.

When Román had started working at the Boca Barra ten years earlier, he was one of just a few fishermen there. Since then, fishing ranchitos had filled both of the sandbars that divided the lagoon from the open ocean. One of them belonged to

Francisco Toledo, whom I had met on my first visit to San Francisco del Mar. On that visit I'd watched Francisco unload his boat after the night's fishing. While the other shrimpers talked and joked quietly, he was exuberant. He pulled the crabs and fish from hundreds of shrimp in his boat's hull, laughing as the crabs spun their useless pincers and the fish flopped desperately. He threw them not to the waiting dogs and pelicans but away from the shore, back to life.

He grabbed a half-dozen of the largest shrimp, each more than six inches long, and offered them to me. He held them by their antennae, as if they were bunches of carrots, and pushed them into my cupped hands. The shrimp flexed their cool, slippery bodies, nearly wriggling from my grasp. It was like trying to hold a bit of the sea in my hands.

"Muchísimas gracias, señor. ¿Cómo se llama Usted?" I said.

"Francisco Toledo," he said, tilting his head in a hint of a bow. The name he gave was that of Mexico's most famous living painter, an istmeño Zapotec from the city of Juchitán.

I laughed, assuming he was kidding, testing my knowledge of the isthmus. "Ah, you are a famous painter."

"I am a pescador," he said, with no hint of irony in his voice. The word *pescador* is used rather loosely in Spanish to mean fisherman, crabber, lobsterman, or shrimper.

When I visited Francisco Toledo at his Boca Barra ranchito I learned more about his profession as a pescador. Francisco had been a water man his whole life. Some of that time he'd worked for others, as in the early 1970s when he fished on the shark boats that came down from the north. For most of his career, he had worked for himself. Like Román, he had done unusually well.

"Fishing is beautiful," Francisco said to me as we sat in the shade of his ranchito drinking orange Fanta and talking about the future. "But the government keeps a really watchful eye on us." His voice trailed off. On that point Francisco and Román agreed, but their agreement ended there. Román wanted to continue fishing as he always had, using small motorboats, hand-thrown nets, and regional markets. Francisco thought that San Francisco del Mar should look toward a bigger, wider future. He was the leader of a small group of local fishermen that favored building a shrimp farm.

The previous month, a union closely affiliated with the PRI—the party that had ruled Mexico from the 1920s to 2000 and still controlled the Oaxaca state government—had taken Francisco and many other Huave fishermen to visit industrial shrimp farms in the northern state of Sonora. After seeing those operations Francisco decided that a similar project would be a good thing for his community. Dozens of istmeño fishermen went on those government-sponsored shrimp-farm tours, taking the thirty-five-hour trip to and from Mexico's northern Pacific coast. Many of them returned with shrimp-farm dreams matching Francisco Toledo's.

The shrimp farms that Francisco had visited were huge; a single tank might cover several thousand acres. Francisco imagined something smaller for San Francisco del Mar: a tank of perhaps 700 acres, built far from the mangroves. "We aren't going to destroy any trees," he said with confidence. The place he had in mind was a bare, sandy stretch several miles east of the Boca Barra. "There aren't any trees there. It's a de-sieeeer-to!"

"So, why a shrimp farm, don Francisco?" I asked.

"The shrimp farm would be a way for the community to work together," he said. An oft-repeated Huave saying goes: *May the resources of the few benefit the many*. "Our dream is that we won't have to bring people from outside to work there. If outsiders come, that means exploitation."

Francisco estimated that a 700-acre shrimp farm would employ around three hundred people. Interestingly, this was almost exactly the same number of employees (308) listed for project number 25 in the Ochoa plan, a document that Francisco Toledo knew nothing about.

"Building the shrimp farm will be hard work, but we can do it. It's a beautiful thing, having the desire to work together. That's our dream. Ojalá, someday it will be a reality," he said, using a common Spanish expression that was once Arabic: *Inshallah*, "God willing."

Francisco wanted the shrimp farm "for the children's sake." He hoped some of his kids might work there. One of them had finished college and the other three were on their way there, if he had anything to say about it.

"So, none of your children will be fishermen?"

"Well, at the shrimp farms all the workers are educated." He spoke as if the shrimp farm were a foregone conclusion. "It takes special training to know how to make so many shrimp grow in such a small place, to know how much nutrients to add to the water, and when to add them."

"What will you do with the wastes from the tanks?"

His eyes darkened with confusion. "Wastes? They didn't say there would be any wastes when we were in Sonora." He had seen the pipes that fed water into the tanks. "They were huge, thirty inches across!" He used the U.S. measurement, not the Mexican one. But he hadn't noticed any effluent pipes.

As he described what he had seen and not seen in Sonora, my heart sank. Francisco Toledo's excitement for the shrimp farm and commitment to his village were both authentic. I considered changing the subject, then plowed ahead. I explained to Francisco that the excess nutrients, the antibiotics that prevented disease, the shrimp excrement, and the oxygen-poor but nitrogen-rich water—had to be removed from the tanks or the shrimp would die. They were poured into the surrounding environment but that process could go on for only so long. Once the farm had run its course there was no going back to the old ways of fishing: the mangroves would have been cut down, starving the natural fisheries. Francisco's expression did not change as I explained the process. We were both silent for a moment, and then I asked, my voice low, "Don Francisco, what's going to happen after ten or fifteen years, when the shrimp farm reaches the end of its life cycle? When you can't use it anymore?"

Francisco repeated my question to himself. "I can't answer as if I were a biologist," he said. "It's a good question. We want to produce, not destroy. Maybe there is a way we can prevent this contamination?" He let the question blow away with the warm breeze. When he continued, sadness tinged his voice. "Yes, man came to earth to destroy." He stretched out the last syllable of the word, *des-truuuu-iiiiiir*. Huave people speak Spanish with a harmonic lilt. Things that are far away, hurt a lot, or are otherwise remarkable are drawn out with a long, high tone when described, like the last note of a sad song.

He turned the conversation to the tropical forest that rises in the mountains north of the Huave region, birthplace of the rivers that flow into the Huave lagoons. "The Chimalapas are very, very rich. But who is destroying them? *Man*. I don't want to ruin the land. We are connected to it."

The day after I talked with Francisco Toledo at his ranchito I went to the office of the State Fishing Council of Oaxaca in the city of Salina Cruz. That government agency had organized most of the Huave fishermen's trips to the northern shrimp farms. The council's name was also on the webpage that Leonel had passed around at the Pueblo Viejo video showing.

One of those pages noted that Oaxaca had "50,000 hectares of salt flats that can be used for shrimp aquaculture."

The council's director, Aziz Curioca, welcomed me into his office. I admired the photographs on the walls, images of various Huave fishing grounds and the "rustic enclosures" that many had built. "I spent the last two weeks visiting all the Huave villages and their fishing grounds," I began. He stopped me. Didn't I know how dangerous that was? I shook my head, dismissing his words. Everyone had treated me wonderfully, I said.

His stare turned from shock to guarded disbelief, as if I'd told him I'd just returned from the moon.

I described Francisco Toledo's dream to him. Curioca's vision for the Huave region was quite different. "Tanks of less than 3 acres would be more appropriate," he said. "Not even one leaf of mangrove will be touched."

"If that's the case, why are you taking them to see the farms in Sonora, which operate on a completely different scale?"

"Well, the purpose of the trips is to show the Huave fishermen that their current system is better."

I swallowed a smile. Most of the schools, medical clinics, and roads in the rural isthmus had been built only after local residents had insisted on them. Mixe villagers from Boca del Monte had marched all the way to Mexico City to get a small clinic built. Did they really need to be told what was best for their villages?

He went on, describing the differences between rustic, semi-intensive, and intensive shrimp farms, and concluded, "You have to teach a child to crawl first, then to walk, and finally to run."

"So, why don't you tell the fishermen who go on the tours to Sonora about the wastes from the shrimp farm tanks?"

He sat silently.

I waited.

He said finally, "You can't give a high-school textbook to a six-year-old child because he isn't going to understand it."

Curioca agreed with me that industrial shrimp farms equaled "total destruction" of the ecosystem. He knew that the Mexican government needed private investment, even for small projects, but he was worried. "Investors don't think long term."

"But don't *you* have to think long term?" I asked. "How are the Huave going to earn a living after the shrimp farms have outlived their usefulness?"

Aziz Curioca leaned across his wide hardwood desk toward me. His voice dropped to just above a whisper. "I'll tell you a secret. I'm not looking forward to the day when shrimp farms arrive here."

# 4

## A Village of Sand

I hadn't moved to the Isthmus of Tehuantepec to learn about education, but I came to realize that I wouldn't understand much else until I did. How istmeños educate their children linked to everything that I wanted to explore: how local buying and selling intersected with global buying and selling and speculation; how istmeños felt about the Trans-Isthmus Megaproject; and how they kept their villages and their landscapes intact, while so many forces pulled them apart.

A few months after Maritza Ochoa, Leonel Gómez, and I wandered the dead mangrove forest at Candelilla, I visited Maritza again, this time in her preschool classroom. I arrived just as class was beginning for the day and wedged myself into a four-year-old-sized chair in a corner of the classroom, nearly eye-level with Maritza's students.

Maritza stood at the front of the room, clapping her hands and calling the class to order. "Ndek müm!" she said to the girls, and then "Ndek teat!" to the boys. Then, to all: "¡Buenos días!" In ragged unison they called back, "¡Buenos días, maestra!" The children's sandals scuffed the cement floor as they swung their legs under the table. Maritza spread her arms wide in a gesture of welcoming. Her thick hair was pulled straight back from her wide forehead

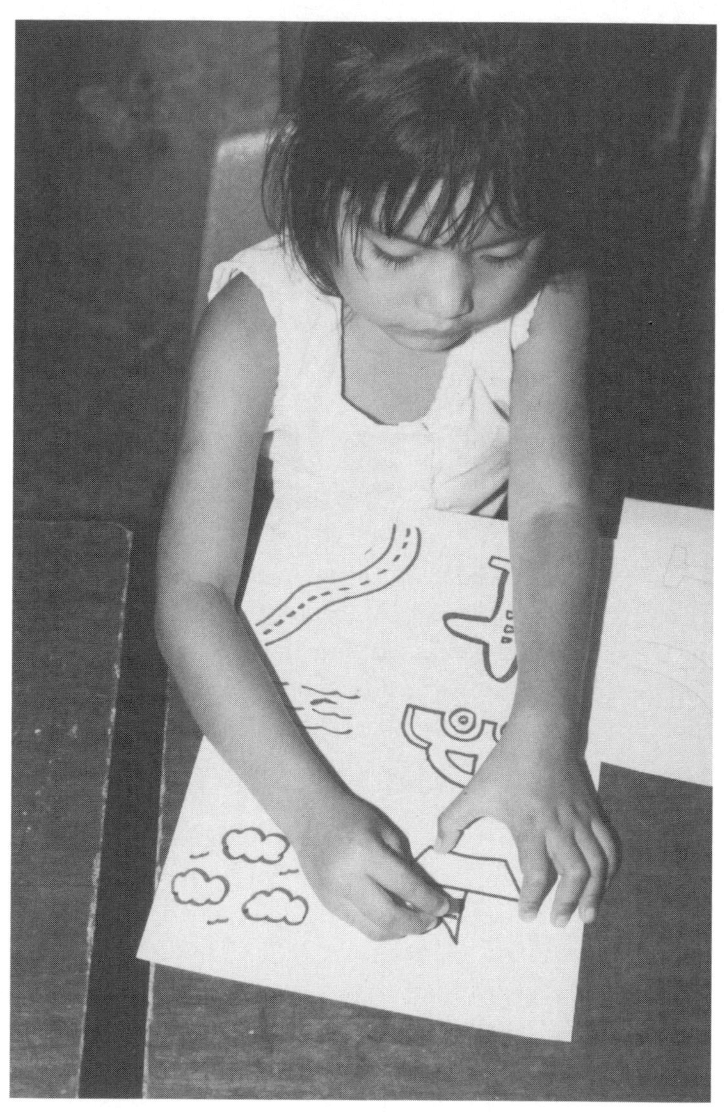

**5.** One of Maritza Ochoa's four-year-old students completes a visual quiz, drawn by Maritza, about methods of transportation (2000).
PHOTO BY THE AUTHOR.

into two ponytails, out of her way. She wore a close-fitting sleeveless top and sweatpants with the Adidas logo above the word "abidias"—a U.S. status symbol jumbled on a Chinese-import version. A tiny dried seahorse hung from a leather cord around her neck.

My first lesson in Maritza's classroom was one in linguistics, woven into her morning greeting. The greetings *ndek müm* and *ndek teat* were not heard as often in San Mateo del Mar as *Dios müm* and *Dios teat*. *Müm* and *teat* mean mother and father, terms of respect for women and men in San Mateo's language, called Ombeayiüts by the people in San Mateo and Huave by most everyone else. To address her children with these words was to greet them as "ladies and gentlemen." Wagging her finger, Maritza told her students not to use the Spanish word dios in an Ombeayiüts greeting. Not that God wasn't important. Maritza went to Mass nearly every week, took flowers to the altar, talked about her faith, and traced the good things in her life back to God. Still, Ombeayiüts was far older and more deeply rooted than Catholicism.

One boy sat in the far corner of Maritza's classroom, tears streaking down his heart-shaped face. He sniffed and shivered, seeming to listen to about half of her words. While this was the second year of preschool for most of her students, Abisael Beltrán had just started school. He had come to Maritza speaking no Spanish; half of her words were unintelligible to him. Maritza treated him gently but ignored his tears. She felt confident that within a month or two he would understand enough Spanish to get along without trouble. No need to affirm his idea that there was something to fear.

Several of Maritza's students had, like Abisael, just begun their formal education. Some parents in San Mateo del Mar delayed sending their children to school for as long as possible.

Why did their children need something they had never had? Why send their children to an institution that was *mol*, that was controlled by outsiders? What if their children forgot Ombeayiüts? The Catholic Church had done a much better job ingratiating itself than the public school system had. So much so, in fact, that the first European language spoken in San Mateo del Mar had not been Spanish, but Latin. Still, four hundred years after the Catholic Church had shown up, Abisael and three of his classmates spoke only Ombeayiüts. Another three, the children of newcomers to the village, didn't speak the local language. Maritza's twenty-one other students were more or less bilingual. Maritza's job, as she saw it, was to ensure that her students became perfectly bilingual and bicultural. Her job, as the Mexican government saw it, was to ensure that her students learned Spanish. In San Mateo del Mar, Spanish was mol and yet it was becoming more widespread. About half of the village's residents had spoken Spanish when Maritza was a baby. By the time she started working as a teacher, two decades later, four-fifths of the villagers spoke it.

After the linguistics lesson, Maritza took a maraca, a drum, and a tambourine from her classroom shelves—a stack of open-ended cardboard boxes wrapped with aluminum foil and old gift wrap. She waved the instruments at the children. "Who wants to volunteer?" she asked twice, once in each language. Three children scraped back their chairs and ran up to her. Maritza clapped a simple rhythm and sang. One child rattled a dried gourd with a few pebbles inside glued to a stick. Another tapped an animal skin stretched over a rusted can. The third child's tambourine, especially, showed the full scope of the job of "teacher" as Maritza fulfilled it: she had cut rectangular holes into the sides of a flat-bottomed plastic bowl, then pounded bottle caps flat and tied them into the holes with scrap wire. Maritza had built or scavenged nearly everything in her classroom except the tables, chairs, chalkboard, and chalk.

After the song the three children set their instruments back on the shelf with deliberate care while Maritza grabbed a spiral notebook from her desk. These notebooks were Maritza's most important teaching supplies: one for each child, filled with drawings she had hand-copied into each one. There wasn't money for printed materials or photocopying, and nothing existed in Ombeayiüts anyway. Later Maritza would tell me that she used Spanish-language materials reluctantly, if at all. "They talk about things like traffic lights, and these children have never seen a traffic light! The people who prepare those textbooks are really well-educated but they aren't indigenous. They don't understand our reality." It is a reality both relentlessly collective and highly individual. Though Maritza spoke in first-person plural more often than singular, she also liked to say, "Cada cabeza es un mundo": every mind is a whole unique world.

During the first week of the school year Maritza had led her students on a walk along San Mateo del Mar's main street. This wide strip of gravel and sand passed just one block from the preschool. It linked San Mateo—via a ninety-minute bus ride of bumps and dust clouds—to the petroleum boomtown of Salina Cruz. The city offered markets for their fish and shrimp, high schools for some of their children, and oil-refinery jobs for a lucky few. It was also the closest source for newspapers and postal mail.

The most common sight along the road was a woman headed to market balancing a round tub of dried fish, salted shrimp, or corn totopos on her head or hips. Old bicycles rattled by; horses and cows ambled; trucks wheezed back and forth. Once in a while a car passed, infrequently enough that people would look to see who was inside. After Maritza's students walked through the streets, they drew pictures of what they had seen. Most drew cars, horses, or buses. One drew a train—which was no more common than a traffic light in San Mateo, though the train to Arriaga, and to Guatemala, passed just a few miles north of the village.

Two weeks after their walk, I sat in front with the students, chins tilted up toward the spiral notebook Maritza held above her head. The day's lesson—methods of transport—reviewed their tour around town.

The lesson might have been the most important one of the school year. San Mateo del Mar lies 13 miles east of Salina Cruz, the southern terminus of the Trans-Isthmus Megaproject and the southern end of the proposed highway. While the men of San Mateo fished with hand nets and herded a few head of cattle, the isthmus economy shifted. Rumors whipped through San Mateo like the northern winds. One went like this: The government wanted to privatize their communally owned beach and allow foreigners to build a tourist resort. Another was identical to the rumor in San Francisco del Mar: foreign investors were going to build a shrimp farm on their fishing grounds. Maritza worried that decisions made by people she didn't know, who lived in cities she had never visited, could come crashing down on her village.

That was the big picture. The little picture was drawn in Maritza's stack of spiral notebooks. Holding one overhead, she pointed to her cartoonish outlines of a bus, a bicycle, and a car. Abisael watched Maritza closely; his tears dried. The children called out the names: *autobús, bicicleta, coche*. There are no words in Ombeayiüts for most of the things that have arrived since the Spaniards did. When Maritza held up a drawing of a helicopter, the children shouted, "Nchilil!" Expecting to hear *helicóptero*, I was startled by their unfamiliar word.

Why would there be a word in Ombeayiüts for helicopter, if there was no word for bicycle? As Maritza finished up the lesson, one boy snapped his head up and named the noise chopping the viscous air. A *nchilil*—a helicopter! Chair legs scraped cement as all the children rushed the door. Maritza and I followed them outside. She squeezed the shoulder of the boy who had named the noise and gently corrected him—it was actually *un avión*, an airplane. The children craned their necks and shouted, excited by their close encounter with the flying machine. *Nchilil* is Ombeayiüts for cicada; from where we stood the word seemed perfect for the speck buzzing past the clouds.

Maritza shuffled her students back into the classroom and began the day's main activity: a test disguised as a game. She handed each child a single sheet with drawings she had repeated twenty-seven times: a boat, a car, and an airplane lined up on the left side; and clouds, waves, and a road on the right. The children passed around a tin can filled with crayon and pencil stubs and settled in, filling the outlined images with graphite and wax, pausing only to ask a classmate to pass another crayon. Once they were immersed in the exercise, Maritza explained its real purpose: connect the method of transport to its medium. Crayons clutched in small fists connected a purple boat with a pink sail to a black sea, or a blue car with green windows to a green road. As the children worked, Maritza took an Exacto knife from the pocket of her sweatpants and whittled sharp points onto pencils, already broken in half to serve twice as many students.

The thin breeze from the open windows flattened itself on my damp neck. The air suddenly stilled and I turned to see a man leaning against the window frame. Abisael's father had come to see how his son was doing. The boy, absorbed in the energy of Maritza's classroom, didn't even notice.

Because fishing is mostly a nighttime activity, several fathers walked their children to and from school. Some of the parents stayed to watch their children do something that probably half of them had never done. Men leaned against the cement walls. Women crouched on the walkway, their long skirts fanning into circles around them. Each woman held a round basket or a baby or both. Many of the mothers were younger than Maritza. They smiled and nodded at Maritza's stories and jokes. In istmeño villages teachers are usually held in high esteem, even if the system that employs them is not.

Abisael crept up to me shyly with his completed test, still not noticing his father outside. He pushed the paper into my hands and smiled expectantly. Everything was orange, except the thing he knew best: the sea. He had colored the waves blue. Careful lines connected car to road and ship to sea, but the line from the airplane led past the clouds, straight off the top of the page: *up*.

I smiled and murmured encouraging words that he didn't understand. "Qué bueno, Abisael. Muy bien hecho y bien bonito, también."

Another boy handed me his test. "What's this?" I said, pointing to the road.

"Una carretera," he said.

I pointed to the other images and he gave me the Spanish names for boat, car, plane. I pointed at the drawing of the waves. "¿Y eso?"

He paused, then said confidently in Spanish, "Where the boats swim!"

I moved my finger to the cumulus puff.

"Nangaj oik." *Oik* means cloud. *Nangaj* is a word used with many elements of the natural world. There is no direct translation into Spanish or English, but its meaning lies somewhere between "supreme" and "honorable."

The Huave worldview is manifest in everyday words. It is a fragile wealth; Ombeayiüts is spoken only in San Mateo del Mar. The name means "our mouth": *mbeay* is the root word for mouth, and the prefix *o-* and suffix *-iüts* together form the possessive "our." The language lives only in the voices of San Mateo's nine thousand residents. That is to say, it's a language in danger of extinction, as are half of the languages in the world. Maritza's task is huge.

The sign painted on the front wall of Maritza's school building reads Pre-escolar Benito Juárez, Escuela Bilingüe. Named for Mexico's first indigenous president, the preschool is part of Mexico's "indigenous and rural" school system, one of two public school systems. There isn't even a pretense of "separate but equal." All the teachers in the other system—called *el sistema formal*—had graduated from four-year teachers' colleges. Until 2001, indigenous system teachers received only a six-month training program after ninth grade, which is how Maritza had become a full-time teacher by the time she was nineteen years old.

Every Ombeayiüts word I learned (to recognize and spell, if not pronounce) opened a window onto another world. The word *iüm*, for example, translates most easily as "house" or "home." *Iüm* also means "the place where we live" in a more general sense and "the unity, or trinity, of people, the natural world, and God." If Maritza's students don't speak Ombeayiüts to their future children, will this concept be lost?

At the time of my first visit to Maritza's classroom, there were only three published books in San Mateo's language: an Ombeayiüts-Spanish dictionary, the Bible, and a first-grade reader. The dictionary, compiled and published by North American missionaries, defines *iüm* as simply, *la casa (edificio)* ("the house [building]"). In an oral language, what repository of knowledge is there but the words in people's mouths? With no written texts, history is housed in the language, each phrase its own small story.

Ombeayiüts is unrelated to the nine other indigenous languages spoken on the Isthmus of Tehuantepec, a rarity among rarities. Most linguists consider the language to be in a family all its own, rather like Basque. When speaking Spanish, most people who live in San Mateo refer to their language simply as *la lengua*, "the tongue." Most mestizo Mexicans refer to languages such as Ombeayiüts as "dialects." With no close linguistic relatives, it surely isn't a dialect. The people of San Mateo del Mar generally call themselves "mero Ikoots," rejecting the term Huave. Like many tribes' names for themselves, "mero Ikoots" means "the real us" or "our true selves." There are several hypotheses about the origin of the word Huave, but by far the most common is that it's a Zapotec word meaning "those who rot from the humidity."

Shortly after noon, Maritza's class wound down for the day and the children squirmed in anticipation of leaving. Abisael looked toward the door. He finally realized his father had been watching him and began to cry.

Before letting her preschoolers go for the day, Maritza asked them, "What are you going to say to your mothers when you get home?" "Ndek müm!" about half of them yelled back. "What are you going to say to your fathers?" More responded this time: "Ndek teat!" Maritza smiled as the children clattered out of the room.

I picked up dropped pencil and crayon stubs as Maritza swept onto a square of cardboard the day's dust, dead insects, scraps of paper, food crumbs, and even bits of metal. The wind that nearly always blows in San Mateo had carried it all over the threshold and sills that day. Maritza glanced up at the stick-and-eggshell mobiles she had hung from the light fixtures (eight fixtures but only one lightbulb). They hung at odd angles, broken. She shook her head. "When the northern winds come, it's impossible to protect things." The Huave lagoons and surrounding land lie at the southern end of the Sierra Madre range in a depression that acts as a wind tunnel. Even the shape of San Mateo's sandy peninsula is determined by those northern winds. As San Mateo villagers explain it, the northern winds, brought by a male deity, shape the environment, while the southern winds, controlled by Müm nij meor, the goddess of marine fertility, bring the shrimp.

Maritza crouched to separate the pile of refuse: paper saved for paper-making with her students, plastic and metal into the garbage can, everything else into a bucket for the composter at the local high school. As Maritza and I stacked the crayon cans on the cardboard shelves, one girl sat at one of the low tables with her transportation quiz still before her. A dimple burrowed deeply into her right cheek as she pressed her lips together and gripped her pencil. Maritza nodded toward her. "She's always the last one working, but she always finishes." After the little girl finally handed in her quiz and skipped out the door, Maritza locked the classroom for the day. She and I walked past the 150-year-old brick church, past the cinderblock municipal building and the metal-roofed, dirt-floored market. At the far end of the market we turned left and headed for the door of the Ochoa-Jarauta home.

Maritza lived with her mother and father, one of her three brothers, a sister-in-law, a niece, and a cousin in a house built by her mother's parents. Maritza's family had moved into it when her grandparents, as she put it, "went to heaven." One of her brothers worked construction in the beach resort town of Huatulco; the other served in the army in Baja

California. Her fifteen-year-old sister had recently married and moved a few blocks away to the home of her husband's family. Maritza, unmarried and childless, was less typical of women in San Mateo than was her younger sister. Soon Maritza would finish her bachelor's degree in education and become even more atypical.

Maritza and I arrived home as her father, Gerardo, was preparing for the night's fishing trip. With the wiry muscled body of a fisherman and no hint of gray in his shoulder-length hair, Gerardo didn't look old enough to be the father of a twenty-three-year-old. Working in the open space between two palm shelters—the kitchen and the bedroom—he rolled up his fishing net slowly, careful not to tangle it. Like most San Mateo houses, the Ochoa-Jarauta home consisted of several small buildings around a central dirt courtyard, all enclosed by a high fence of woven reeds. Buckets and baskets, tucked in the low branches of almond trees and husky bark of the coco palms, were stuffed with dishes, toothbrushes, and tools. On the far side of the yard, alarmingly close to the well, two large pigs snorted and whimpered in their pen.

Gerardo smeared kerosene on the outside of his wheelbarrow so the sea salt wouldn't corrode it. He twisted lengths of salvaged string into ropes the diameter of his forefinger, making wicks for his tin-can lanterns. It took more than two hours to walk to the Boca Barra, the Huaves' most prized fishing grounds. It was a long haul through the sand, pushing a wheelbarrow filled with nets, lantern, knife, three days' worth of drinking water, corn totopos, and salt. Gerardo didn't feel like making the trip that night, so he planned to fish at the San Mateo beach—a smaller investment with a smaller payoff. One good day at the Boca Barra could yield twenty-eight dollars worth of fish. If his night on the San Mateo beach went really well, Gerardo might earn six dollars—half what Maritza had earned that day. But a bad day at either location, "when the catch is sad," as they say in San Mateo, would leave him with about two dollars to show for his work.

Maritza's teaching salary had transformed their home. Her family had built a new two-room building with cement walls and a corrugated metal roof. One of its windows looked out onto the town square, just across from the market's public bathrooms. Children often gathered by the window to watch Maritza's large television. They would stand for hours, eyes and expressions blank, as snowy images trembled on the screen. Maritza had saved for a long time to buy the television even though she believed that the black box was *newaïich*—it told lies. She had bought the television to show videos in her classroom but she hadn't yet saved the money for a VCR.

In a sense Maritza had been working toward her teacher's salary since she was eleven years old. She had left home after the fifth grade to attend secondary school in Juchitán, three hours away. She stayed with a Zapotec family, working in their house and at their photography studio to earn her room and board. Maritza mentioned the years she had spent in Juchitán to me several times. It wasn't until I had known her for four years that she described how difficult it had been for a Huave girl to live in a Zapotec city, in a place where many people looked down on the Huave. She still remembered the day she received the highest score on a test and the teacher congratulated her in front of the entire class. Sitting near the back of the room, fear inched up her throat as all her classmates turned to stare at her. *That* girl? The highest score? *¿Una huave?* How could that be?

After middle school, Maritza won a scholarship to a Catholic Marist boarding school near Juchitán. She rarely returned to San Mateo del Mar; she could afford to make the 45-mile bus trip home only once or twice each year. She dreamed of attending college in Mexico City and becoming an anthropologist. She was enchanted by "the idea of exploring: to see, to go, to seek, to get involved in things." Even with a scholarship, though, how could she possibly afford to live in Mexico City? An aunt tried to convince her to get a job at the PEMEX oil refinery in Salina Cruz—these were the best-paying jobs imaginable for people in San Mateo del Mar.

After Maritza finished high school and returned home to live in San Mateo, she continued to think about college. One day a teacher asked Maritza to fill in and teach her classes so she could attend an out-of-town training course. The local schools were understaffed that year so Maritza found herself, at age seventeen with no training as a teacher, standing before seventy first-graders. That first day she looked around the room and thought to herself, "What am I going to do with all these children?" She threw herself into the tumult of the crammed classroom. She played games with them, told stories, and taught them letters of the alphabet. She didn't have enough time for all the children in the four-and-one-half hour school day, so she invited them to come to her house in the afternoon. Those two weeks made her think hard about the intersection of her dreams and her community's needs. Within a few months she had registered for the training program to become a bilingual elementary schoolteacher.

In the 1940s Mexican linguists began to challenge the policy of teaching indigenous children exclusively in Spanish, believing that young students should first learn to read and write in the languages they learned and spoke at home. Thirty years later, public primary schools began to employ indigenous people as teachers. By the time Maritza began her training in the late 1990s, in some parts of Mexico the problem had become indigenous people *not* knowing their language, rather than knowing *only* their language. "It makes sense to learn another language," Maritza often said of Spanish, "but we shouldn't forget our own." When I asked Maritza the Ombeayiüts names for the Mixe and Zapotec peoples—San Mateo del Mar's neighbors since before the Spanish conquest—it alarmed her that she could not remember. Maritza worried that language loss and external pressures—like those exemplified by the Trans-Isthmus Megaproject—would combine to create her greatest fear: cultural extinction.

Every other weekend Maritza attended a teachers college that was a three-hour bus ride from San Mateo. Most of the students were indigenous istmeños: Chontal, Mixe, Zoque, Huave, or Zapotec. Until recently, many of the teachers in indigenous schools had only finished secondary school, the equivalent of ninth grade. Now some had completed *normal*, a two-year post-secondary teachers' training program, or *bachillerato*, the equivalent of a high school diploma. When Maritza graduated she would be one of the few indigenous teachers in San Mateo del Mar with a college degree. After paying tuition and covering expenses for in her household of six, she didn't have much left from her paycheck, which totaled about two hundred seventy dollars a month.

"But, that's how things are in our country. This is what poverty is like," she would say, without a hint of irritation or sadness. "They say they are going to wipe out poverty in Mexico—but what they're going to wipe out are the poor people!" Her black eyes registered both humor and pride, as if to indicate, *Somehow we'll survive this, too.*

One month after Maritza's transportation quiz, I returned to San Mateo del Mar to spend more time in her classroom. The other times I'd visited San Mateo del Mar I had been a passenger in someone else's car. This time I traveled alone by bus. I reached Salina Cruz and realized I didn't know where to catch the bus to San Mateo del Mar. The two communities were 13 miles and half a world apart. Few people in the city would have noticed the sputtering bus at some roadside, and almost none would have ever taken it. At 6:00 in the morning I wandered Salina Cruz's downtown streets; San Mateo del Mar was close yet far away. Finally it occurred to me: there was one place in Salina Cruz I was sure to find people from San Mateo del Mar. I headed for the seafood section of the central market and immediately found a group of women gathered around wide plastic tubs of fresh and dried shrimp, easily recognizable in their doll-sized huipils and wide ankle-length skirts.

"Good morning, excuse me," I said to the five women. "Where can I catch the bus to San Mateo?"

Ten eyes turned to stare at me.

"You are going to San Mateo?"

"On the *bus*?"

I nodded, yes.

Their stares shifted from confusion to surprise. A *güera*, a white girl, going to San Mateo on the same bus on which they carried their shellfish? Through their giggles they drew me a map with words and gestures.

"You just walk past the parque central, then take a left."

"Then a right at the bank."

"The Banamex."

"Así es. El Banamex." They repeated the directions, arms and wrists miming the path.

I thanked them, nodding to each one. I could still hear them giggling as I left the market.

I knocked on Maritza's front door two hours later as she was getting ready for work. She pulled a small wooden table into the shade, filled a bowl with boiled shrimp, balanced several totopos on top, and offered it to me.

"No thanks, I already ate breakfast." It was a lie, but I wasn't hungry and food wasn't always plentiful in San Mateo del Mar.

Maritza sat down, leaving her hands in her lap as we chatted about her family and her students and my trip from Salina Cruz. Finally she said, "Bueno, with your permission," gesturing toward the bowl.

It was another moment in what I could only assume was a long series of such moments: a gringa's social gaffes in rural Mexico. It had taken me several months to understand that guests would stand in my living room until I repeated, "please, sit," several times, and then would deny thirst until I thrust glasses of water into their hands. I added Maritza's request to my mental guidebook to istmeño etiquette: even when in other people's houses, remember to give them permission to eat. Maritza, like every other istmeño I knew, showed no concern over my apparent thoughtlessness. Her easy generosity smoothed over my blunder.

Our conversation wandered through mutual friends, Mexican politics, and happenings in San Mateo del Mar. We finally paused, realizing at the same moment that Maritza was late for school. We jumped up, left half her breakfast in the bowl, the bowl on the table, and the table in the middle of the yard, then rushed out the door. When we walked up to the school's locked gate, just minutes before classes were to begin, five children waited there quietly. Maritza was the first teacher to arrive. She smiled at the students as she pulled the padlock from the chainlink fence. "Lazy teachers!" Her words hissed out in a voice too low for the children to hear. It annoyed her to see the children more excited than the teachers to start the school day. Her irritation passed, left behind as we stepped over the chainlink threshold onto the school property. A moment later Maritza stood in the middle of the schoolyard and banged a rock against a rusted cowbell, calling the village's children and teachers from their homes.

After her four-year-olds settled into their seats she told them a story in Ombeayiüts, acting out the emotions. Abisael, who still cried when his father dropped him off in the morning, sat with his wide eyes fixed on Maritza's face. It seemed his tears had become little more than habit; he now paid attention to both the Ombeayiüts and Spanish lessons.

While the Ombeayiüts sentences passed by me in a jaunty tumble, the Spanish words told their own story. They offered a catalog of things that have come relatively recently to San Mateo del Mar: school, doctor, injection, garbage can, painting. Two of those words, *basurero* and *pintar*, related directly to the day's project. Twelve papier-mâché barrels were scattered around the schoolyard. When Maritza had taken her class out for the "transportation tour" of San Mateo at the beginning of the school year, it surprised her that they noticed the garbage as much as the cars and buses. Plastic bags and bottles littered the roads, fields, and waters of San Mateo; dead fish dotted the beaches. "The fish are dying," the children had asked her, "Why?"

Their question thrilled her, but "Why are the fish dying?" was hard to answer. (The occasional petroleum smell of the fish in their nets led her to suspect PEMEX's oil refinery.) She took their question as opportunity. Maritza had long faulted her school system for not teaching San Mateo's children the things they needed to know, such as how to plant and harvest crops; how to fish; and how to avoid polluting the water, land, and air around them. She suggested the children start with smaller questions. She organized a school-wide children's assembly for them to decide what to do about pollution. The preschool meeting mimicked San Mateo's local government. As in most of the villages and towns in the state of Oaxaca, all major decisions had to be approved by San Mateo's community assembly. There were no local elections; officials were also chosen at assembly meetings by consensus.

When the Benito Juárez Preschool's three- and four-year-olds gathered for their assembly, Maritza made sure the boys and girls got equal time at the megaphone. In this way it was unlike San Mateo's assembly, which was led and attended almost exclusively by men. Maritza posed the first question: What could they do about the garbage?

"We can sweep all the streets," one child said.

What about garbage at their school?

"We'll buy wastebaskets for the whole school."

But they couldn't afford to buy anything, and all trash collected had to be burned. With nudging from Maritza, the group decided to start a school recycling program. Students from the local high school—run by Catholic Marist volunteers, the new school was the only one in town—helped the four-year-olds make papier-mâché barrels: three for each of the school's four classrooms, to hold paper, compost, and trash.

Today they would color code them: yellow, red, blue. Every afternoon Maritza would gather the banana peels, fish bones, mango pits, and almond fruits from the red barrels and carry them to the high school's composting bin. Maritza divided her class, along with the school's other classroom of four-year-olds, into small groups and led them to the courtyard. "Three!" she yelled. The children scrambled into trios. Four! They dropped hands, then reformed in circles of four. Five! Six! Here the game ended. Each group of six received one barrel, one jar of paint, and six brushes. They crouched around the barrels, running their paintbrushes over the nubs and ridges of glue-sculpted newsprint. After the paint had been cleaned up and the children dismissed for the day, Maritza and I sat down to talk, our legs bent double as we hunched on the small chairs. One of her students hovered nearby as Maritza unrolled large squares of newsprint on the floor, showing me the records the children had made of their assembly. Hand-drawn plastic bottles and bags floated across the sheets of paper through piles of dead fish, expanses of blue lagoon, and shakily drawn beige beaches.

Maritza turned to her student, Zairet. "What did we see when we walked along the streets?"

"Ba-suuuu-ra." Zairet pulled out the syllables of the word, savoring her correct answer.

"What kind of garbage did you see?"

"Jars, plastic bags," Zairet paused, trying to think back to that day, many weeks earlier. "Bottles!"

"Who is leaving all that garbage?"

"People."

Maritza pressed her. "Is it men? Or women?" Zairet hesitated. "Or children?"

"No! It's the big people." She was sure of that. Zairet turned to me, pointed to her group's drawing and gave me a tour of the map of devastation. "There's a lot of garbage in the streets. The drunks throw it there. There are lots of fish in the water, but they've died because the water is dirty."

The three of us sat in silence, looking over the children's pictorial records. The children were following a long Mexican tradition, handed down from the ancient Aztecs, Zapotecs, and others. In those people's pre-Columbian codices, both scrolls and books, pictures told stories of royal lives and land transfers and long journeys and important discoveries. Those documents, on the cusp between narrative and map, told stories in a visual language that included images, glyphs, and text. There have never been Ikoots codices; their history is contained in the stories they tell and the language they speak. As Leonel Gómez's older brother once said to me, "We never did calendars and astronomy and shit like that; we're just fishermen."

Maritza patted the girl's arm. "Your mother will be worried about you, Zairet. It's time to go home." Disappointed, Zairet took her bag and said good-bye. Maritza rolled up the drawings and shifted our conversation from the little picture of her classroom back to the big picture. "People here don't really know what's happening with the Megaproject. I don't know a lot, but I've talked to other people, community elders and teachers. It's clear there's a lot behind it." As in: a lot of power, a lot of money, and a lot of special interests that Maritza couldn't quite identify.

"So if the Megaproject happens, how do you see the future?" I asked her.

"The future," Maritza repeated, doubt in her voice.

"Say, in fifty or a hundred years?"

"Little by little, it will end," she said, her tone oddly pleasant. "We won't see an end to the various megaprojects, but an end to indigenous communities. So maybe we will have more millionaires and more mines, but where will all of this leave our people? We'll have work for a while, but afterward? The work is temporary. If it harms the sea, what are we going to eat? How is my community going to survive? The Megaproject is a break from our roots, from everything we have sown." Maritza made the gesture of breaking a thick branch, and then she shrugged.

I nodded, not knowing what to say. Maritza kept talking. "We might live in paradise for a while, but what happens after that? It's like Carlos Salinas de Gortari said. He told everyone, 'Six years of heaven.'" She quoted the campaign slogan of Mexico's president from 1988 to 1994. The one who had signed NAFTA. The one whose staff members went on to develop the Trans-Isthmus Megaproject. The one so unpopular by the time he left office that he'd gone into exile in Ireland. Maritza laughed at Salinas's old slogan, then answered it: "But then, eternal hell!" She repeated it three times: eternal hell. She paused. "It's the same with the Megaproject."

Maritza told me a story about running a long-ago errand in Salina Cruz. She went to a government office to pick up a check for her school. When the clerk learned she was from San Mateo del Mar, he told her, "Your people are dumb."

"Why are you calling us dumb?" she replied. *Why* was an important word for Maritza. When she came up against someone's resistance or criticism, it was usually the first word from her mouth. She spoke it in an insistent but still friendly way, using it to avoid anger or discouragement, instead looking for the reason why someone was challenging her or her community.

"You had the opportunity to build a shrimp farm in your community and you didn't do it," the man said. The proposal, to lease one of San Mateo's lagoons and build an industrial shrimp farm, had come before the village assembly, which rejected it. Maritza took pride in that decision. She had heard enough about shrimp farms to know that sort of development offered no solution to San Mateo's poverty.

It seemed the storeowner had been one of the businessmen hoping to invest in the project. He told her: "We were going to grow big, huge shrimp, not like you all, who kill the tiny little shrimp."

"In the end, all the benefits of this project would leave with you," Maritza said. "What would be left for us?" He told her the investors had wanted to help the people of San

Mateo. This annoyed Maritza. "I've heard this story before," she told him.

Now, recounting the story to me, she sighed, adding, "They always say they are coming to help, help, help. It's never true."

# 5

## Worshipping a Wooden Cross

Sometimes, when the catch was sad, the Ikoots fishermen would hang up their nets and head out of San Mateo del Mar. Maritza's father, Gerardo, often headed west, away from the Isthmus of Tehuantepec, to the Huatulco, Oaxaca, beach resort, where he played saxophone in a band. He earned a lot more money than he did at the San Mateo fishing grounds, or even at the Boca Barra, but little of that money found its way back home to Maritza's family.

On one of the first afternoons that I sat with Maritza in her classroom, she had brought up the subject of Huatulco while we talked about the changes that might be coming to San Mateo del Mar. "What about *our* beach? What if someone wanted to come and build a big hotel there, like they did in Huatulco?" she asked, her voice urgent, as the scent of sun-warmed sand and sea gusted into the musty room. "The indigenous people in Huatulco were the owners of that land. It was theirs, but the truth was they had no guarantees."

Carlos Beas had told me several times, "You want to see why people fear the Megaproject? Go visit Huatulco." It was the ultimate example, he said, of what happens "when a rich man comes with his highway." Huatulco, a small fishing village turned big beach resort, came up often in conversation

**6.** Laurentino Cormona tells of fighting the federal land expropriation in Huatulco so that he may keep his family farm (2001).
PHOTO BY THE AUTHOR.

with istmeños. They told me various iterations of the same story, their voices heavy with pity: Pobre Huatulco, where the local people lost their land, a few of them ended up rich, a few ended up as taxi drivers, and many ended up with nothing. The lamentations over the Huatulco resort called to mind some of the word's other uses: We had to resort to this. It was our last resort. I went to Huatulco to find out what, exactly, istmeños meant when they worried aloud that the Megaproject could mean the "Huatulquization" of the Isthmus of Tehuantepec.

Sometimes—but only sometimes—one bus traveled all the way from Matías Romero to Huatulco. I decided to make the trip on a morning in early November. The clerk at the Matías Romero bus station told me there wasn't a *directo*, but I could ride as far as Juchitán and there perhaps be able to change to a Huatulco-bound route. Perhaps? It's "servicio de paso," the clerk said. The isthmus had many *hoteles de paso*, which rented rooms by the hour, but I didn't know what a *servicio de paso* bus might be. I headed to the main bus terminal in Juchitán, an hour's bus ride south of Matías Romero, doubtful but open to possibility.

The woman at the Juchitán bus terminal confirmed that a bus headed from the colonial city of San Cristóbal de las Casas to the beaches of Huatulco would pass by that afternoon. She wouldn't know whether I could buy a ticket for the bus until it arrived. Finally, I understood. A bus from San Cristóbal headed toward the Pacific beach resorts would be filled with tourists. The bus company wouldn't want to reserve seats for people boarding in Juchitán, who would probably be going only to sell hammocks or visit children and grandchildren working at the resorts, when they might be able to sell those seats to dollar-spending tourists leaving San Cristóbal's chilly mountaintop for a few days in the sun.

Hours later the woman's voice boomed from the steel rafters: "Servicio Cristóbal Colon anuncia, servicio de paso a Salina Cruz, Huatulco, Pochutla y Puerto Escondido." I hopped up from my plastic chair and rushed into line with the old women balancing huge knots of hammocks on their heads, or baskets of totopos and cheese on their hips. I got the last ticket, then settled into my seat on the reeking bus. Tourist routes were always the worst. Penny-pinching backpackers used the long bus rides as mobile motels, wedging dirty underwear between the seats, shunning Dramamine and then vomiting the whole way, abandoning their toddlers' soiled Pampers on the floor, smoking pot in the bathroom, dribbling sandy trails from the crevices of their backpacks.

I tried to ignore the travelers' detritus and concentrate on the view. As the bus rolled west, blue sky, ivory cement houses, tan thatched huts, and green hills blinked by, the windows framing the landscape at odd angles as the bus grumbled up hills and tilted around curves. About four hours after we left Juchitán, the first of Huatulco's nine bays stretched before me: pearl white curled around a blue jewel. Seconds later, the poster-perfect image was torn away. The bus lurched around a sharp curve, descended, and huge hotels appeared: a flat-topped pyramid, a sand castle with palm-frond awnings, and a square-block fortress. Out the bus windows that faced inland, hills reached up toward thin, dry forest. Beachside hotels clumped along the promontories, angling for the best view. More buildings stood half-constructed than finished. Manicured strips of lawn and curb flanked the smooth, wide-shouldered road. I had traveled only 60 miles from the Isthmus of Tehuantepec, but I felt as if I had returned to my childhood home, southern California.

The superhighway planned for the Isthmus of Tehuantepec, part of the Trans-Isthmus Megaproject, would go to

Huatulco as well. It would begin 200 miles northwest of the isthmus in the state capital, Oaxaca City. Halfway between that city and the isthmus the route would split, with four lanes heading south to Huatulco and two continuing southeast to Salina Cruz. The local government and many Huatulco residents wanted the superhighway as desperately as the istmeños were fighting it. The highway's two paths pointed toward divergent futures: the istmeños farmed, fished, traded, or went to the United States; the *huatulqueños* gave up the farmland, baited sport-fishing lines, and hoped the United States would come to them.

Until the 1980s, Huatulco had been—like the Huave region still was—a string of fishing villages along pristine Pacific beaches. Over many centuries, indigenous people had trekked long paths from Oaxaca's highlands to Huatulco. They came to harvest the famous *caracol púrpura,* a conch whose aubergine ink had decorated formal clothing for thousands of years. The dye from this sea snail is yellow when first excreted, turns to green, then blue, and finally a royal purple-red when exposed to sunlight.

In 1984 the Mexican government announced that Huatulco's seaside enclaves would be replaced by a tourist resort "on the order of Cancun" . . . Cancun, but without all the raw sewage pouring into the ocean, without so much pavement, without all the drunk college students on spring break. Cancun, that is, but *not* Cancun. With that decision, *de la noche a la mañana*, more than 51,000 acres of beach, field, and forest became federal government property, controlled by FONATUR, the national tourism development agency. Just inside the border that divides FONATUR-controlled Huatulco from the locally controlled land surrounding it, a trio of highway signs punctuated the roadside: "Huatulco is . . . ECOLOGY." "Huatulco is . . . PLANNING." "Huatulco is . . .

QUALITY." Each all-caps word appeared inside a stylized outline of the land that had been expropriated in 1984. The west, north, and east borders of the property were razor straight; the southern edge was the jagged Pacific coast. The sign portrayed Huatulco's bays, jetties, and outcroppings so schematically that the expropriated land looked like a handsaw. Federal government officials told Huatulco's fishermen in May 1984 that the land was no longer theirs, slicing it indelicately, even violently, from the coast of Oaxaca. Government funds built a first-world sewer system, a world-class golf course, and paved roads with neat curbs and smooth sidewalks. Club Med snapped up a prime peninsula and illegally fenced the beach (by law, all Mexican beaches are public), then hired armed guards. European and Mexican companies put up hotels and dug swimming pools.

And the original residents of Huatulco, the huatulqueños? Some left. Some stayed and later wished they had left. Some stayed and made new lives for themselves with the money they received as compensation for their land and homes. Some never stopped fighting the expropriation. Life, work, and even the seasons changed for the huatulqueños. There had been just two seasons—wet and dry—but now things were much more complicated. Suddenly the weather didn't matter; the weather somewhere else mattered. Huatulco's tourism workers waited all year for the stretch from Thanksgiving to Easter, "American season," when the foreigners came to spend their dollars, euros, and yen. There were several shorter and less lucrative "Mexican seasons," including summer, Easter, and long weekends in autumn. Then there was *septihambre,* "hungry September," the stretch from late August, when Mexico City's middle-class children returned to their private schools, until the long weekend in late September that marked Mexico's independence day.

The *bus de paso* from Juchitán dropped off the tourists, hammock-sellers, grandmothers, and me in La Crucecita, Huatulco's largest town, several miles from the ocean. The central plaza was typically Mexican, if uncommonly well-scrubbed. Cement benches dotted pathways lined with lollipop-shaped bushes and trees; women sold chile-powdered mangoes, sugared tamarind, and popcorn. A bougainvillea-tangled, whitewashed church towered over the whole tableau. A few blocks past the church, La Crucecita's few restaurants and shops gave way to tiny cement-block houses. I peeked into the doorways of humble homes that opened directly onto the street, spilling out tinny music, drying laundry, and the smell of old frying oil.

All this felt familiar and similar to life in most of southern Mexico, but other details seemed oddly out of place. Many of La Crucecita's stores sold things that no one really needed: hundred-dollar plastic coolers, titanium fishing rods, and swimming-pool chemicals. Street signs bore names like Guanacastle, Ocotillo, and Pochote—named for trees, as in the United States, rather than for important historic personages and dates, as in most of Mexico. Strangest of all, La Crucecita was *finished*. There were no stacks of cement blocks and corrugated metal waiting to become houses, no forests of rebar jutting from rooftops waiting to become a new floor. Perhaps this was why La Crucecita seemed profoundly un-Mexican. In Spanish the verb *esperar* means both "to wait" and "to hope": to stop doing one was to stop doing the other.

The town of La Crucecita, "the little cross," was built from the ground up in the late 1980s to house both the huatulqueños kicked out of their waterfront huts and the workers who came from elsewhere to build the tourist resort. It was Huatulco's largest population center though that hadn't been FONATUR's plan. Even sixteen years after the expropriation there were more service workers and huatulqueños than newcomers rich enough to afford real estate along the beautiful bays. By this measure the new Huatulco was an abysmal failure.

I arrived in Huatulco just as American season was rolling to a lazy start. I stayed at the edge of town in a hotel that charged thirty dollars a night for stark white sheets, walls, floors, fans, and stairways. That was the most I'd ever paid for a hotel in southern Mexico even though this one had no pool, no beach, and no waterfront view. On my first morning at the Hotel Amakal, a man in the lobby wanted to sell me a boat trip. Only three hundred pesos, a private boat, five hours.

"No thanks," I said. I wasn't looking for a boat ride, I was looking for huatulqueños. "But, are you from here?"

"No, I'm an indio."

"But there are indios here, the huatulqueños."

"I'm from Chiapas. I'm not indio-indio," he said, sweeping his hands up and cutting the air next to his ears, as if indicating a hairdo. "I'm from the city, but I consider myself an indio." He had come to Huatulco ten years ago because he liked nature and because there was no violence here.

I nodded, smiled, and moved on, wondering at his gesture. Only later did I realize he was indicating a Mohawk haircut. I imagined the gesture's context: the man had spent enough time with the sort of people who conflated Mohawks and Mohawk haircuts that he thought the association would explain something to me.

I stepped outside Hotel Amakal's glaring white lobby into the glaring sun and hailed a cab to the nearby town of Santa Cruz Huatulco. One of the concessions FONATUR had made to the huatulqueños was giving them taxi licenses. As more huatulqueños left to work illegally in the United States, the hackney licenses fell to people who had moved to Huatulco from elsewhere in Mexico.

"How do you like Huatulco?" the *taxista* asked as his eyes swept over my light hair, light eyes, and backpack.

"The beaches are lovely, but this place looks more like San Diego than Mexico," I said.

"And where are you from?"

"I grew up in Alta California. I'm living on the isthmus right now."

His eyebrows and voice rose in surprise. "I'm from the isthmus." I didn't know whether to believe him. "San Francisco del Mar," he continued. Only a true istmeño would even know that name.

"Such a lovely village," I said, smiling at the thought of Leonel and Román's hometown.

"I used to be a fisherman." Looking at him more closely, I could see the lean fisherman's body hiding under his baggy taxista clothing. He had used the indefinite past tense to describe his former profession—*me dedicaba a la pesca*—as if to hint that he might one day return to it.

Arriving in Santa Cruz Huatulco, the taxi hadn't even rolled to a stop when someone pulled open the door. I tried to be polite as I shook my head "No" to a dozen offers: Did I want a tour boat to the beaches? Did I want a guide? Did I want to go SCUBA diving? Snorkeling? Sunbathing? Deep-sea fishing? On the short walk from the marina to the town plaza, the tour-hawkers greatly outnumbered the visitors.

I wandered away from the marina, then up and down each of Santa Cruz's few streets. Roads that appeared on my two-year-old map, printed by FONATUR, led to dead ends or to empty grass lots, or they didn't exist at all. Partly constructed buildings looked long-abandoned with tall grasses growing up around half-built walls. At least as many signs said "For Rent" as "Welcome."

Had I landed in a town slowly on the rise or one that had become a premature ghost town? Huatulco's function-follows-form model, which seemed to have stalled at form, stood in unsettling contrast to most Mexican cities. Usually people moved into a new area and threw up houses; public services and roads eventually followed. In the Bays of Huatulco the process had been reversed: the sewage system and electrical grid had been installed but the buildings, residents and visitors were still missing.

I followed a patchwork of empty lots back to what the tourist map called the "main plaza"—just a small espresso stand in the middle of a huge cement slab, half-surrounded by cyclone fencing. I was there to meet Enrique LaClette, who had been Huatulco's first SCUBA instructor. For two hours I shouted questions and nodded, while Enrique strained to be heard over the rumble and blur of heavy machinery as workers built a new dock.

An accent, too faint for me to identify, laced Enrique's near-perfect English. I spent the first half-hour of our conversation thinking he was French because of his light eyes and hair, straightforward manner, and last name. I realized he was Mexican only after he asked me how to translate several words from Spanish into English. "How do you call it—¿Censo? ¿Presidente municipal? ¿Meta?" Enrique was from Celaya, Guanajuato, a city often described as one of central Mexico's ugliest. He had left as soon as he'd finished school, backpacking through Europe and Africa before finally realizing that he wanted to return home, but not to his hometown. "I was looking for something new and fresh for starting my life and I hear about this Huatulco thing: on the Pacific Ocean, a tourist development that will grow, with a national park, a beautiful area. So I just come with my backpack." He leaned forward as he talked, so wired with energy that his legs, rather than his chair, seemed to bear his weight. After he arrived in 1988 he lived in a palm hut and offered SCUBA lessons right on the beach. All his personal belongings fit in one box. "It was good, but not *that* good." Enrique was just a couple of years older than I; I could see in his eyes the younger beach-bum idealist battling with the older pragmatic businessman. The beach bum seemed to be losing. Was life in Huatulco getting better or worse? Enrique grappled with that question.

Past the growling cement mixers, fat pylons squatted at the mouth of Santa Cruz Huatulco's petite port: a six-million-dollar cruise-ship dock in the making. Enrique was anxious for those passengers to pour into the languishing Santa Cruz marina "because they can fill the hotels the fastest."

I doubted his optimism. Cruise ship passengers tended to stay in the room they'd already paid for, onboard. And what about the invisible costs of the new dock? What about the coral-reef dredging? What about the tons of waste that pour from those cruise ships into the sea?

Enrique's face hardened into a bored glaze; he'd already thought about all those things. "It is a sacrifice that we must make," he insisted. By "we" he meant all of Mexico. "In the sixties we had the world's elite tourism in Acapulco. In the seventies we had it in Puerto Vallarta. In the eighties we had it in Cancun, and in the nineties it was gone. We are becoming a third-class country for tourism." In the 1950s Hollywood stars had flown private charters to vacation homes in Acapulco. These days, mobs of *springbrekers* jammed cut-rate flights to Cancun then piled into hotel rooms or rented hammocks on the beach, spending their money on cheap booze.

In the first few years after the federal land expropriation in Huatulco, many *licenciados* and *gente preparada*, such as Enrique LaClette, had moved to the former fishing village. "It was very funny watching people with a university education getting together with the people who used to live here." Before 1984 some of them had lived right *here*, their huts located exactly where our wrought-iron chairs scraped freshly hosed pavement. "The mayor, he didn't know how to read and write, and he was giving orders to the engineers, architects, chemists." Enrique's tone conveyed both amazement and disdain. In the microcosm of Huatulco, Enrique observed a Mexican dynamic as old as the European conquest: "Oaxaca is a state with a lot of resentment. There is a big difference between the conquistadors and the conquered. I have a lot of friends who are fishermen or gardeners. One of them told me once that he was mad because the managers of the hotels are foreigners. So I told him, 'Yeah, you should go and manage Club Med. With your education, I'm sure you can do it easily.' What I said was a big shock to him; he didn't know if I was joking or serious." His tone shifted from flat to fatigued. "My generation is getting tired of Che Guevara and the guerrilla and all that." Tired of the huatulqueños because, Enrique said, "They don't want to be prepared to manage anything."

I walked with Enrique back to his small dive shop, Buceos Triton, squeezed between a Bital cash machine and a sundries shop called Super Coco Solo, or "Super Lonesome Coconut." As we said good-bye, he introduced me to a huatulqueño who happened to walk by. This was someone who did, in fact, manage something: a cooperative tour boat company. Francisco Hernández was about to go home for the day but seemed happy enough, in the way that Mexicans usually are, to invite me into the cooperative's small office. Before introducing me to Francisco, Enrique had warned me that, like all huatulqueños, he would tell me how much better everything was before (as in, "before the 1984 expropriation").

But Francisco said nothing like that. Instead he talked about the challenges of the new Huatulco and what was required of him.

In the cooperative's small, perfectly organized office, a fourteen-volume set of books and audiotapes called *Inglés sin Barreras*— "English without Obstacles"—filled one shelf. "The tourist development is nice, but you have to know how to negotiate really well," Francisco said. In a high-quality denim shirt, cuffed khaki shorts, and lug-soled deck shoes, he looked every bit the tour-boat operator he had become. As he talked, though, I could hear glimmers of the indigenous fisherman's son underneath, speaking about the ocean in a wistful tone. Francisco knew that he needed to become one of the gente preparada ("well-educated people") ready to handle all the changes. *Gracias a dios* his mother had made him finish high school, Francisco said, even though he hadn't wanted to bother.

The tourists wanted bigger, fancier boats, so the cooperative had to fix up its catamaran. Tourists spoke only English, hence the collection of books and tapes. Tourists liked to buy things, so they had just purchased a video camera to record and sell mementos of every boat tour.

"Everyone should benefit from Huatulco," Francisco said, referring to both past and future. He explained that there had been a small group of huatulqueño fishermen who had long refused to leave their beachfront huts and their stubbornness had helped the entire community. The long and complicated negotiations over compensation for lost land, lost homes, and lost livelihoods continued, in fact, more than sixteen years after the expropriation. Some had long since received their money: some continued to fight.

Francisco's cooperative had been founded shortly before the expropriation by some of the fishermen who would later be evicted from Santa Cruz Huatulco. They had planned to run a fishing operation but ended up ferrying around government officials and, much later, tourists. Now the cooperative's twenty members managed fifteen boats. The largest, a catamaran called the *Huatulco Fiesta*, could carry 140 passengers. He invited me to join the inaugural trip of American season that coming Saturday.

The cooperative members had adapted in the mid-1980s, and they continued to adapt. When I asked about the new cruise ship dock, Francisco shrugged and said, "We need the cruise ships because we need the work."

Behind the co-op office the sun dissolved into the Pacific; it was time to go home. As Francisco slid the bolt on the office's front door, he asked, "Do you want to see our church?" I already had, but he seemed anxious to show it to me. We walked down the marina toward a pink-and-salmon-stuccoed building that recalled Arizona more than Oaxaca. It was built on the beach with walls opening toward the Pacific on each side of the spare altar, giving every worshipper a waterfront view. Behind the pulpit on a brick pedestal stood a cross. It was rough-hewn and chunky yet somehow elegant and commanding, standing alone rather than surrounded by figures of saints and miracle workers and Virgin Marys, as in most Catholic churches in Mexico. The altarage—unusually minimalist for a Mexican church—consisted of baskets of orange marigolds marking the recent Day of the Dead. Francisco pointed to a smaller cross, crudely cut, that hung at the center of the large one. "That is all that's left of our original cross," he said.

Growing up on the Santa Cruz beach, Francisco had heard the story many times. When Thomas Cavendish dropped anchor in Huatulco in 1587 he was astonished to find the local people venerating a tall cross that appeared far older than Spanish colonization. The name Huatulco comes from a Nahuatl phrase meaning "place where the people worship the wood." The name carried the community's history. The local story, carved into a large wooden plaque in the church's sanctuary, goes like this:

> Nearly two thousand years ago . . . the Indians from these lands saw coming from the sea, as if from Peru, an old, white man, of long hair and beard, a long, tight-fitting tunic, and cloak. This man—who in the millennial tradition of the village, is recognized as Saint Thomas and in Mexican history as Quetzalcoatl—came bearing a beautiful, decorated cross. Scared by this wondrous miracle, many locals gathered on the beach to see it. The white man greeted them benevolently in his own language and was there several days, teaching them many things. He remained there, kneeling. When he wanted to leave them, he told them he was leaving the wooden saint with them, as it was so large and heavy. He himself placed it on the beach. And Indians from all over came to worship the wooden saint.

Thomas Cavendish, whom the British remember as an explorer and the Mexicans remember as a pirate, decided that a non-Christian cross could only be the work of the devil. How could Christianity have arrived before the Christians? He ordered Huatulco's "wooden saint" destroyed; but his men's hatchets could not cut it, their flames could not burn it, even their ships could not haul it into the sea.

Four hundred years later the village of Santa Cruz Huatulco would prove easier to destroy than the old man's cross had been. In the early 1990s the huatulqueños demanded that a church be built on the spot where their homes had been. Carlos Beas had told me about the violence that followed the arrival of FONATUR: two Santa Cruz residents who refused to leave their homes had been murdered. One of them had lived next to what would become the church. "They killed someone here, didn't they?" I asked Francisco. "One of the people who resisted the longest?"

Francisco stared at me for a long moment, as if trying to figure out how I knew about that. A ribbon of brined air floated through the sanctuary, and for just a moment I could picture Santa Cruz Huatulco as a village of palm huts, hammocks, and small boats—not a marina crowded with yachts and stores selling wetsuits, fried fish, and daiquiris.

"Yes, right over here," Francisco said, his voice calm, gesturing toward the west side of the church. "They killed him right here."

In late 1989 Alfredo Lavariega had been shot dead while lying in his hammock in front of the hut where he still lived. By that time most Santa Cruz residents had moved from their hand-built beach huts to cinderblock houses in prefab La Crucecita. Next to the church a large palm tree grew from blank spaces in the paving-stone patio. Nearby, two other palm trees arched between sunbathers' wooden umbrellas. "See those palm trees? He planted those."

The arching palms and the weary look of loss on Francisco's face were the only traces of that decade-old act of violence. Much of the history had been paved over just as surely as the beach huts had been leveled, but scraps of physical evidence remained for those who cared to look. In this way, Huatulco was like the rest of southern Mexico: even a tree could hold political and historical meaning.

At noon the next day I sank into a doughy waiting-room chair at the Huatulco FONATUR office and leafed through a coffee-table book. On the cover the title glittered in silver-foil Spanish above beryline waves: *Twenty-five Years of the National Fund to Promote Tourism.* The office felt more like a travel agency than a government agency, with overstuffed furniture, brochures filled with beaches and bikinis, and the hollow air of a place with more infrastructure than activity.

Jorge Ayanegui, the only Mexican government official I'd ever seen wearing an open-necked, short-sleeved shirt, welcomed me to his office with a wide smile. The eleventh person in sixteen years to hold the job of Huatulco FONATUR director, he leaned against an almost-empty desk in his wood-paneled office. Within a few months of our meeting he would be gone, called back to Mexico City. Rather like a travel agent, he peddled a place more perfect than the one that actually existed. Behind his desk a large, rainbow-colored map showed FONATUR's master plan for Huatulco: three golf courses, dozens of resort hotels clustered around three bays, an international airport, a first-class bus station, three marinas, a zoo, and a national park.

At the time of the expropriation in 1984, FONATUR set out a vision for the Bays of Huatulco by 2000: nearly nine hundred thousand tourists each year visiting a newly urbanized region that is home to one hundred thousand permanent residents, half of them tourism industry workers. As of November 2000, Jorge Ayanegui told me, the real Bays of Huatulco had 2,130 hotel rooms (with a dismal 50 percent occupancy rate) and eighteen thousand permanent residents. He couldn't tell me how many people had visited Huatulco over the last year nor how many jobs the development had created, but the coffee-table book (his gift to me) reported that fewer than two hundred thousand people had visited the Bays of Huatulco in 1998 and, in all, fewer than fifteen hundred jobs had been created.

I asked Ayanegui about water use. Though Huatulco receives about thirty-eight inches of rain annually, nearly all of it falls in July and August. The rest of the year, including all of American season, the water comes from the rivers that run down from the hills to the north. By early November those hills looked parched. "As the tourist development grows, where will the water come from?"

He laughed off my question. "We're only using 50 percent of the water that's available. There's no problem with water here."

Strange math. Huatulco, home and host to one-fifth of the hoped-for population, was already using half the available water, yet to him that meant "no problem." I'd also asked Enrique LaClette about rumors of water shortages. He had looked at me quizzically and replied, "Water is something that we can assume."

To assume plentiful water is, of course, to assume forests. Many of the trees in the forests north of Huatulco had become framing and furniture for Huatulco's hotels. In the past, the peasants who lived in those forests had carefully tended farm plots, improving the soil. They were judicious about the number of trees they cut down to make sure they protected the aquifers. In the last few decades, though, they had traded in traditional practices for slash-and-burn farming—a hopeless attempt to keep one step ahead of falling prices for their corn, beans, and coffee (triggered in large part by the North American Free Trade Agreement). By 1998 more than half of the region's original forests—the basis of the local economy and ecology—had disappeared.

Feliciano García, a huatulqueño farmer, had once tended the exact spot of land on which Jorge Ayanegui's office had been built. García had cultivated corn, sesame, hibiscus flowers, and peanuts. I would not have guessed the earlier use of the long-since-paved plot of land, but Feliciano García's daughter, as it happened, was a friend of Carlos Beas. Beas led me to Marina, who introduced me to her father.

Señor García spent most of his time sitting on a cement

porch in La Crucecita. The day after I visited his former farm I went to visit him on his front porch. Living in a stuffy cement house made him ill, he was sure, so he stayed on the porch day and night. About the size of a bathroom, the porch held a daybed, a box radio, and a folding table. As the old man sat on the bed's faded floral sheets, his knees almost grazed the floor-to-ceiling chain-link fencing that separated porch from sidewalk. There was just enough room for me to sit on a narrow chair borrowed from the dining room. Viewed from the street, the space looked less like a porch than a zoo cage. Because cataracts had transformed señor García's world into foggy outlines, he couldn't see the people who stopped and stared at us. But he knew they were there.

Feliciano García and his wife had moved to La Crucecita in 1987. His adult children, seven sons and three daughters, lived there too, with their own families. "They all have businesses," he said. "And I stay here, like this." He crossed his arms in front of his barrel belly and sat motionless. The García family had received a good sum for the land they had once farmed, enough to start several of those small businesses: a restaurant, a handicraft stall in the market, and a shop that sold Taiwanese beach trinkets. Señor García's children tended to shrug when asked about the expropriation—the past was past.

His daughter Marina had warned me that I would need to be extremely patient when talking to her seventy-nine-year-old father, but he spoke with razor clarity. He gave me a narrative more linear than I usually heard in Mexico, where stories would often start in the middle and move backward and forward at the same time.

In 1959 the García family had been one of twenty to build houses in Santa Cruz Huatulco. "Before that, no one lived in the lowlands," he told me. They had come to the coast only to harvest turtles, clams, and oysters, spending most of their time farming the hills to the north. His map of the coast of Oaxaca included far-off ports, which at that time were the closest market towns. "We went to Puerto Angel by boat to sell our products. Then we got the money to go to Pochutla to buy what we needed. We went by water. We didn't go by land because we couldn't. We couldn't get across the large rivers and gullies. That's how it was. Then the highway was built and the cars came in." After that, FONATUR came in too. The beach *palapa,* where the Garcías had lived, had been replaced by another, a restaurant called Frente al Mar that is now managed by one of his sons.

The Garcías and the other Santa Cruz residents learned they were losing their land when the governor of Oaxaca visited their community on May 28, 1984. "Some people said that the governor was coming to expropriate, but we didn't believe them. No. But then they came. We suffered a lot, señora. They threw us out. It doesn't matter. Everything has its end." He shrugged and turned his vacant gaze away from me.

On Saturday morning I joined Francisco Hernández, nine other cooperative members, and fourteen tourists for a day aboard the *Huatulco Fiesta* catamaran. The co-op members dashed around the spotless desk—helping the guests into their life jackets; pouring them generous drinks from new bottles of brandy, rum, tequila, and mescal; announcing the day's itinerary; pointing the video camera in all directions; handing out iced bottles of beer; and untying the boat from its mooring—all at once and with giddy energy. American season had begun though I was the only North American on the nearly empty boat. Maybe *this* would be the year that Huatulco would fulfill its promise. Twenty dollars bought a ticket for the day's trip (plus all you could drink) and another four dollars rented a snorkel, mask, and fins (no lesson provided).

Even on the *Huatulco Fiesta*, managed by huatulqueños, the beaches we glided past seemed just like every other tropical beach where I'd snorkeled or swum. The first moment I'd seen Huatulco's bays, they had seemed heartbreakingly perfect: a single boat cutting the lapis water, a few figures walking across a curl of white sand. Why did those bays now fade into mediocrity? Was it because as tourists, we all see the same things, from the same vantage point? I couldn't decide whether the day aboard the *Huatulco Fiesta* met my expectations or if I could only see what I had expected to find here. Perhaps my expectations—the same as everyone else's—left an unavoidable impression that was reflected back at me.

"Would you like something to drink?" Francisco asked me, cutting into my thoughts. "A rum-and-Coke?"

My stomach lurched though I'm not prone to seasickness. Francisco didn't push it. Skilled tour guide that he was, he hit on something that would interest me more than a mixed drink before noon: "That's Cacaluta Beach," he said in a buoyant tone, pointing at the glowing crescent as the catamaran motored past. "The name means 'where the black birds are' in Zapotec. Thirty families lived there before the expropriation." He paused as the beach glided by, showing no trace of those families' former homes. "And that's Arroyo Beach; there's a seasonal river that meets the bay there. It's a good place for watching deer. If you walk over the mountain between Cacaluta Beach and Arroyo Beach you'll find lots of artifacts, pottery and stuff." The catamaran floated west, passing colorful striations in rocky cliffs that rose up at sharp angles from luminous sand. "And this is Chachacual." Francisco's voice turned reverent and faintly sad. "It's the most pristine, the most isolated. The only way to get there is by boat."

We motored past Chachacual, then Francisco's tour ended as we arrived at our destination, San Agustín Beach. It was exactly like every other Mexican tourist beach I'd visited: rustic, open-air restaurants selling seafood; young women selling dyed coral necklaces and lacquered shells; children selling candy, cigarettes, and plastic bottles of soda. Each receding wave littered the beach with broken bits of dead coral.

Francisco sent us out to snorkel over the reef. We stayed together, like fish in a timid school. Fins slapped other people's masks, flailing arms bumped soft bellies; frantic splashes rained down on my back. The tide was too low; we kicked up sandy clouds as we battered the top of the fragile reef. The sediment smoke parted briefly and I caught glimpses of a few pale yellow tangs, a blue-and-white polka-dotted fish, and black sea urchins with eight-inch spines. Maybe our innocent havoc didn't even matter. Local ecologists referred to San Agustín's beach as "a garbage dump," a lost cause.

After leaving San Agustín we visited Bahía Maguey. Huatulco's most visited bay, Bahía Maguey was named for the agave used to make tequila and mescal. No one bothered to snorkel at Maguey anymore; the coral had long since been choked to death by outboard motors. Our group filtered into a beachside restaurant, also owned by the huatulqueño cooperative. I sat at the outermost table where the tide nearly reached my bare feet. Three men in jeans and cowboy hats see-sawed their pointy-toed boots through the sand. One carried a drum, another an accordion, and the third a massive string bass. The woman at the next table pointed and stared, open-mouthed. "A mariachi, at the *beach*." Actually, it was a *banda norteña*: a drum and accordion had replaced the mariachi guitar and trumpet. The banda seemed to have landed here by accident, as arbitrarily as we had arrived. A family hired them to play as the waiter lowered a wide platter before me: *pescado a la Veracruzana* (grilled fish swimming in tomato salsa).

Just offshore, a teenager with a large cross glinting at his throat toured small children around on a wailing Jet Ski. The kids sat on the seat as the boy stood over them, gripping the handles and steering jerkily. The Jet Skier's buddy approached me, his black hair dripping saltwater onto my table. "Want to go?" he said, pulling out the vowels of the English words. "Only thirty pesos." His expression hovered between cool and imploring.

"No, gracias."

"But it's very safe," he said, switching into Spanish. "And only twenty-five pesos for four minutes." Theoretically that meant the jet skiing pair—one buzzing the tables, the other the waves—could earn thirty dollars an hour, a colossal sum.

"It's not the cost. Those things create a lot of pollution."

We both looked out over the blue pearl bay. "But," he said, "you can't see it."

The discomfort that had been lapping at my toes all day—no, from the minute I'd arrived in Huatulco—broke over me like an unexpected wave. *That* is the essence of tourism: only what is visible matters.

*Only what is visible matters:* the idea haunted me, several months later, when I returned to Huatulco for another visit. I made the trip from Matías Romero to Huatulco again so that I could talk to Laurentino Cormona. He didn't seem happy to see me the day that I showed up at his farm. From La Crucecita I'd taken first a bus, then a collective taxi filled with people and groceries and sweat, then waded across the wide, shallow Coyula River. Three buzzards circled overhead as I pulled off my shoes and stepped into the insistent current.

Mid-river, two young girls scrubbed a wheelbarrow's worth of laundry on flat rocks. They crouched next to a teepee of sticks and palm fronds that shielded their bare heads and bony shoulders from the flaying sun. When they saw me they both jumped up, shouting and waving. We were only 15 miles from La Crucecita, still on the land that the government had expropriated in 1984, yet the sight of a gringa was something out of the ordinary.

I waved back as I curled my toes around smooth river stones, trying to not lose my balance in the rushing water. Nearly every inch of Bajos de Coyula, the river's floodplain, shimmered with life, even at the peak of the dry season. Palms heavy with coconuts bowed overhead; glass-green cornstalks shimmered in the breeze; papayas the color of sunset bulged from skinny trees.

During Christmas and Easter holidays, exceptionally skilled taxi drivers maneuvered their sedans over the hilly dirt road that connected Bajos de Coyula to the coastal highway. Mexican families came and bought baked fish, fresh coconuts, and beer, sleeping in hammocks hung inside open-air palapas. The post-and-palm structures were rebuilt each year; it was less work than trying to construct something that could withstand the hurricane season's rage. Foreigners rarely visited Bajos de Coyula. FONATUR representatives didn't go there either. The local residents had marked a line across the road heading to the village and told FONATUR not to cross it.

I climbed between two strings of barbed wire and finally arrived at a cluster of banana trees poking from low grasses: the edge of the Cormona family farm. A boy, one of Laurentino Cormona's sons, stared at me silently from a long way off, then turned back to summon his father. Señor Cormona appeared fifteen minutes later. After a few more minutes of explanations, nods, and long pauses, the farmer told his oldest son, Guillermo, to fetch coconuts. Guillermo tied a machete to his waistband then shimmied up, his hands and thighs gripping the smooth trunk. Perhaps thirty feet overhead he balanced at the palm's crown and wrestled a large cluster of coconuts into a pulley harness. His father eased the bunch to the ground and separated one fruit from the gnarled branch with a confident machete swing. One more *thwack* let loose a mist of coconut hairs and opened an inch-wide hole in one end of the fruit.

I nodded a thank you and hefted the coconut in both hands, pressing the sheared side to my mouth. The cool, sweet-sour liquid ran over my tongue. Until that moment I'd thought that I disliked coconut water. Once I handed back the empty shell with an effusive gracias, Cormona was finally ready to talk to me about his seventeen-year conflict with the Mexican government over the fate of Bajos de Coyula.

The Coyula River meets the Pacific Ocean at a deep-water beach. When I walked along the Coyula beach later that day, the waves crashed into the land with such fury that I could feel the tremors sent through the concrete-hard sand. Because of that immitigable fury, FONATUR didn't plan to fill the beach with four-star hotels, sunbathers, and SCUBA divers. I never could get anyone at FONATUR to tell me exactly what they wanted to do with Coyula—only that it would be part of the "second phase" of Huatulco's tourist resort development. The local director of the federal environmental agency told me that the most important thing about Bajos de Coyula was its river, by far Huatulco's largest source of fresh water.

Rather than invite me into his home, Laurentino Cormona thought for a long time about where we could go to talk. I followed his bleached-white shirt and chalk-colored jeans like a beacon through the baking streets. We trudged past Coyula's general store, a cantina, a small restaurant, another cantina, the homes of the town's wealthiest residents, and a third cantina. Buzzards still circled overhead. More than one-third of the families in Bajos de Coyula belonged to the nonprofit organization Cormona had founded to fight the government expropriation, and many others were quietly supportive. But he still had to be careful about who might overhear a conversation about his fight with the federal government. Just as my patience began to stretch thin, Cormona decided on an open-air bar not yet open for the day.

He began his story by telling me about his neighbors' new houses. FONATUR had told the people of Coyula to stop building because they no longer owned the land. They kept building. He couldn't remember exactly what he had been doing the morning of Wednesday, May 30, 1984. He was probably somewhere on the 5 acres of land that he has farmed his entire life. One thing he remembered clearly: a neighbor came by midafternoon and showed him a newspaper with an article announcing that the Mexican government was taking control of all the coastal land—including his 5 acres—in the municipality of Santa María Huatulco.

The article that appeared in the Oaxaca City newspaper on May 30, 1984, probably the one that Cormona saw, quoted the state's governor: "This great project becomes a reality for the people of Oaxaca today, with concrete actions to strengthen their future." Cormona insisted he was happy with the future that he'd had before the expropriation. He refused the small indemnity he was offered by FONATUR for his home and farm—accepting the money would mean accepting the expropriation. By the time he spoke to me, he and the others in Bajos de Coyula had been saying *No* for sixteen years, insisting they would one day regain legal title to the 8,000 acres they had owned communally. They found lawyers in Oaxaca City and Mexico City willing to help them pro bono, "because we don't have a single lawyer or licenciado here." The people of Bajos de Coyula did have reason to be hopeful. According to Mexican federal law, expropriated land must be developed within five years, and the government had missed that deadline three times over.

I told Cormona that I'd spoken with the director of FONATUR. "He mentioned only two communities still fighting the expropriation. He didn't mention Bajos de Coyula."

"Well, he has already forgotten us," he said with a small smile. He'd spent the better part of the previous sixteen years making sure that FONATUR didn't forget about Bajos de Coyula. Laurentino Cormona remained hopeful. "With God's help we will succeed. We have faith that, in the end, we will get out of this expropriation."

"So far, things are going well," he told me calmly, as if he were talking about a situation that had lasted just a few months. "We keep living here; we keep sowing our fields and building houses."

After visiting Bajos de Coyula and the man leading the fight against FONATUR, I could finally leave Huatulco. I hoped never to return. The next day I happily checked out of my hotel and chose a sunny seat at the bus station's streetside waiting area amidst middle-class families from Mexico City and blond backpackers from elsewhere. So much money spent, so much forest leveled, so many lives changed to make their tourist experience possible. The people sitting around me didn't seem particularly happy to be in the Huatulco that FONATUR had built for them. No happier than crowds of people pushing through a city street to get to work on a weekday morning or at a shopping mall on a Sunday afternoon.

Once I arrived home to Matías Romero—where the only tourists I ever encountered were lost—Huatulco seemed so far from the isthmus that I couldn't imagine the same thing happening in San Mateo del Mar. But, then, Feliciano García and Laurentino Cormona had never imagined it could happen to their villages either. I had asked Enrique LaClette, the dive instructor, why he supported the tourist development and the cruise-ship dock even though he considered himself an environmentalist. He wanted Huatulco to grow, he explained, even as he feared that growth. "There will be more people, more concrete, more boats, more everything," he had said. "It is very, very hard. Sometimes you just have to hold your stomach and realize that it is better to protect people than nature. There is a poem, by the emperor Nezahuacoyotl, on our hundred-peso bill." That poem, he explained, exemplified his feelings.

I pulled a hundred-peso bill from my wallet and looked at it, but I didn't see a poem. Then I saw a tiny smudge at the bottom of the bill—could that be it? I dug through my desk drawer for a magnifying glass and stepped outside into the midafternoon sun. The text was so minute that even with the magnifying glass focusing bright rays onto the worn bill, it took several minutes to decipher the five short lines by the Aztec king.

Amo el canto del zenzontle
Pájaro de 400 voces
Amo el color del jade
Y el enervante perfume de las flores
Pero amo más a mi hermano el hombre

I love the song of the mockingbird
Bird of four hundred voices
I love the color of jade
And the intoxicating perfume of flowers
But I love man, my brother, more.

# 6

## Isthmus Defended

Carlos Beas decided I should spend my first New Year's Day at Guiengola, the most important ancient ruin on the Isthmus of Tehuantepec. I needed the history lesson, he insisted, because there was a connection between UCIZONI resisting the highway and what had happened at Guiengola centuries earlier. Istmeños had been fighting invasions for a millennium and Guiengola was a monument to that struggle.

The ruin was also the most important tourist attraction—to the extent that such a thing exists—on the Isthmus of Tehuantepec. Miguel Covarrubias, author of *Mexico South*, had gone there as well. Though Guiengola wasn't as well known as the Aztecs' Teotihuacán, or Monte Albán in Oaxaca City, or the Maya sites of Tulúm and Chichén Itzá south of Cancun, it told an equally important story about ancient Mexican history.

Beas, his partner Mirna, and I left Matías Romero early on New Year's Day 2001, with severe hangovers and not nearly enough bottled water. After an hour's drive southwest from Matías Romero, we came to the turnoff for Guiengola not far from the city of Tehuantepec. A military checkpoint blocked the highway exit. Young soldiers sweating in heavy

**7.** Maximina Martínez celebrates at an isthmus fiesta in San Francisco del Mar (2002). PHOTO BY THE AUTHOR.

fatigues gazed dully from a hut built of sandbags and palm fronds in the middle of the road. Next to the road was a large pile of boulders, a sort of handmade ramp that spanned the sharp drop-off between the highway and the road toward Guiengola. Sitting in the back seat of the Volkswagen Beetle, I looked down at my feet as we passed the soldiers, our small car pitching and heaving over the rock pile off-ramp. Turning away from the soldiers was an automatic response after having passed through so many military checkpoints. Avoiding eye contact somehow reduced the chances of being stopped and asked a long series of questions. Where was I from? How long I had been in Mexico? How did I know the other people in the car?

Once safely past the soldiers, the Beetle spiraled slowly around the mountain on a road that matched the highway off-ramp: no pavement, cement, gravel, sand, or clay—just rocks. Through the flexible skin of the Volkswagen's belly I felt the rubble sliding under the soles of my sandals. Out the window, low bushes gave way to scrub forest, dry as matchsticks. The name Guiengola, which in Zapotec means "large, old rock," seemed perfectly appropriate.

The road widened out to a dirt parking lot. Beas swung the car into the only circle of mottled shade, passing by a faded sign that instructed us to find an official guide to accompany us. The three of us climbed a boulder-strewn hillside toward a pathway that led sharply up. The path, bare and white, stood out from green trees with long spines. Judging from the lack of trash it seemed few people had visited Guiengola recently. Some istmeños believed the site haunted and refused to visit it. We passed a second rusted sign suggesting we hire a guide, then a third that insisted we not continue alone. One of the only tourist guidebooks to mention Guiengola notes that visiting the site without a Zapotec guide from the city of Tehuantepec "could get you in mucho trouble with the authorities."

We passed a fourth sign that said only "Please ask permission." Beas laughed. "First they told us to get a guide. But they figure if you've made it this far, you aren't turning around." He leaned back on his heels and yelled, "We ask permission to continue!" We waited as his voice echoed away from us. Mirna and I raised our eyebrows at one another, Beas shrugged, and we all started hiking again.

As we plodded along the path, up and down, then more steeply up, the heat glared down, dulling the colors of the marbleized limestone and quartz boulders along the path. We had chosen the coolest month of the year but the warmest time of day for our pilgrimage. An old saying from India, often repeated in European travel narratives about the isthmus, marched through my mind: *Only mad dogs and Englishmen go out in the midday sun*. In our case it was dogs, foreigners, and people with New Year's Day hangovers.

We crested the first peak and the path leveled out, the land dropping off to one side. The isthmus lowlands stretched far below us. One of the most dramatic landscape changes in all of Mexico—a country replete with geographic contrast—occurs here, where the humid hills of the central isthmus plunge toward the southern dry plains. The earth and leaf tones of irrigated farmland, tended by Zapotec farmers, stretch hazily toward the Huave lagoons on the Pacific coast. The land extends almost perfectly flat, interrupted only by trees scattered in knots and wavy lines. The view lifted my spirits despite my throbbing temples.

Mirna began to gaze, eyes filled with doubt, at the steep path before us. Beas shook the half-empty water bottle, reminding us that we needed to reach the top before the temperature rose too high. We continued trekking, grim eyes trained on the rocky path underfoot. Though Guiengola Mountain would hardly count as a hill in most of Mexico, it is the isthmus's highest point and steepest climb. A folded landscape runs from Alaska's Mt. Denali all the way to Guiengola, continuing south into Guatemala. The mountains run down the continent from the Alaska Range, through the Cascades and Sierra Nevada, to Mexico's Sierra Madre. The ridge dips below 800 feet at only one place: the Isthmus of Tehuantepec. The Guiengola outpost was built at the southern end of more than 4,000 miles of rugged terrain. In a sense it's the last North American mountain.

The rocky path finally flattened out, the cacti giving way to long-needle pine and nanche fruit trees. Mirna, Beas, and I stumbled into a tangle of leaves and rocks and earthen mounds. Grayish white succulent leaves, like two-foot-long arrowheads, whorled from the center of Guiengola agaves—a species of succulent that grows only on this mountain. Squat *biznaguitas*, barrel cacti that are also native to Guiengola, wedged themselves between rocks and sand. Quietly regal, Guiengola made every other ancient ruin I'd visited, carefully rebuilt and scrubbed of time's markers, seem Disneyesque: Here the steep charcoal walls of the pyramids seemed set within the landscape rather than looming above it. Despite centuries of looting, Guiengola still held small treasures. Beas plucked a C-shaped bit of pottery, probably the handle of an old pot, from an indentation in a boulder. As Mirna and I turned it over in our hands, Beas told us about pre-Columbian soldiers who camped out at Guiengola, about how this place had protected the isthmus from invaders. I was reminded of the job that had brought Beas to the isthmus in the first place: teacher of anthropology. Beas returned the pot sherd to the crevice where he'd found it. Mirna and I wandered the plaza between the two pyramids, straining to move a disc-shaped rock propped in a small entryway. To our surprise we found the narrow opening to an underground chamber. Protected from light, wind, and rain, the walls of the entryway were perfectly intact. The dark recess, probably a tomb, exhaled cool breath from far underground. We looked at each other, both knowing we weren't brave enough to enter, and pushed the stone disk back into place.

Guiengola's main buildings sit 1,300 feet above the Tehuantepec River, about halfway up the mountainside. Perched high over the valley floor yet between Guiengola's twin peaks, there's almost no way enemy troops could surround the site. Workers or slaves or penitents—no one is sure which—moved limestone rocks and tons of soil from the mountainside to fill in the hollow between Guiengola's two mountain peaks. They created an artificial plateau of 64,000 square yards, the equivalent of more than eight soccer fields. Siting the fortress here hid it from invaders. The Zapotecs built a 100,000-square-foot palace, with sixty-four rooms, eleven patios, thirty-eight columns, twenty-five stairways, several grain silos, a swimming pool, and a burial crypt for their king, Cosijoeza. They carved large depressions in the limestone rock to collect rainwater for drinking.

Aside from a few wooden supports propped against collapsing walls, Guiengola had been left to rain, wind, and the will of the gods. Tree roots pressed apart stacked and stuccoed walls, sending stones avalanching to the ground. Muscular agaves grew out of near-vertical pyramid faces, threatening to pull away large sections of the wall. Still the site was remarkably intact. Guiengola's builders had mixed sand and clay to create stucco, black and rough as asphalt but far tougher. Earthquakes and hurricanes and tidal waves have obliterated so much of what ancient istmeños left behind; Guiengola is a singular treasure.

As we wandered around the pyramids, plazas, lookouts, and ball courts, a comforting quiet surrounded us. Since passing the soldiers we had not encountered a single other person. A lizard sat motionless under a tree while I stroked its tail. A yellow-bellied bird with iridescent green wings watched us carefully with a blue-ringed eye. This bird, a citreoline trogon, seemed calm, not moving until we stood just a few feet from it. Though it was a military fortress, Guiengola felt strangely peaceful. Its current inhabitants seemed watchful but not fearful.

As the scant cup of water left in our bottle turned hot, we turned back to the trail, wending our way past mesquite and liquid amber trees. We passed a wall, built halfway between trailhead and fortress, that I had not noticed on the way up. The long curving wall, ten feet tall and five feet thick, was built without mortar, held together only by tight-fitting stones. The wall had once surrounded most of the mountain, offering further fortification against invasion. On top it flattened out to a platform wide enough for soldiers to watch for approaching enemies. My gaze landed on a baseball-sized stone, almost perfectly round. As I turned the rock over in my hand, Beas said, "They used these rocks as ammunition."

I laughed, thinking he was kidding. How could those loose stones have been there for more than five hundred years? He gave me a look that had become familiar. It meant, You think I'm just making this up, but you'll see. We reached the bottom of the trail just as the sun reached the peak of its New Year's Day arc.

Later I learned that archeologists who had written treatises on Guiengola agreed with Beas: the river-smoothed stones still found there had been carried up the dry mountainside to become catapult projectiles. Fifteenth-century Zapotec soldiers lobbed river rock ammunition at Aztec armies that had marched south from central Mexico. In hand-to-hand combat the Zapotecs wielded flint-encrusted clubs and rock-headed hammers. Undeterred, the Aztecs attacked over and over again. Their king wanted the isthmus for himself, just as the Zapotecs' king had. The Zapotec soldiers had invaded the isthmus from Oaxaca's central valley, snatching southern isthmus lands from the Huave people.

Before anyone called this continent "America," three decades before the Spaniards arrived, the Zapotecs built Guiengola as a military base and palace for their king, fending off invasions from the Aztecs. That's one version of the story—the one told by most Zapotecs and, with less confidence, most historians. Another version goes like this: An eon or two before the Zapotecs and Aztecs fought over the isthmus, an unknown people, perhaps the ancestors of the Maya, came to Guiengola and built the black and gray pyramids. That's the version of the story Beas tells. After burrowing through a library's worth of books I still can't say which version edges closer to the truth.

These days, when istmeños organize roadblocks of the trans-isthmus carretera or demand retribution when PEMEX spills oil on their land, they often invoke the long-ago battles at Guiengola. The ruin is a monument to strategic genius and evidence of the very long tradition of istmeño ingenuity. Aztec troops invaded the southern isthmus but failed to conquer the Zapotecs, confounded by Guiengola's labyrinthine walls. They made camp and tried to wait out the Zapotecs barricaded at their mountaintop garrison. They seemed to assume the soldiers *had* to leave the fortress at some point. Their mistake. At night, small groups of Zapotec soldiers descended the mountain and attacked the Aztecs, who were already suffering from the brutal heat of the southern isthmus. The standoff at Guiengola wore on for seven months.

The mountaintop had no streams or springs, so the Zapotecs carved hollows in huge rocks to catch rainfall. Several istmeños told me that, as one nineteenth-century historian had put it, the Zapotec soldiers at Guiengola "made the flesh of all the dead Aztecs into dried meat." Three times the Aztec king sent reinforcements from Tenochtitlán. Finally he declared a truce and called home his weakened troops.

The story of the last Zapotec king is one that many have studied, many more have told, and none can verify. Here is one version culled from many: In 1502 King Cosijoeza's third child—the one he had decided would succeed him—was born. He named his successor "Wind of Lightning," or Cosijopii. It was a slighter version of the king's own name, which could be translated as "Lightning that Inspires Trembling in the Ether of the Clouds." Little Cosijopii came into the world on one of those isthmus winter nights when a stiff wind raises bumps on your skin and the horizon blazes orange and red. A Zapotec priest told King Cosijoeza that the weather was a bad omen; the prince's reign would be unlucky and the man himself unhappy. The boy's name foretold his sad life: he would begin his royal tenure with the might of a lightning bolt but his power would fade away with the wind. At the age of fifteen, as the story goes, Prince Cosijopii became King of Tehuantepec while his father continued to rule the rest of the Zapotec kingdom near what is now Oaxaca City.

The year after Cosijopii ascended to the isthmus throne, the Spaniards invaded the Aztec capital, far north of the isthmus. On November 8, 1519, Montezuma and Spanish conquistador Hernán Cortés faced each other for the first time in a meeting that would have a profound effect on Cosijopii's life. Montezuma climbed down from his sedan chair,

Cortés from his horse, and they stood nearly eye-to-eye. By allowing Cortés, a common man, to look him in the eye, Montezuma bestowed a gift on this visitor. The significance of this concession was lost on Cortés, who noticed only that he wasn't permitted to touch Montezuma. The Aztec king offered the Spaniard a necklace of shells and gold, food for his nearly 400 soldiers, fodder for their horses, women to grind corn for them (or so said Cortés), and comfortable lodgings in Montezuma's father's palace. The Spaniards took these things as gifts of welcome but the intended message was probably something closer to: *Here are some things to placate you. May you soon go away.* Or maybe those gifts weren't offered, but requested. In the Aztecs' account of the meeting Cortés and his soldiers demanded the food and fodder, then gold, and they were provided grudgingly.

Cortés wrote to the king of Spain, Carlos V, that he had asked Montezuma about good land to farm and safe harbor for his ships. For some reason he didn't ask the real question on his mind: Where might his ships pass from Atlantic to Pacific for travel from Europe to India? As Cortés told his king, this was "the one thing in the world which I most desire to discover."

Montezuma did not know where Cortés might find safe harbor, so he ordered his cartographers to paint a map. With this map the Aztec cartographers painted a new future for the Isthmus of Tehuantepec. "On the following day," Cortés wrote to King Carlos, "they brought me a cloth with all the coast painted on it, and there appeared a river which ran to the sea, and according to the representation was wider than all the others." Cortés needed an indigenous map to find what his own eyes had missed. Before landing in Mexico his ships had prowled the Mexican Gulf Coast, searching for an inlet that would lead toward the Pacific Ocean. When they passed the Coatzacoalcos River delta at the Isthmus of Tehuantepec they hardly noticed it, though it was precisely what they sought.

Cortés sent off ten Spanish explorers with the map and Aztec guides. The Aztecs led the Spaniards to the Coatzacoalcos River even though it coursed through land inhabited by Montezuma's enemies. According to Cortés, the explorers returned to the Aztec capital, where the conquistador awaited them, with great news: the answers to all three of his burning questions. Cortés later told the story this way: Lord Rabbit, the leader of the northern istmeños, enemies of the Aztecs, had given them more than one hundred canoes to navigate the waterway. Paddling upriver, they had found fantastically rich farmland—soils that would eventually offer vanilla, indigo, corn, cotton, cacao, sugar, and beef cattle to colonial Mexico. Even more important, the Coatzacoalcos delta would make an excellent port for trade between Mexico and the Caribbean.

Thrilled by the news, Cortés sent 150 men to found a military garrison on the northern isthmus. On Easter Sunday 1522 the Spaniards stormed a village on the banks of the Coatzacoalcos, 14 miles inland from the river's mouth. They renamed the site Villa del Espíritu Santo, or "House of the Holy Spirit." The depopulation of the indigenous residents happened relatively easily, to hear the chroniclers of the Spanish conquest tell it: they claim the local people fled at the sight of Spanish military garrisons being set up around their adobe and palapa town.

Meanwhile, other Spanish troops prowled the southern coast of the isthmus, sailing the treacherous waters of the Pacific Ocean and searching for an inlet, or delta, or bay—a promising place for a path across the isthmus for shipments between Europe and Asia. The group planted crosses in the sands at what is now Salina Cruz. Cortés made the great salt flats there part of his *marquesía*, the land he claimed for himself. There are still towns on the southern isthmus whose names end in de Marqués, "belonging to Cortés." The Spanish conquistadors decided the Isthmus of Tehuantepec was the best site for their transcontinental path, as so many foreigners have decided since then, over and over again.

Meanwhile, the Zapotec king, Cosijoeza, learned of the Spaniards' arrival and sent them gifts. Unlike the Aztecs' gifts, whose intended message was probably along the lines of, *Please don't bother us*, Cosijoeza wanted to convey something different: *Let's talk, we might be able to help each other*. Cosijoeza thought an alliance with the Spanish troops might allow him to finally vanquish the Aztecs, who, he predicted, would fall to the Spanish because of the Aztecs' fear, as a nineteenth-century historian described it, of "the lightning they held in their hands": gunpowder. Cosijoeza was right about the Aztecs, more or less, but Tehuantepec ended up more vassal than ally of the Spanish crown. Cosijoeza battled the Aztecs so that his people would not have to pay tribute to them. Instead, the Zapotecs ended up paying tribute to the Spanish crown.

After the death of the elder Zapotec royal, Cosijoeza, Cosijopii, his son, converted to Catholicism. Now called Juan Cortés, he went on to wear Spanish-style robes (this, along with carrying a weapon, was considered an honor) and to order a great Dominican church built in the city of Tehuantepec. Juan Cortés Cosijopii accepted Spanish rule and Catholic doctrine by day but continued his traditional religious practices at night. In the end his collaboration with the conquistadors would be his undoing: twenty-three years after he allied himself with the Spanish they arrested him for participating in a Zapotec religious ceremony. Depressed and ill, he made the grueling trip to Mexico City to face trial. He died, unhappy and unlucky—just as the Zapotec priests had predicted the day he was born—while traveling back, only 60 miles from home.

After my visit to Guiengola I came to see more clearly the layers of history that blanketed isthmus lands; the stories began to seep into me. I saw the deep antecedents of the Zapotecs' tendency to incorporate outside custom into local culture—Catholic churches, velvet dresses, global trade—rather than reject such things. I began to appreciate the long, still-relevant histories behind things I had wondered about, or had hardly noticed. As my senses opened more fully to the place I realized that I had spent my first seven months on the isthmus blocking much of it out. Like the noise.

Though it was a small town, Matías Romero rattled and buzzed, squawked and blared. I went to sleep each night wearing earphones, turning up music over my neighbors' thumping stereo, over the booming sermons from the nearby evangelical church, over the incessant clucking and crowing of the chickens and roosters in the frontyard.

During the day I concentrated on my computer screen's cursor until the sound of my fingers tapping the keyboard was the only thing I heard. I learned to block out the distractions but I missed the important sounds, too. When the gas tank feeding my stove reached empty, I didn't hear the banging of a wrench on metal, signaling the gas vendor's truck in front of my house. When I had just a few sips of drinking water left in my five-gallon jug I didn't hear the forlorn cry of "¡Aguaaaaa!" from the water vendor on his tricycle cart. Trash bags piled up outside my front door because I didn't want to burn my trash and I missed the weekly jingling bells indicating the garbage truck would pass by soon. The bags remained, growing fetid. More than once the neighbor's son tapped on the living-room window to tell me the garbage truck was out front, while his mother burned piles of plastic bottles in our shared frontyard.

Behind the human buzz of the isthmus hung another curtain of sound. Each night after my neighbors went to sleep, this curtain rose around me: thousands of tiny creatures rubbed hard calcium wings, their collective hum rising and falling with a tone somewhere between the wind's whistle and a hooting owl. Down an octave, other insects pealed an on-and-off bizert bizert bizert. Under the insects' calls, fat drops of water knocked softly against warm rocks, against waxy leaves, against the moss-softened roof. These sounds of the isthmus had not changed through millennia.

Most of all, it was smells that reminded me of the history of the Isthmus of Tehuantepec, of invasions wrangled into cultural intermingling. At fiestas, corn tamales steamed in banana leaves, beer spilled on dry dust, firecrackers fizzled in the warm air, velvet dresses wilted with sweat, and pineapple juice dribbled from foam cups. I attended fiestas in Mixe and Huave villages that mixed Catholic iconography, Zapotec dress, Aztec food, Spanish prayers, and mestizo music, even as villagers remembered with acrimony the invasions of the Zapotecs, Aztecs, Spanish, and mestizos. Battles and coronations and vanquishings recorded on ancient walls and in five-hundred-year-old codices linked to contemporary events and resentments and alliances. On the Isthmus of Tehuantepec time did not stretch out in a straight line but curled back on itself in surprising ways.

As I began to grasp isthmus history, my understanding of those events and resentments and alliances changed too. On one of my early visits to the Boca Barra, San Francisco del Mar's fishing grounds, Román Cruz had asked me, "How do you feel here? Do you feel safe?"

He and I were sitting in his fishing hut a few yards from the lagoon. The sun had long since slid below the horizon and soon it would be time for Román to drop his fishing nets into the warm sea. We drank Nescafé and ate pastries; the only sounds were the wind, the lapping lagoon, low voices from other huts, and an occasional crowing rooster. How could I possibly feel unsafe?

Registering my surprise with an arch smile, Román continued. "Lots of people won't come to the isthmus because they say it's dangerous. They say we're rebellious."

It was true. I'd had numerous conversations with middle-class urban Mexicans in which they asked me questions such as: How can you go there by yourself? Aren't you scared?

Román leaned forward into his words, his light brown eyes both playful and proud. "I think it's healthy, a lot healthier than other places." Román took pride in the lives his people had built for themselves. Maybe he was a bit too proud. "Now that you have been to all the Huave communities, which is the most advanced?" he asked me. Three Huave towns, San Francisco, San Mateo, and San Dionisio, all surrounded the pair of lagoons where the Huave fished. Rough water and harsh weather had separated the three communities for many centuries, and each had its own dialect of Huave, its own subculture. I knew Román's question was rhetorical; I leaned back in my metal chair and waited out the silence.

"San Francisco has advanced," he continued, "because it has intermixed. Look at my family. My father came from Unión Hidalgo. My mother is Huave, but her parents came from Salina Cruz and Tehuantepec."

His words hung in the salt-sharp air. Had I heard wrong? Unión Hidalgo is a Zapotec fishing town on the other side of the lagoon. Tehuantepec is a Zapotec city and Salina Cruz is a port-and-petroleum boomtown where most residents are mestizo. The statement was too simple for me to have misunderstood.

Simple words, but not a simple idea. I realized Román was no longer telling me about his village or his own family history. He was telling me about the nature of identity and what it meant to him to be indigenous. Later I asked him again about the conversation. Yes, he confirmed, I'd heard him correctly. "So, your grandparents are all from Zapotec communities? Your blood, so to speak, your lineage, is 100 percent Zapotec?"

He smiled and gave a shrug of acknowledgment. "But I feel 100 percent Huave!" Román had been born in San Francisco del Mar. He didn't speak Huave, but hardly any San Franciscans younger than fifty did.

Román had chosen as his community of origin one whose own origin is unknown. No one knows where the Huave people came from originally, though linguists and archeologists place their arrival on the Isthmus of Tehuantepec sometime between eight hundred and three thousand years ago. That makes them relative newcomers; the Mixes, Chontals, and Zoques have lived in the region several thousand years. That's as much as anyone can say for sure. The Huave probably arrived by boat, perhaps from what is now Peru, possibly with a long stopover in what is now Nicaragua. That's one hypothesis; another—one that I heard from several Huave villagers—is that they came from outer space.

A few nights before my first conversation with Román about his Zapotec heritage, his nephew, Vicente Gómez, Leonel's younger brother, had asked me, "Hey, have you seen the OVNIs near the lagoon? Let's go, maybe I can show them to you."

At that point I'd only spent a couple of weeks in Huave communities, but at least half a dozen people had asked me whether I'd heard about the *objetos voladores no identificados* (UFOs). My queries (never clearly answered) about the ancient history of the Huave people seemed to prompt these questions.

Vicente, his girlfriend, Carolina, and I piled into the Gómez family's pickup truck. I turned to Carolina. "What do you know about the history of the Huave people?"

Before she could reply, Vicente said, "She's not Huave," as if to indicate she were unqualified to answer. I turned to him. "What does *that* mean?"

"Her father's not Huave." Vicente's father is Huave and his mother is whatever Román is. Carolina is the daughter of a Huave woman and a man from the neighboring state of Chiapas.

I turned back to Carolina. She stared out the window, saying nothing.

An older woman I knew in San Francisco del Mar, Maximina Martínez, had yet a different perspective on what it meant to be Huave. Maximina, a distant cousin of Vicente's, was in her late fifties. Like Leonel and Vicente, her father was Huave. Her mother was Zapotec. Maximina grew up speaking Zapotec with her mother and understood quite a bit of Huave because her father spoke it. She had lived in San Francisco del Mar her entire life and usually wore the wide flowing skirt and short embroidered tunic that made Huave women recognizable wherever they went. Still, she thought of herself as Zapotec because that was her language.

The categories that the people I knew in San Francisco del Mar had drawn for themselves, and for others, sprang from complex and divergent definitions of identity: Maximina, who is half Huave, is Zapotec; Vicente, who is half Huave, is Huave; Carolina, who is half Huave, is not Huave; Román, who is not Huave, is.

Before moving to the Isthmus of Tehuantepec, I had thought of indigenous people in Mexico as those descended from communities already there when the Spanish arrived. But what does "descended" mean? Whenever I mentioned to an istmeño that a person in the United States considered Native might have only one great-grandparent who was Native, they would look at me dumbfounded, often laughing out loud. "Well, by that definition nearly everyone in Mexico is indigenous!" they would say.

Might that not be close to the truth? The first time I had that conversation, I realized that the word *indígena* conjured something very different for me than it did for most Mexicans. What was it?

Until the Europeans showed up, of course, there were no "indigenous people" in the Americas. There were only *people*—at least twenty-five million of them, speaking more than three hundred different languages, playing out long histories of battle, conflict, negotiation, imperialist expansion, cultural florescence, and military retreat. This history is embedded in the name many Native tribes use for themselves: words that often translate as "the real us" or "the people."

For nearly three hundred years the Spanish tried to gain control over Mexico's indigenous peoples by assimilating them into Spanish colonial culture. At least superficially, Mexican national culture has long celebrated *mestizaje*, while the United States has only recently begun to do so. Most of the United States still marks Columbus Day each October, while Mexico celebrates its indigenous origins with El Día de la Raza. Nonetheless, among most of the istmeños I know, mestizaje is an ambiguous or even negative concept, laced with a deep sense of loss: of land, autonomy, language, traditional arts, and vocations. A person could lose all of those things and still be indigenous, not mestizo. As many istmeños explained it to me, the way a community approaches the division of power and labor makes it an indigenous community. Hence the definition of who is indigenous relies on the collective more than the individual: Román Cruz was Huave because he came from a Huave community.

# 7

## We Come Here to Name Ourselves

At the stark intersection where the trans-isthmus carretera and the Pan-American highway diverge, hundreds of ragged plastic bags flutter from brittle branches. Brought by the stiff wind that nearly always blows here, such castoffs are usually the only movement and color in this vast triangle of brown grass and leafless bushes. On this day though, February 25, 2001, a brass band performed. The clarinetist, trumpeter, tuba player and drummer stood in a tight circle and played with all possible force, but the relentless gusts yanked the notes from the instruments and scattered them unpredictably. On this day banners, music, laughter, and anticipation crowded this space at the edge of La Ventosa, a small town whose name means "the windy place." UCIZONI members, teachers, students, farmers, and fishermen fastened huge banners to hand-whittled poles and stood in their scant shade. At the edge of the bare triangle nine women planted a banner that read "¡Fox, entiende, el istmo no se vende!" ("Hear this, Fox: The isthmus is not for sale!"). They braced the banner's poles with small boulders, then crouched low into the wide circles of their skirts, cupping hands over their eyes and sitting in pairs so that one sheltered the other from the sun and wind.

I had spent a lot of time in this windy triangle, an inter-

**8.** Zoila José Juan speaks on behalf of UCIZONI, the Association of Indigenous Communities in the Northern Zone of the Isthmus, welcoming the Zapatistas to the Isthmus of Tehuantepec (2001). PHOTO BY THE AUTHOR.

section both literal and metaphorical of highways and travelers, boredom and expectation. At La Ventosa the *transístmico* heads south to the city of Juchitán and the Pacific Ocean, while the *panamericano* peels east past the turn-off for the village of San Francisco del Mar, across the state line into Chiapas, past the train station in Arriaga, then southeast across the Guatemalan border, stopping only when it reaches Darién rainforest in Panama. I had sat for hours at the La Ventosa intersection waiting to change buses, waiting for Leonel to arrive for another trip to San Francisco del Mar, waiting for a rainstorm to pass, waiting for the protestors who had organized a roadblock to go home for the night, waiting for the chance to use the single phone at the gas station, just waiting.

On the morning of February 25 a group of men from UCIZONI hammered together a rough wooden stage at the Pan-American's gravel shoulder. At some moment that afternoon the Zapatista comandantes would stand on it. Seven years into their conflict with the Mexican government, the rebels in Chiapas had achieved folk-hero status around the world and throughout Mexico—but most of all among indigenous communities. As more cars and pickup trucks and buses arrived from all over the isthmus, people I had met in far-off classrooms, corner stores, adobe kitchens, and fishing huts waved and called to me. A group of teachers from San Mateo del Mar told me that Maritza had wanted to come but had to devote her Sunday to preparing for the coming week at school. Several teenaged boys smiled, nodding shy hellos; they were members of the youth arts group Leonel had started years earlier in San Francisco del Mar. The youth group's name was Mi Kual Xa Kambaj, ("All the Children of My Village") in the language that hardly anyone in San Francisco del Mar still spoke. Their banner read, in Spanish only: "The Huave Cultural Group supports the Zapatista caravan."

Leonel, at twenty-seven the elder statesman of Mi Kual Xa Kambaj, stepped out of their self-conscious knot to greet me. I congratulated him for organizing the group to come and he rolled his eyes. "The bus was only half full." Just like Leonel, to focus on the empty seats on the bus rather than on the dozens of teens who had chosen to make the long trip. We both knew that without him there would have been no bus at all. The teenagers had brought their flutes, turtle-shell drums, and hand-sewn white costumes. They would perform centuries-old Huave songs and dances while the crowd awaited the Zapatistas. We knew only that the Zapatista comandantes had left the city of San Cristóbal de las Casas that morning. We didn't know how long it would take them to get here, only that they would arrive sometime in the afternoon.

It was too early in the dry season for the *jëmpoj*, the Mixe "fire wind," but it seemed to be blowing all the same. As the afternoon wore on, the loose clusters of people drew into tighter groups, as strips of shade contracted into slits. Women draped white towels over their heads to deflect the sun, lifting the corners to wipe sweat from their foreheads and cheeks. Children crouched in the cool spaces behind adult legs. Three thousand people stood waiting in the brown bowl. I crouched under a tent improvised from two banners with a group of young women from the UCIZONI office. Most of the women were from Boca del Monte; their parents were the farmers demanding retribution for the PEMEX oil spill. They were life-long UCIZONI members, having been essentially born into the organization, and now they were becoming *gente preparada*, a new generation of UCIZONI membership—formally educated yet continuing to live and work in their home villages. Many of them attended school in the evenings or on weekends and worked in the UCIZONI office during the day. The women were surrounded by piles of water bottles and burlap bags of oranges. It was their job to make sure that no one fainted from dehydration and also to dispel any conflict that arose. This desolate highway intersection had been chosen precisely because it was far from any town or city and therefore far from the center of influence of any particular istmeño organization. Party and ethnic politics made such choices delicate ones.

One of the women handed me a peeled orange harvested from a grove not far from her village. The juice ran down my arm, still holding the coolness of that village's shaded valley, even in this sun-parched space.

The hours slid by. Shortly before 4:00, as I chatted with Leonel and the teen members of Mi Kual, the stout man on stage holding the microphone announced in a formal tone, "¡Ya viene la representación!" ("The representatives are here!"). Fatigue lifted away from my shoulder blades. The late afternoon sun glanced off a white, first-class bus that had pulled up next to the stage. Vans full of journalists trailing the Zapatistas' bus had parked and released their passengers, who now swarmed around the door of the white bus. Standing far below, right in front of the stage, I could see only the top half of the bus and the microphones and cameras jostling like puppets around the door. I pressed forward into the crowd as the tangle of journalists high above us suddenly parted. Three Zapatista leaders—comandantes Tacho and David, and subcomandante Marcos—appeared center stage. A young woman near me bit her fingers anxiously as the middle-aged woman next to her screamed, "¡Todos somos Marcos! ¡Viva el EZLN!" ("We are all Marcos! Long live the EZLN!"). The fat of her upper arm flapped as she waved furiously, then a man stretched his arms in front of her face to snap a picture of the comandantes. I had never seen anything that quite compared to the happy hysteria that surrounded me in the wind-whipped bowl. The closest parallel would be something I know only from scratchy, faded newsreels: British teens screaming for John and Paul. Subcomandante Marcos and the other Zapatista leaders had become both pop-culture heroes.

On December 2, 2000, nearly three months earlier, the day after Vicente Fox had been sworn in as Mexico's president, subcomandante Marcos had sent the new president a letter that read in part: "It is my duty to inform you that, as of today, you have inherited a war in the Mexican southeast, one that the Zapatista National Liberation Army [EZLN] declared on the federal government on January 1, 1994, demanding democracy, liberty, and justice for all Mexicans." The same day Marcos sent a second letter addressed to "the people of Mexico" and to "people and governments of the world"—essentially, everyone on the planet except for President Fox and his administration. The letter announced that twenty-four Zapatista leaders would travel from their mountain villages to Mexico City to ask the nation's congress to ratify the 1996 government peace agreement with the Zapatistas. Since the San Andrés Accords, as they were called, had been signed, the government had completely ignored the agreement. And no wonder, since the accords guaranteed Mexico's Native peoples collective land rights, the ability to elect local governments through traditional means (without elections), and recognition of tribal judicial systems. All reasonable, but this had been agreed to by a government that had been anything but reasonable in its dealing with indigenous Mexicans. These demands stretched back to the sixteenth century. As it was worded nearly five hundred years ago: "Los dejarían vivir en la ley que tenían" ("that they be allowed to live with the laws they had").

The Zapatistas invited the people of the world to accompany them to Mexico City, and several hundred journalists and several thousand supporters did, on what came to be called the Zapatista Caravan. Before arriving in Mexico City two weeks later the comandantes spoke at seventy-eight public events like the one in La Ventosa.

As the two comandantes and Marcos stood on stage, arms and cameras and microphones pressing in around them, Zoila José Juan took the microphone and told the crowd, "Compañeros, please, stay quiet for a moment." Zoila, a forty-four-year-old grandmother and UCIZONI member, would be the one person to represent all three thousand of us who stood in the audience.

While the Mexican women cheered for the Zapatistas, I cheered for Zoila. Born and raised in Boca del Monte, she was one of the people who had been most vocal in the battle against the highway. I had met Zoila three years earlier, when she had been a new volunteer in UCIZONI's Women's Commission. "That woman is unstoppable," Beas had told me, his voice knowing and admiring. Like all gifted organizers, Beas was a shrewd judge of character. Zoila was a traveling market vendor with a third-grade education and the financial supporter and emotional nurturer of her family of six. When her husband had fallen ill years earlier and become unable to work, she had turned to UCIZONI for support. The Women's Commission, she said, "helped me a lot, not with money but with many hands."

The crowd's screams subsided as Zoila drew a deep breath, clamping the microphone in one hand and her typed speech in the other. The short script had been blurted by committee onto the UCIZONI computer that morning; Zoila had been asked to read it only a few hours before she climbed up onstage.

She hadn't even planned to go to La Ventosa that day. There was too much work to do at home, "too many problems to attend to," as she put it. But at the last minute she had asked herself, *How can I not go?* How could she let the Zapatistas pass through the isthmus, her land, without welcoming them? She had changed into her best huipil—black with red and orange flowers—and tied a blue bandanna tightly around her hair. Now that bandanna, high on her unlined forehead, kept her hair out of her eyes as the smoke from Marcos's pipe lassoed over his balaclava. The wind electrified the multicolored ribbons hanging from the brim of David's traditional Chamula Tzotzil sombrero and lashed Zoila's two-page speech around her wrist. The emcee, a barrel-bellied man who had been onstage for hours, just stood there, not offering to hold either the microphone or her speech. Finally Zoila managed to pull the sheet taut between one fist and two fingers and began to read: "We welcome you to these lands of the Isthmus of Tehuantepec. For many years, these lands have been the home of ten Indian nations."

It would only be the next day when she was described in the newspaper, "Zoila, a woman with a wide isthmus-style skirt and a good voice," that she would realize she had not even introduced herself. Even more distressing, she had forgotten to greet the Zapatistas in her first language, Mixe.

Her speech continued:

> We have come down from the mountains, we have left the jungle, we have traveled hours to be here with you, to say that you are welcome in our homes. We want to tell you that your struggle is our struggle. In January 1994 when we learned of your efforts, we redoubled our own. Before your uprising, we lacked clarity. We knew that we had to fight, but we didn't know which path to follow.

Though Zoila had not written the words, her voice, resonant with authority and emotion, made them her own. Later she would tell me that watching the conflict between the Zapatistas and the government was how she "had begun to understand the problems of indigenous communities" and their conflictive relationship with the Mexican government. She said of those who governed, "It's such a shame because they are well educated, but they just stomp on us. And our communities are important because without our natural resources, what are they going to do? There they are up there governing, but I would have to say that their education didn't do them much good." Her speech for the Zapatistas continued:

> Seven years have passed since those days, and the government has been unwilling to give us a fair deal. Our communities and our organizations have been persecuted by the *malgobierno*.

The two words, *bad government*, were usually spoken and written as one, as if the government's villainy were intrinsic. Zoila paused, then continued,

> We also want the soldiers to stop harassing the communities in Chiapas, and throughout the country. They should return to their barracks and serve their legal purpose.

The pause before she read those lines held the heartache of a woman who was both activist and mother. Years earlier, as Zoila had watched the conflict between the Zapatistas and government soldiers spiral in Chiapas, her two oldest sons had grown into teenagers and joined the military. The Mixe nation, a warrior people famous for never having been truly conquered by the Spanish, sent many of its sons into the armed forces. Zoila's sons' decision horrified their mother but she didn't see many other work options for them.

On a visit home during a military leave one of Zoila's sons tearfully told her that the military often "did bad things" to people—like his own mother—who had the Zapatista flag hanging in their homes.

> Because this struggle is just and is our struggle as well, we have decided to join this caravan. Humbly, we ask your permission for our journey to accompany yours.

Zoila paused, seeming to gather herself for a moment before she wrestled the first page of her speech behind the second. The microphone caught the paper's rattle, sending it echoing out over the crowd. Screams and chants rose to fill the open moment. ¡EZLN! ¡Viva los Zapatistas! ¡Marcos, Marcos, Marcos! The subcomandante raised his hand a few times in a shy wave. Zoila continued:

> We want to tell you that our land is in grave danger because the rich and their government want to impose a Megaproject on us . . . We ask for your support, and that our struggle in defense of the isthmus may also be your struggle.
>
> Courage, sisters and brothers, the path we must travel is long, and the dangers that await us are immense, but our courage, and our desire for peace, justice and dignity is immense, as well. ¡Viva los pueblos indios! ¡Viva el EZLN!

Zoila drew a deep breath as she finished her speech, then turned and handed the microphone to subcomandante Marcos.

As he began to speak, a thumping descended from above, the sort of noise felt in the ribcage before registered by the ear. A military helicopter swooped low over the crowd. Marcos, his tone slightly unsure, said only, "I'm going to ask you to listen to comandante David for a few minutes."

David's speech lasted less than three. He explained the

reasons for the caravan and its goals, then reiterated the Zapatistas' invitation: "We invite you, we ask you, to accompany us, to support us, so that together we can demand our rights as indigenous peoples."

David handed the microphone back to subcomandante Marcos, reaching up to the light-eyed man who stood nearly a foot taller. "Brothers and sisters," Marcos said, "just to say farewell. We want to tell you that we agree with that banner." He pointed to the words lettered in black, flapping on the far side of the ecstatic crowd: "Fox, entiende, el istmo no se vende." Behind the banner a long line of tractor-trailers moved along the highway, making the 120-mile trip between the two oceans. The Megaproject, transformed by President Fox into the Plan Puebla Panama, would transform that old highway into a high-speed, four-lane thoroughfare useful only to through-traffic. Marcos promised the three thousand people gathered that he would take the banner's message to President Fox—"The isthmus is not for sale!"—all the way to Mexico City. And then, nine and one-half minutes after the bright white bus had nudged the garbage-strewn triangle, the Zapatistas were off again.

The next morning I bought a ticket on a bus that left the isthmus before dawn. I arrived in Oaxaca City late morning, well ahead of the Zapatista Caravan, which was scheduled to arrive in the afternoon. Leaving the bus station, still a bit groggy in the mile-high city, I headed immediately for one of the urban luxuries I had craved ever since moving to Matías Romero: a newspaper stand with current copies of every major Mexican newspaper. I bought three. In *La Jornada* the words of the UCIZONI banner, lip-synced by subcomandante Marcos, appeared as a bold headline on page five: "The isthmus is not for sale!"

As I hopped a bus to Oaxaca City to accompany the

Zapatistas, Zoila also decided to join the caravan. The rush of energy she felt welcoming the Zapatistas in La Ventosa and her anger about the Superhighway inspired her. She packed a small bag and said good-bye to her husband, grandson, and the youngest of her four sons, the only one still living at home. UCIZONI had organized a delegation of six—representing nearly twenty-thousand members—that would drive a truck all the way to Mexico City; she squeezed in with them. Her husband supported her decision, Zoila said, "because he is a sensible person." The Zapatistas had promised to carry their anti-Megaproject message all the way to Mexico City and Zoila wanted to be there to witness it.

Early in the afternoon the entire Zapatista delegation arrived in Oaxaca City and stood in front of a billboard-sized banner that announced in a gaudy rainbow-palette, "Bienvenid@s EZLN." The "o" enclosing the "a" de-gendered the Spanish greeting and welcomed all the leaders of the Zapatista National Liberation Army, both male and female. That afternoon subcomandante Marcos spoke last in a long line of speakers, as he would throughout the caravan. He saluted the indigenous communities of Oaxaca, the only state in Mexico poorer than Chiapas: "We have marveled at your organizing capacity, your fighting spirit, your sincere pride in the roots that give both name and color to these lands. The indigenous people of Oaxaca have made it possible for all of Mexico's indigenous peoples to be proud of who we are."

He spoke of the only ones in the world not invited to join what the Zapatistas called the "March for Indigenous Dignity": the Mexican government. "The powerful ones call us 'ignorant' and say that our beliefs in communal work and mutual well-being are the products of foreign, communist, subversive ideas. Perhaps they are unaware that collective work and benefits already existed in these lands long before some foreigner 'discovered' us."

At the end of his speech Marcos ad-libbed, including something that wouldn't appear in the prepared version of his speech. "There will be no plan nor project, by anyone, that does not take us into account. No Plan Puebla Panama, no Trans-Isthmus Project, nor anything else that means the sale or destruction of the indigenous peoples' home. I am going to repeat this so that they can hear us all the way in Cancun."

As Marcos spoke, representatives of the Mexican government joined their global counterparts in Cancun at a meeting of the World Economic Forum. It seemed that Marcos's words did echo all the way to the Yucatan peninsula, more than 1,000 miles from Oaxaca City. The following day President Fox replied that only those who really understood the details of the Plan Puebla Panama had the right to criticize it. With these words Fox dismissed most Mexicans as legitimate critics, since the government had made public almost nothing about the plan.

Outside the hotels hosting the World Economic Forum meetings, police officers who had been bussed from all over Mexico tear-gassed, beat, and kicked young people, students, and other activists protesting the forum. For two days newspapers and television screens across the country transmitted a montage of incongruous but inseparable images: the dark faces of thousands at the Zapatista Caravan rallies, the pale faces of men in dark suits at World Economic Forum press conferences, the bloodied faces of stunned *globalifóbicos* on Cancun sidewalks. Those who questioned the sort of global economy promoted by the World Economic Forum had been christened "globalphobics" by the Mexican media, even though they tended to wear t-shirts with slogans such as, "More World, Less Bank" and "Another World Is Possible." In this series of images, narratives of globalization and identity politics braided together. Those in the meeting halls of the World Economic Forum imagined a world made much smaller by globalization, while the Zapatistas envisioned, as they put it, *un mundo donde quepan muchos mundos* (a world with room for many worlds).

A Mexican state governor who had participated in the meeting would later write in one of the country's major newspapers, "Without being present, Marcos set the framework for the meeting of the [World] Economic Forum in Cancun, and the topics of Chiapas and the EZLN passed like ghosts through the hallways of the Westin Regina Hotel. Someone said: 'Marcos is one of the global leaders of tomorrow who should be here.'"

At the end of the Zapatista Caravan, when subcomandante Marcos spoke in Mexico City's Zócalo, his words included this refrain: "Aquí estamos, y un espejo somos" ("We are here and we are a mirror"). The Zapatistas wear ski-masks; their faces cannot be seen. As Marcos said that day, March 11, 2001, in the Zócalo: "We are here to see ourselves and to show ourselves so that you can look at us and at yourself. So that the other can see himself in our gaze. We are here and we are a mirror. Not reality, but merely its reflection." Each of us in the audience saw a reflection, not the person behind the mask.

I spent four days traveling with the Zapatista Caravan in loops and circles, slowly winding toward Mexico City. As we traveled that winding path, observers and well-wishers lined nearly every kilometer of roadside. Thousands upon thousands of people bore witness to the caravan, to the struggle of the Zapatistas and their own belief that Mexico could become a better place. Many of them remain in my memory. A woman stood in front of her small roadside restaurant waving a white handkerchief. Three generations of a family lined up on a stone wall, their eyes and hands wide open. A shrieking group of middle-class, middle-aged women tossed brown-bag lunches to us through the open windows of our dented, second-class bus. A man in a freshly pressed button-down shirt stood silently, clutching a small camera. Clusters of blue-uniformed students crowded in front of their private school. Two men in a field of dry crumbling earth straightened their backs and raised their hands as we passed. As all those people watched the shiny bus with the Zapatista comandantes; the battered buses with spray-painted slogans in Spanish, English, Italian, and German; and the rattling pickup trucks dangling banners in Zapotec, Nahuatl, and Tzotzil, they also saw themselves.

The Zapatistas' strategies and messages have shifted and morphed since 1994 when they first blasted their way into newspapers and onto computer screens around the world. Still, some of their statements have remained unchanged. Since the beginning they have said, *Detrás de nosotros, estamos ustedes*. Ungrammatical and almost untranslatable, the phrase means, more or less, "Behind us, are all of you (who are us, too)." During the march to Mexico City they said these words into crackling microphones, into stiff winds and driving rain, and over internet signals and radio wires. People all over the world, but mostly Mexicans and most of all, indígenas, replied: *Todos somos Zapatistas* (We are all Zapatistas).

Constantly, over and over, the Zapatistas have said, "Nunca más un México sin nosotros" ("Never again a Mexico without us"). And how could it be any other way? Without them, without Mexico's indigenous communities, there never could have *been* a Mexico.

When the Zapatista comandantes finally arrived in Mexico

City, seventeen days after leaving their mountain villages, one hundred thousand people greeted them in the capital city's Zócalo between the National Palace, the National Cathedral, and the Aztec Templo Mayor. Marcos had given speeches at seventy-eight public events as the "March for Indigenous Dignity" had made its way from the highlands of Chiapas to Mexico City. Each presentation was different. In Juchitán he told a fable. In Oaxaca City he recited a homage to the Oaxacan indigenous movement. In the northern city of Querétaro he reeled off a long string of one-liners, challenges, and insults directed at those who opposed the Zapatistas. Here in Mexico City he did something completely different: he recited a poem that began, *To those who, being first, appear and perish last. . . .* The poem, which most listeners did not even recognize as such, named all of Mexico's fifty-six Native peoples in this way:

> We hold so many years in our hands. Maya.
> We come here to name ourselves. Kumiai.
> We come here to say "we are." Mayo.
> We come here to be seen. Mazahua.
> To see ourselves being seen. Mazateco.
> Our name is spoken by our passage. Mixe.

Zoila José Juan and I both stood in the Mexico City Zócalo on March 11, 2001, as subcomandante Marcos recited his poem before the enormous crowd gathered and the millions more watching on television. Zoila was away from her hometown of Boca del Monte for more than a month accompanying the Zapatistas. Shortly after they arrived in Mexico City, she was chosen as one of three hundred people to provide security and counsel to the twenty-four Zapatista leaders. As much as she disliked being away from home, she had decided she would stay in Mexico City as long as the

Zapatistas did. As she explained it to me later, "My idea was to stay there, to see what reaction the governments and congressmen would have. It was very important for me to see for myself how they responded *personally*, whether they took responsibility."

While she was in Mexico City, camped out at a university, a national newspaper interviewed her. When asked why she had devoted a full month to accompanying the Zapatistas, she replied by talking about the Plan Puebla Panama:

> We are still living on our land because we have fought for it. The Trans-Isthmus Megaproject disappeared and turned into the Plan Puebla Panama. They are changing the name so that the indigenous people won't understand it. But we understand; we know why we are fighting for our land. Some of my neighbors on the isthmus say that the Plan is a good thing . . . that there will be work and all that. But that is nothing more than fooling yourself. The effects of the companies, the machinery, and the filth they will bring are deadly . . . .
>
> This expansion of the highway, the expansion of the train. Are the indigenous people really going to use it? Are the indigenous people really going to go back and forth in their cars? What cars do we have? We only have our animals to carry our corn . . . There is no way we are going to teach our horses and burros to go up the stairs [of the overpasses] to carry our firewood.

On the day after the Zapatistas' feted arrival in Mexico City, the federal government formally unveiled to the media the Plan Puebla Panama. With the country still focused on the Zapatista Caravan, the media turned unusually skeptical eyes on the development plans. Even *El Financiero*, Mexico's version of the *Wall Street Journal*, was less than generous in its coverage. Complementing an article about the official press conference, it printed an illustration that echoed—though with condescension—Zoila's critique: A thin woman dressed in a pauper's rags sat on the ground with one palm upturned. A landing strip crossed her outstretched palm with a tiny plane zooming above.

# 8

## Peregrination

A group of women, boys, and girls stare at the camera, their faces smudged, tired. A sepia-toned early 1900s world stretches out stark and angular behind them: a cluster of simple shacks, a few mule-drawn wagons, blank dirt to the horizon. In spite of the women's tight-waisted long skirts and puff-sleeved blouses, they know hard labor. The girls' A-shaped frocks and the boys' knickers are practical, ungenerous.

Charles B. Waite took this photograph, titled "Mujeres Retrato del Grupo." I'd never heard of him, but Waite is almost single-handedly responsible for my mental image of rural Mexico at the turn of the last century. A gringo who traveled throughout the country, Waite reached the smallest villages and farthest outposts via oxcart or mule, capturing images that would become some of Mexico's first picture postcards. Even when they first appeared, the power of his images was understood—and resented. In 1901 he was arrested and jailed for sending what the authorities called "indecent" material through the mail: a photograph of "two dirty, absolutely wretched boys, wracked by disease." In the century since then Waite's work has been celebrated.

Maritza Ochoa held up a poster of "Mujeres Retrato del

**9.** Maritza Ochoa takes a motorboat ride to Candelilla, part of Santa María del Mar's traditional fishing grounds (2000).
PHOTO BY THE AUTHOR.

Grupo" for her preschoolers. It met the strict criteria by which she decided whether government-issued, Spanish-language teaching materials could enter her classroom: there wasn't any text and it wasn't any more relevant to the lives of mestizo kids in Mexico City than to the lives of her preschoolers in San Mateo del Mar.

The back of the poster included a list of suggested questions: "Where have the men gone? Why didn't the women go with them?" Maritza ignored them, of course, instead asking her students what questions formed in their minds as they absorbed the image's details.

"Is that your family, maestra?"

"Are those three people who are wearing dresses and holding cigarettes men or women? They are men, aren't they, maestra, because they're smoking."

When Maritza related their first question to me, I laughed. How could that be *her* family? Later I realized the question's logic. In their homes, photographs were valuable and rare; if people had them at all they were of the family members closest to them. Occasionally people would look at the photos on the walls of my casita in Matías Romero—of dancers at a fiesta, a fisherman mending a net, children playing—and ask me, "Why do you have photos of people you hardly know?"

Maritza asked her students about Charles B. Waite's photograph: "What is this group of people doing?"

Well, since they're all gathered around, they must be telling stories, the children decided.

Maritza told me all this hours later. By the time I arrived at her classroom that day in mid-April, the students had settled into their next activity: drawing portraits of their own families. I walked across the schoolyard and waved to Maritza, who stood at the front of the room. She nodded ever so slightly without waving back, not wanting to distract her students.

Abisael noticed her gesture. He ran out of the room, anxious to see who had arrived. His eyes widened with recognition when he saw me. Unlike the mothers and fathers who came and went from the schoolyard barely noticed, I always drew attention. Several other children followed Abisael into the breezeway and waved at me. Maritza hustled them back to their drawings as I settled into my usual place, a small chair near the door.

How quickly things change in the life of a four-year-old. Abisael, who had sat crying in the corner early in the school year, was finally ending the tug-of-war with his teacher over bilingualism. At first, when Maritza pushed him to speak Spanish, he would say only, "Ngomin!" ("I don't want to!") or "Ngondum!" ("I can't!"). She encouraged him to just scribble even if his pencil couldn't form the letters that spelled Spanish words. He refused to mark up the spiral notebook that Maritza had filled with images and exercises for him. "My father is going to get mad at me," he told her, because books were special, not to be written in. Maritza and Abisael reached a compromise: she gave him a blank sheet of paper and he scribbled. Eventually he began to pronounce Spanish words and string them slowly into sentences. "Mi tarea, lo voy a hacer." Whenever he said something in Spanish, like "I'm going to do my homework," he ended up giggling. The unfamiliar words seemed to tickle his mouth.

Now, Abisael swam midstream in the two-language current of Maritza's classroom—a long way from the little boy who had once told Maritza, "No, maestra, I don't want to speak Spanish. It's mol, and I'm not mol." Even at the age of four Abisael understood the Ikoots perspective, which divides the world's population into three parts: the mero Ikoots; the *mixiig*—meaning indigenous istmeños, the word translates literally as "people who wear *enaguas* and huipiles," the traditional women's embroidered tunic and long skirt with a pleated underskirt beneath it; and everyone else in the world, the mol. As was so often true, these categories drew the boundaries of the isthmus by culture, not by geography.

Maritza wandered around her classroom, labeling the stick-and-blob people in the children's family portraits: *xi teat*, my father; *xi teat xeech*, my grandfather; *xi müm*, my mother; and *xi teat nchey*, my grandmother. Many of the children referred to their grandfathers as *xi teat vida*, another example of encroaching Spanish. *Xi* means "my" and *teat*, "man." In Ombeayiüts, *xeech*, which indicates the relationship of grandfather, has been replaced by *vida*, the Spanish word for "life," as in, "the man who gave me life."

Once the children finished their drawings it was time for a snack, then a soccer game. By the time they again sat in their plastic chairs the sun had hoisted itself directly overhead. April and May brought the year's most unrelenting heat. The winter winds had stopped but the rains hadn't yet begun, so there was no relief from the sun. It was simply too hot for the children to keep their attention on Maritza's voice and too hot for her to coax them into listening. There were only a few more days until Semana Santa and a two-week school vacation. By the time the children returned from the Easter holiday perhaps their bodies would have adapted to peak dry season. Today, though, Maritza gave in and bade the children good-bye early. They drained the classroom faster than usual, and finally the space seemed to contain enough air. Maritza and I stacked and swept, preparing to lock up. She turned to me and said in a serious tone, with no preamble, "You know, a lot of people come here and they ask us about our stories and our history."

A shudder of self-consciousness ran through me. I was one of those people, those mol, who did the writerly version of what Charles B. Waite had done: taking away images and records of life, destined for a foreign audience. I tried not to act like so many of the journalists, anthropologists, folklorists, and sociologists whom I'd encountered while living on the isthmus. They tended to come for just a few hours, days, or weeks, blurting out questions before their bodies had even warmed a chair. I tended to follow people around silently for quite some time before asking questions. Often after I followed someone around for a couple of days, as he or she went to work, ate dinner, or attended meetings, the person would turn to me and say, "Thanks for accompanying me." To simply *be* with someone, even if I did nothing else, somehow carried value.

I took a long breath, wondering how to explain myself. But Maritza kept talking. "They know more about our culture than we do." This was not what I'd expected to hear next: "Because they do the research."

Maritza and a few of her friends had decided they should do their own research into local customs, arts, legends, and pastimes. Even as Ombeayiüts persisted, she could feel San Mateo's traditions and historical memory eroding like the sand from their beach. The anthropologists seemed to know more about San Mateo's history and traditions than many residents did. Maritza believed this was because outsiders asked the questions of the elders, took the notes, made the recordings, and published the books. (Those books rarely found their way back to San Mateo del Mar, she was quick to point out.) Maritza described the volunteer group that she and several friends had formed. They had received a small grant from the government's Institute of Indigenous Affairs and had begun to gather as many of the books and articles written about the mero Ikoots as they could. Even if the information the books contained was wrong, at least they would know what others were saying about them.

Maritza's description of the new volunteer group made it seem that she was the driving force behind it. "So the group started at your initiative?" I asked.

The hint of a grimace passed across her face; my effort to attribute individual credit pained her. "Well, I think it was everyone's initiative."

Maritza said the group's mission was "cultural defense," something more urgent, she thought, than language preservation. "Our language is doing more or less okay. The children still speak it." Nonetheless, Maritza told me, because language is the vessel that holds and protects culture, the group called itself Ikoots Mikual Iüt Nieng Apmapaüechran Ombeayiüts ("All the Children of San Mateo Defending Their Language"). Maritza used one of the same criteria that linguists use: a language is unquestionably in immediate danger of extinction when young children no longer learn it as a mother tongue. Another measure, however, considers endangered any language with less than one hundred thousand speakers—ten times the number of Ombeayiüts speakers.

Ikoots Mikual Iüt planned to publish a series of booklets for all the schools in San Mateo del Mar. Their next meeting would be April 18, Easter Monday, when everyone was on vacation. She invited me to attend. "Perhaps you would also like to visit during Holy Week. Lots of mol come then because of our traditions." The invitation sounded offhand but I knew it had been carefully thought out. I had heard many in San Mateo complain about the mol incursion during the religious celebrations of Candelaria, the end of Epiphany, and Semana Santa; for Maritza to invite me was to invite criticism from other villagers. When I thanked her for the invitation, we both knew I was thanking her for the willingness to take that risk for my benefit.

Nearly five centuries after the first European mol arrived on the isthmus during Holy Week to found the Villa de Espiritu Santo, Mexican society still consisted of stitched-together cultures. People like Maritza found themselves living on the seam. As a schoolgirl, stepping into a classroom had meant leaving Ombeayiüts behind. As a bilingual teacher she was part of a movement to insert San Mateo's language into the classroom, to live purposefully in the overlapping borderlands of Ikoots culture and mol culture.

After deciding to become a teacher when she was seventeen, Maritza had attended a six-month teacher training in San Baltazar Yatzachi, a mountain village more than 100 miles from her hometown. Though she appreciated the training, Yatzachi had terrified her. The students lived in bare concrete dormitories and paid elderly women to cook for them. The grandmothers were some of the only people still living in the village; nearly everyone else had left for El Norte. "There wasn't anyone there; only our souls walked its streets," Maritza remembered. She wondered at the difference between San Mateo del Mar and Yatzachi. Her family members and neighbors might work in Salina Cruz or Huatulco or join the military, but few crossed to El Norte, the United States. Was that because San Mateo was poorer and going to the United States so very expensive? She doubted that true economic necessity had emptied the hills around Yatzachi. Many people there grew agave cactus for the mescal industry, earning a decent living. No, it wasn't abject poverty that had turned that community into a ghost town. Maritza thought Yatzachi was dying because, in her words, "La idea del indio ya se fue" ("The idea of Indianness is gone"). How could she stop this loss in San Mateo del Mar? For Maritza this question was bound up with questions of how to stop the most damaging aspects of the Plan Puebla Panama. The Megaproject, the chahuixtle, was both cause and effect of the departure of *la idea del indio*.

Not so long ago Mexican teachers had slapped hands and pinched ears when their students spoke the languages they used at home. Teachers were taught what Maritza called the "banking approach" to education: the child was an empty, silent container to be filled, like a piggy bank, with facts. Maritza considered this approach abusive. She wanted her preschoolers and their families to speak up because education was a collaborative venture.

She used the language of Paulo Freire, the Brazilian who had pioneered popular education, though she did not recognize his name. Maritza's ideas mirrored Freire's critique of the "banking approach" to teaching. Almost a decade before Maritza was born, in 1968, Freire had written of the "bank clerk" teacher's dismal role: "His task is to 'fill' the students with the content of his narration—contents which are detached from reality, disconnected from the totality that engendered them and could give them significance." To give one example: the traffic lights that Maritza complained about in the preschool textbooks from Mexico City. More than three decades later, Maritza brought Freire's legacy, if not his name, into her classroom.

Her ideal school would have nothing to do with the banking approach. In fact, it wouldn't even be bilingual or bicultural; instead, as she put it, "intercultural." It would work like this: "When teachers come from other regions, they can share their language with their students. When Zapotec teachers work in a Huave school, they can share Zapotec and learn Huave."

Mexican public-education administrators—against all logic—frequently assigned indigenous teachers to a village where their language wasn't spoken. The daughter of a Zapotec teacher at the Benito Juárez preschool was in Maritza's class. The girl spoke Zapotec and Spanish and was learning

Ombeayiüts. Maritza pointed to her as proof that multilingualism was possible.

These ideas made Maritza somewhat unusual among istmeños. Over and over people explained to me that they hadn't taught their children their own language—Mixe, Zapotec, Huave, or Zoque—because it was essential that they learn perfect Spanish. When I asked why their children couldn't learn both at the same time, they would look at me quizzically. Sometimes they pointed to my imperfect Spanish as a case in point: true bilingualism was impossible. The fact that I'd waited until I was in my twenties to begin learning Spanish didn't interest them.

On Thursday of Holy Week, Maritza and I stood at the back of the San Mateo church, our shoulders against the wall's cool white tile. Overhead, sky-blue paint flaked from the arched ceiling. Dark fabric covered the statues and paintings of Christ; they would be revealed three days later on Easter Sunday. The hum of murmured prayers filled the sanctuary. About two hundred people sat in the pews; many more filed in and out of the church, bringing bowls, bags, and scarves filled with flowers or petals or herbs. Two elderly men piled chrysanthemum, gardenia, bougainvillea, and calendula at the front altar, as if constructing a burial mound from the offerings.

Maritza leaned toward me. "I don't know who that priest is," she whispered into my ear, as a line of sweat trickled down my neck. "I've never seen him before; maybe he's new. The last one was *Mexican*," she said with pride.

"They usually aren't Mexican?" I whispered back.

"Oh, they come from all over, from Canada, Spain, Belgium." Most of San Mateo del Mar's teachers, and even one doctor, had grown up there, but a local priest had never officiated at the church altar.

A brass blast cut into Maritza's explanation. "Now they'll do the Last Supper procession," she said, as the saxophone and trumpet notes faded away. One older man and twelve younger ones filed out of the church through enormous blue wooden doors that faced the sea. Many of the parishioners continued whispering their prayers; Maritza and I followed the thirteen men across the courtyard to the municipal building's breezeway. The young men sat at a table covered by a lace tablecloth on chairs decorated with flowers. Places were set for twelve; each plate held a slice of watermelon and a roll, and each glass was filled with creamy white horchata. Behind the table, local government officials kept watch.

At San Mateo's Last Supper no one ate. Each man wore a fabric sling around his neck. They hunched over and their eyes darted around, not landing on anything, as each one pressed his hands together in prayer, inside the sling.

In all my years of Protestant Sunday School I'd never encountered this sort of Last Supper. "What are they doing?" I whispered to Maritza. She gave me an alarmed look. I imagined her thought: *You never could guess what a mol wouldn't know.* As always, her reply was patient and polite. "The man who removes his hands and eats will reveal himself to be Judas." In the version of the Last Supper story I had learned, all the disciples ate and shared communion.

Several mol, college students from Mexico City, stood near the Last Supper table, their expensive cameras clicking and flashing. The mechanical light and noise seemed to add to the heat pressing up from the cement floor and down from the colorless sky. An older man walked up to the students. I couldn't hear his words but gestures made his message clear. He pointed to the cameras and then tapped his fingers on the open palm of his left hand: If you want to take photos, pay up. Most of the students lowered their cameras; a few complained.

Even Maritza had run into trouble taking photographs in her village. She'd once taken a borrowed camera to a dance ceremony and a village elder had approached her, demanding to know why she had it. She met his question with another: "Why do you ask?"

He was worried that she would sell her photographs.

Maritza was shocked. "Of course not," she told him. "Culture isn't for sale."

While in San Mateo del Mar, I was careful to focus my questions, attention, and camera only on Maritza, her classroom, and her family. The longer I lived in the isthmus region the more I had to push myself to take photographs. I continued to pour words into my notebooks but was increasingly reluctant to train my camera lens on the world around me. Part of my discomfort stemmed from some istmeños' beliefs about photography. Once I asked a woman if I could take a picture of her young daughter. She nodded, I snapped the shutter, and then she said, "Now my daughter is going to get sick." She was saying what many others thought but were reluctant to tell me as my camera shutter trapped their likenesses.

Countless anthropologists, journalists, travel writers, and other chroniclers had wandered the same roads as Charles B. Waite. Their words, for the most part, had been relegated to seldom-seen library shelves while Waite's photographs lived on through postcards, posters, magazines, and book covers. They continued to shape the world's impression of rural, poor, indigenous Mexico more than a century later. The sensitivity of San Mateo del Mar residents to the gaze of foreign eyes is born of long experience. For nearly two hundred years anthropologists and folklorists and linguists and sociologists have come to the village, anxious to see the community long considered one of Oaxaca's most isolated and extraordinary.

Miguel Covarrubias was part of this tradition. *Mexico South*'s short section on the Huave tosses off small fictions: "They worship the cheap prints of Catholic saints on their home altars," and "Other than the traditional designs woven into the napkins, they have no arts worthy of the name."

During my first few visits to San Mateo I replayed numerous iterations of the same conversation. A stranger would approach me in the market or on the street or at the bus stop and say, as more statement than question, "You're an anthropologist."

"No, actually, I'm not," I would reply.

A flicker of surprise would cross the person's face. The next question would be, "Are you a missionary?"

"Oh, no. I'm a journalist," I would say. That wasn't quite right, either, but the label came closest to what I was actually doing. Usually the response would be a confused "Ah," with a polite nod of the head. End of conversation.

I thought of all those moments as I watched the Mexico City college students shove their cameras into their backpacks.

Maritza touched my shoulder and nodded in the direction of the beach. We slipped away from the Last Supper reenactment, passed her house, and followed the long straight road to the sea. We walked without speaking, both of us knowing our destination; our skins hungered for the ocean's breeze. We sat on opposite ends of a curved driftwood tree trunk: Maritza at the bow, I at the stern. As the sun dipped low in the sky, cooler air whistled over our damp bodies. We sat quietly for several minutes, letting the wind cure our Holy Week fevers.

Maritza broke our silence. "We don't tell the anthropologists the whole truth. We would never tell them everything."

"Do you tell them partial truths, or do you make things up?" I asked.

"Well, some people tell them more than others, but we have to keep something in here," she said, pointing to her heart. "We have to keep something for ourselves."

As we sat at opposite ends of a wave-tossed tree, I could feel the fragile balance between the two of us. I wasn't an anthropologist but I looked and acted like one. San Mateo residents had a word for people who paid more attention to visiting mol than they did to their own people: *cual mitcats*, literally, "missionary's child."

The tide came in, rushing around our feet as they dangled from our arboreal boat. I took Maritza's words as both a confidence between friends and a gentle warning. I walked a careful line in San Mateo del Mar but Maritza walked one far more treacherous. While I kept my attention on her, she kept her sights within her classroom. Though her aspirations swept wide, the scope of her actions was narrower. She thought a lot about the impact of the Megaproject, the nature of community in her village, and the relationship between the two. Both topics connected directly to the village assembly. There had been much talk in San Mateo of abandoning the community assembly in favor of political parties and regular elections. Maritza understood the problems with the traditional system but she believed political parties weren't the answer. In her opinion, they lived up to their name. She liked to repeat a common saying: "Partidos nos dejan partidos ("Parties leave us divided"). For Maritza, division meant death. She saw San Mateo del Mar on one side of a theoretical playing field and global economic forces on the other. "What they don't want is for us to unify ourselves."

The community assembly meetings, at which all important decisions were made, represented this unity or, at least, the aspiration for it. Maritza desperately wanted to participate in the meetings, but she did not. In a town of almost ten thousand, only a few women actively participated. Many men regarded the youngest women who attended—two sisters in their thirties—as troublemakers. The older sister had even been named town treasurer until some men complained that only a man could be trusted in that role and she was removed. The sisters were occasionally kicked out of assembly meetings for speaking. A woman's voice, regardless of the words spoken, was disruptive. Maritza promised herself that she would attend the assembly once she finished her college degree, when she was a little older and could claim a bit more authority.

"It's the same with men," she explained to me. "They wouldn't let a young man, say, one who is seventeen or eighteen, state his opinion. It's the men's maturity that brings respect." But she was twenty-four, older than many of her preschoolers' parents. It probably wasn't Maritza's age but the fact that she had neither husband nor child that mattered. Regardless of the specifics, she knew she would face comments like those she often overheard: "She's a woman—what could she have to say?"

After the San Mateo del Mar celebrations reached their peak on Easter Sunday, another week of school vacation followed. On Easter Monday, Ikoots Mikual Iüt held a meeting in Huazantlán del Río, a hamlet in the western reaches of the municipality over an hour by bus from Maritza's home. Huatzantlán had once been the center of San Mateo, but as the Zapotec communities expanded eastward and took more land as their own, the center of the Huave community moved east to accommodate them.

I arrived in Huazantlán at the time Maritza had told me to meet her, then waited well over an hour on the town's main road. Several buses stopped but no one I knew got off.

Finally, a group jumped from the back of a pickup truck. It took me a moment to realize that one of them was Maritza. Dressed in a tight lapis-colored huipil and a long flowing skirt, her hair pulled tightly into a bun, she was transformed. I'd never seen her in the traditional Ikoots women's clothing and hairstyle.

I kissed her smooth cheek. "How pretty," I said, tugging on the edge of her huipil and winking. She laughed. My surprise faded away as I remembered a conversation we'd had during my Holy Week visit. Maritza had been researching traditional weaving and tailoring in San Mateo del Mar, interviewing a master weaver. There was a word the woman kept using that Maritza didn't recognize: *meed*. Maritza finally figured out, to her chagrin, that it was the Ombeayiüts word for huipil. The Spanish word, borrowed from Nahuatl, was the only one that she knew. How could that be? She was losing words in the language of her thoughts and dreams, replacing them with words that, as she put it, "came from outside." The word huipil was a relic of the triple colonization of the Huave communities. Brought to them by the Aztecs, then adapted to refer to the Zapotec-style tunics they wore, the Spanish word had been adopted to refer to any indigenous woman's handmade blouse.

The Ikoots Mikual Iüt meeting would be held just a few blocks from the main road at the home of an older man, a grassroots linguist, a keeper of Ombeayiüts. We reached his house and shouted a greeting over the high fence of woven reeds. An older woman, thin and bent, opened the gate, "Buen día, buen día," she said, her Spanish heavy with a throaty Huave accent. She gestured to a picnic table, then turned back to a metal tub filled with suds and laundry.

As we sat down, Maritza introduced me to the rest of the group. "This is Bety," she said, her voice filled with pride. I'd been hearing about Bety Gutiérrez for months: one of the two sisters who insisted on attending the community assembly even after being kicked out, the woman who had struggled to become fluent in Ombeayiüts because her Zapotec mother didn't speak it, the elementary schoolteacher who refused to use any Spanish in her classroom. "She was in Congress with the Zapatistas," Maritza said, with a touch of awe in her voice.

Three weeks earlier the Zapatistas had invited two representatives from each of Mexico's fifty-six indigenous peoples to attend their Congressional testimony—one result of the Zapatista march to Mexico City. Maritza was deeply impressed by the Zapatistas because it was the first time, as far as she knew, that a group of indigenous people had risen up successfully against the federal government. Yes, it had been a thrilling experience, Bety said, then waved the subject aside. She was more interested in talking about the work at hand. Supporting the Zapatistas was important, of course, but they were there to talk about Ikoots Mikual Iüt.

Maritza, Bety, a middle-school student, and three men—two teachers, Guillermo and Constantino, and San Mateo's only Ikoots doctor, Elías—had come for Ikoots Mikual Iüt's fourth official meeting. Tereso Ponce Villanueva came out of his small house and Maritza introduced me. I thanked him for hosting me and asked if he had grown up in Huazantlán.

"Yes. This is where I started throwing the net." He had learned how to fish at the age of nine, nearly half a century before. He sat at the head of the table, his muscular arms resting on weathered wood and his rough hands folded in front of his chin.

For two decades, don Tereso had worked with U.S. missionaries to complete the first (and, so far, only) Ombeayiüts-

Spanish dictionary. In 1967 he'd even spent seven months in Baltimore, working with the American missionary couple who compiled the dictionary for the Summer Language Institute. While in the United States he had been able to do things he'd never imagined, such as attend a Billy Graham revival and see Boston's old city center. The 1981 dictionary, 483 pages bound in thin blue paper, doesn't credit him as a coauthor. It merely lists him as one of several "collaborators" and notes that he illustrated the book. His drawings show things difficult to render in Spanish words: the parts of a backstrap loom, the anatomy of a fish, the different words for bottle gourds from the same tree, depending on their shape and how they have been cut. Those images represent tiny bits of what Maritza and the others feared losing as Spanish took hold in San Mateo del Mar.

Don Tereso opened his notebook and began to read a story about a competition between a blue crab and a ghost crab. "Tajlüy noik künch al chiük tiül ndorrop mal mbas ten, kiaj chiük ajngot noik pilaw" ("There was once a blue crab. She lived in a very deep hole behind the tallest plum tree. Suddenly an old ghost crab happened by"). The tallest plum tree was a place that all San Mateo children would know: it was the place the fishermen stopped to rest on the long walk to the fishing grounds at the Boca Barra.

The four teachers, middle-school student, and doctor wrote down don Tereso's words. The old man's handwritten lines stretched across his notebook in a long slanting script: a practiced hand, even though he had attended school for only two years. In Mexico, usually only college graduates had such fine penmanship. A focused silence fell over the group as don Tereso murmured the sounds of Ombeayiüts: soft-popping P's, throaty U's, and nasal NG's. He told the story slowly while pencils scratched notebook paper, each person copying down the story. Maritza and the others interrupted don Tereso several times, making sure they were using the correct Ombeayiüts words and clarifying fine points of grammar. The story ended with a moral: *Leaw neyamb yamb, nej ndoj wüx omal.* Or, as Maritza explained it to me, "Don't make assumptions."

Story finished, the discussion turned to a logo for their booklet series. After months of work their first booklet was almost ready for printing. Someone suggested a *tej*, the tiny shell that composed their beaches. Or what about the clam shells they ground up to add calcium to their tortillas?

"How about a turtle? Because we move so slowly," Maritza said, giggling. Everyone knew that choosing the sea turtle wouldn't really be self-deprecation. Turtle meat and eggs were traditional foods; turtle shells made their traditional drums. The *danza de la tortuga* was one of San Mateo del Mar's best-known dances, even though the Zapotecs sometimes claimed it was *their* dance.

"What should we call the bulletin?" someone else asked.

"What about 'Ikoots Forever'?"

"Unless the Megaproject comes," Bety said.

Everyone laughed.

A month later, the first Ikoots Mikual Iüt booklet appeared in an edition of five hundred, photocopied and hand-stapled. Maritza asked Leonel Gómez to deliver a copy of the booklet to me. Unlike every other istmeño indigenous-language publication I'd seen, this one contained no Spanish translations; it was *only* for people who spoke Ombeayiüts.

The group had solved their logo dilemma perfectly. The

image on the front cover was a talking stick, the ceremonial baton used at many meetings. It is passed from hand to hand; anyone can hold it and speak, then pass it on, deciding who speaks next. A turtle, shrimp, crab, stalk of corn, and the sun rising over the water all decorated the carved staff.

# 9

## Outpost of the Poor

Good morning, Wendy. Did I wake you?" Leonel Gómez's voice jumped from the phone upbeat, without regret. Early dawn light seeped, tentative, from the living room window.

"Buenos días, Leonel. Sí, pero no importa." Leonel was the only person who called me so early, but when he did it was always important. Almost every phone call I received at my casita was important—calls were expensive, after all.

Leonel was several steps into his story, something about a column in *La Jornada* called "Destructive Farms in Oaxaca." Iván Restrepo, Mexico's best-known environmental journalist, was writing about the threat of shrimp farms on the Isthmus of Tehuantepec—and one planned for Unión Hidalgo. With the mention of this town, halfway between Matías Romero and San Francisco del Mar, I startled awake. Unión Hidalgo and San Francisco del Mar did not share a language or a culture but they shared a lagoon, an economy, and a way of life.

"Wait, Leonel. This is about *Unión Hidalgo*, and you first heard about it in *La Jornada*?"

"¡Síííí!" He said, exasperated. I didn't know whether he was annoyed that he'd not known what has happening in his

**10.** A dugout canoe is stored by a fishing hut at the beach near Unión Hidalgo (2002). PHOTO BY THE AUTHOR.

own backyard or that I was catching on to his point so slowly. I imagined the path of this bad news: from Unión Hidalgo northwest to Mexico City, then back to San Francisco del Mar, passing right by Unión Hidalgo. Later I learned the path had been more complicated than that. Iván Restrepo didn't know anyone in Unión Hidalgo; he'd heard of the shrimp farm plans from Francisco Toledo, the famous painter who had grown up in Juchitán.

The day before Leonel's phone call to me, he had visited Unión Hidalgo to find out what was going on, and how the chahuixtle had floated into this town as well. Someone, or perhaps a group of someones, had bought nearly 250 acres of marshland with plans to buy five times more. This was all quite impressive because Unión Hidalgo's land was communally owned. Technically, land purchases required the approval of the town assembly, but the fishermen Leonel talked to hadn't agreed to this sale nor even known of it until after the fact.

Leonel was making plans for a longer visit to Unión Hidalgo and the supposed new shrimp farm site for sometime the following week. "So, I'll let you know what day we'll go, Okay? Adios." The oh of his good-bye stretched out long, as if I were hearing it from a boat leaving shore. The quirk of San Francisco del Mar Spanish made me smile.

Ten days later Leonel and I walked into a dim storefront in Unión Hidalgo. Haphazard piles of canned sardines and chiles, fishing nets, cooking oil, and bars of pink soap filled shelves and covered tables and crates. A man with a soiled t-shirt, its graying fabric stretched tight across his wide belly, stood behind the counter. We introduced ourselves and he, Carlos Cruz, smiled, extending his hand to us.

"Welcome to Ranchu Gubiña. That's what we call our

town. Gubiña means 'very poor people' in Zapotec. Do you know why it's called that?"

Leonel and I shook our heads.

"One hundred and fifty years ago there was an influenza outbreak in Juchitán. You got the fever and in three days you were dead. They gathered all the sick people and moved them out of town, here." At that time Unión Hidalgo had been just a bare patch of coastal land, more than an hour from Juchitán by horse-drawn cart. "Only the strongest survived—our ancestors. So welcome to the Tierra de las Muchachas Bonitas. Did you see the sign as you came into town?"

We nodded. I'd wondered about it: "Land of the pretty young women"?

"That's because of our abundance of homosexual men. We have them, and then we have the ugly guys, like me." Finishing the introduction to his town, he led us out of his shop and down the street to the home of Carlos Manzo and Sofía Olhovich.

A group was just starting to gather in the living room of the old adobe home. The paint peeled from the double doors, which opened like a pair of tall, narrow shutters right onto the street. The space inside was cool, sheltered by a high terracotta roof. The chairs, bookshelves, and table were simple and made by hand, like the front door, and glowed with a weathered patina. The room looked like a film set, one in which poverty is rendered artistically, full of beauty.

Manzo had grown up in that house; Sofía had lived there with him for three years. Her eyes were light brown, but her skin and hair were about the same color as mine. Her last names, Olhovich Filanova, hinted at her family's history: the daughter of a Ukrainian woman and a second-generation Russian immigrant to Mexico, she'd grown up in Mexico City. Carlos Manzo was Zapotec, like everyone else from Unión

Hidalgo. He had left home as a teenager to attend high school in northern Mexico, in the city of Guadalajara. He stayed there for college and several years' work, earning a master's degree from a university in Mexico City along the way. By the time he returned to Unión Hidalgo to live, he'd spent more than half his life *afuera*, or outside, as they said. Sofía and Manzo had met in 1997, at the National University of Anthropology and History in Mexico City. She was a student there and he was visiting with a delegation of Zapatistas. In 1998 Sofía came to live with him in Unión Hidalgo.

When Carlos, Sofía, Manzo, and the others learned about the shrimp farm plans, "We called everyone we could think of, even maestro Toledo," Sofía said. Of all the things they tried, the phone call to the famous istmeño painter seemed to have had the biggest impact. Events became a little more real when they appeared in national newspapers, but only rarely did the names of indigenous towns like Unión Hidalgo appear in those newspapers. Iván Restrepo's article had led to our visit to Manzo's living room with several fishermen and other concerned residents of Unión Hidalgo.

"I think what we need is a regional coalition against shrimp farms," Manzo said abruptly, ending the introductions. He spoke as if he needed to convince the rest of the group gathered in his home. I glanced at Leonel, who had been trying to organize that very thing for more than two years. He caught my eye and smiled weakly, then nodded at Manzo.

"And what's the situation in San Francisco del Mar?" Manzo asked Leonel. The question itself was revealing: though the two communities were only 18 miles apart and their survival depended on the same lagoon, people from one village rarely visited the other, rarely even knew one another. Though there were occasional exceptions (one of Leonel's grandparents had come from Unión Hidalgo), miles of brackish water, language, and history separated the two communities.

Leonel described the conflict in his village between the few who wanted a shrimp farm and the many who did not. So far the latter were winning. In Unión Hidalgo they had skipped over the sort of debate that bubbled in San Francisco del Mar; the pro-shrimp-farm group had leaped directly to selling shares in their business venture and buying land.

Manzo said, "They say it costs fifteen thousand pesos to become a shareholder in the shrimp farm. If you don't have that then you can only join the group as a peon."

"That's what they call social privatization," Leonel said without humor.

Carlos Cruz nodded. "The shareholders with the money are people with master's degrees from up north; the local people are in the group just so they can buy the land."

To understand his comment is to untangle a web of legal and political issues reaching back one hundred years. Unión Hidalgo became a municipality politically independent from Juchitán in 1885, a generation after the founding residents survived the flu epidemic. One generation after that, the railroad opened, connecting Unión Hidalgo to Juchitán and to the cities in Chiapas, to the east. The town thrived. While the political line between Juchitán and Unión Hidalgo was clearly drawn, control of the land had never been so straightforward. Because Juchitán's and Unión Hidalgo's land rights had been granted together in a single declaration by the federal government, the latter relied on the former for land tenure administration. The land in both municipalities is classified as *ejido*, meaning that community members can either sell usage rights for their plots to other community members or bequeath that right to their children, but can't sell to any private business or *los de afuera* (people from outside).

That's how it should have worked, but didn't. In 1978 the person in Juchitán who was responsible for making sure land wasn't sold to outsiders, the Communal Lands Commissioner, disappeared. Most istmeños believe he was killed by the Mexican military in an attempt to silence upstart Zapotec peasants. Istmeños never stopped talking about that commissioner. A few years after his disappearance Juchitán became the first city in Mexico to throw out the PRI, the Party of the Institutional Revolution—which had ruled the country since shortly after the Mexican Revolution—and elect an opposition party to city government. Poems and songs still honored their fallen lands commissioner, but a combination of fear, cynicism, and apathy had left his position vacant for more than twenty-five years.

So, as Carlos Cruz explained, the shrimp-farm group needed local members so that it had access (even if illicit) to local land.

Cruz turned the conversation to Armando Sánchez, the person responsible for the local shrimp farm plan. "This all started because he wants to be municipal president. Maybe it's just a way to get money for his campaign." The issue wasn't party politics; Carlos Cruz, like Armando Sánchez, was a PRI member. This time, though, Cruz thought the PRI members had gone too far: planning an industrial shrimp farm next to the lagoon that most of the town relied upon. The Guie'e Estuary, the small inlet from the Laguna Superior that separated Unión Hidalgo from Juchitán, was more important than party loyalty. "How are we going to feed ourselves? Normally we make a living from the firewood, from the palms," he said.

Unlike San Francisco del Mar, Unión Hidalgo residents didn't rely only on the shrimp, red snapper, blue crab, sea bream, and catfish that filled their waters. They gathered mangrove and mesquite branches for firewood; they harvested hearts of palm for food; they cut palm fronds for roofing material, baskets, and mats. "The shrimp farm isn't for the fishermen, or the palmeros, or the peasants. It's for los de afuera."

The line separating the locals and "those from outside" might have been clear, but that line moved depending on who drew it. For Carlos Cruz, los de afuera were the ones who had never visited Unión Hidalgo, never sliced the shaggy bark from a cool heart of palm, never organized one of the famous local fiestas with the muchachas bonitas. According to others in Unión Hidalgo, people like Sofía, who grew up in Mexico City and spoke Russian, maybe even Manzo, were los de afuera. Although he had been born and raised in Unión Hidalgo, in that very house, Manzo had lived outside the community for more than two decades. He was, in fact, one of those "people with master's degrees." As Manzo himself explained it, "We are from here, and then we go away, and when we come back they think of us as outsiders."

Months after my first visit to Unión Hidalgo, I talked to a woman from Unión Hidalgo who had invested in the shrimp farm. She would say to me, her voice angry and bitter, "Carlos Manzo is just trying to get money out of us. He needs money to support that foreigner wife of his, that European woman." I would explain that Sofía wasn't a foreigner: she was born and raised in Mexico City. The woman would snap back, "What? I don't think so. You can tell that she's European."

At that meeting in Manzo's childhood home, the locals, los de afuera, and those somewhere in between outlined a collective strategy.

"There are so many different aspects to this problem: economic, legal, and ecological," Manzo said, leaning back in his chair and staring at the burnished ceiling beams. He spoke in a low monotone, purposefully calm, the sort of voice that few would ignore. "We need an assembly meeting."

When something is related to everything, it must be turned over to everyone. At the community assembly the loose strands of conflict, crisis, and sudden change could be woven into a collective response.

So far, in response to the shrimp farm, Manzo and Sofía had done the things that licenciados tend to do in such situations: they asked the federal government's environmental protection agency, PROFEPA, to investigate. The pair traveled to Oaxaca City, seven hours away, to visit PROFEPA's regional office. They placed many long-distance calls begging the PROFEPA director to send an inspector to Unión Hidalgo, telling anyone they could think of about the problem. Two months after their trip to Oaxaca City, the day we sat together in Manzo's living room, they were still waiting for a PROFEPA inspector to show up.

The discussion circled back to the idea of an assembly. Carlos Cruz tugged it in that direction because he thought the heart of the problem was not los de afuera, nor political aspirations, nor even the shrimp farm itself, but this: "the individualism that doesn't let us defend what is ours." Carlos Cruz floated a proposal: "We need an assembly meeting for the people who earn their living from the iguanas, the palms, and the firewood. It needs to be in Zapotec and in Spanish. I'll do the translation. We should hold it in the Fishermen's Church, in the neighborhood where those people live."

Yes, they all agreed, they would do that. First, though, everyone needed to see the shrimp farm site. The group had been relying on reports from the fishermen, firewood gatherers, and palmeros, but we all needed to see it for ourselves. We would go the next day, leaving town at nine in the morning.

The next day Leonel and I arrived in Unión Hidalgo early

so I could visit Armando Sánchez before our trek through the mangrove swamp. I had called señor Sánchez on the phone weeks earlier, but he'd not wanted to answer any of my questions, save one.

"Why a shrimp farm?" I had asked him.

"It's very simple," he'd replied. "What we see is the poverty of the fishermen. We want to get them out of poverty."

I knocked on the front door of the Sánchez home and his daughter answered, talking to me through the metal grating. She summoned her mother, who stared at me through the black iron bars, then yelled my name to her husband. He yelled back to her and she opened the door. She finally addressed me, offering me a chair at their dining room table. Few houses in Unión Hidalgo had dining rooms. Armando Sánchez joined me at the dark-lacquered table, our elbows sticking to the stiff plastic over the lace tablecloth.

Now he was willing to answer more of my questions. "Here in Unión Hidalgo *all* the fishermen are poor. They live in extreme poverty, as they always have. If we could visit some fishermen's houses, we could verify that fact. The children are malnourished and their families live in vile circumstances. And the sea isn't as rich as it once was."

I thought of the saying so common in San Francisco del Mar, "Here, everyone eats." As far as I had seen, that was true in the villages around Laguna Superior. Still, Armando Sánchez was right to say that there were fewer and fewer fish to fill more and more nets.

In the early 1990s he and several others in Unión Hidalgo had convinced PEMEX to donate several boats and outboard motors to them. But that just meant more fishermen could pull in their nets faster with fewer fish in each one. The fishermen grew discouraged, the outboard motors broke down, and the boats sprang leaks.

In 2000, he happened to read an article about a shrimp farm in the state of Sonora, which borders Arizona. He heard that the person who had started that shrimp farm was visiting Oaxaca City, so Sánchez went to see him. "I told him about the poverty of our fishermen, and he told me, 'We're going to see what we can do about aquaculture in the Isthmus of Tehuantepec.'"

By the time Armando Sánchez went to Oaxaca City for that meeting in May 2000, numerous Mexican government agencies, private companies, and even the World Bank had devoted years to that very goal. El plan de Ochoa devoted several pages to plans for shrimp farms.

The organization responsible for the shrimp farm in Sonora, a PRI-affiliated union known by its acronym UGOCEM, invited señor Sánchez and others to visit. The shrimp farm was huge—more than 2,500 acres. "It's an ejido; the direct beneficiaries are the fishermen there. We were able to see how they cultivate the shrimp. They pull more than 3 tons of shrimp per hectare."

An annual harvest of more than 1 ton of shrimp per acre of artificial pond *does* sound impressive. But that's not the whole story. Each acre of pond needs many acres of natural lagoon, river habitat, and mangrove forest to support it. No one is sure exactly how much; these sorts of ecological calculations are a relatively new and inexact science. If *all* the land a shrimp farm depends upon (and eventually destroys) is taken into account, the long-term productivity is not nearly so grand.

"We saw that the fishermen there live in really different conditions than the fishermen here. It's quite miraculous," Armando Sánchez continued. That was true, but it was no miracle. The Sonoran fishermen's living conditions are different in part because there are so few of them. A shrimp farm employs only a few workers per acre of pond.

As Armando Sánchez talked, I realized that I'd already heard about this trip to Sonora: the previous June, when I'd sat with Chico Toledo (the other Francisco Toledo) in front of his fishing hut at the Boca Barra. Toledo, Sánchez, and probably many others who had taken that thirty-five-hour bus trip returned with matching dreams of shrimp farm miracles. Unlike Sánchez, Toledo was a fisherman and would be directly affected by whatever a shrimp farm brought to the isthmus lagoons.

"We want to get a shrimp farm going in Unión Hidalgo and advance from there," señor Sánchez said. "We're also thinking about Huamuchil and San Francisco del Mar, God willing. We're hoping one day to get up to two harvests per year, because we have the optimal climate here."

I asked how large the shrimp ponds would be.

"We're thinking of individual tanks that are four to eight hectares."

I told him that I'd read in *La Jornada* that the plan for Camarón Real de Pacífico was 300 hectares of tanks.

"Well, the overall proposal is for 300 hectares, but obviously we're not going to start with that much; we can't afford it. For now we're thinking of 100 hectares."

"So, this is still at the planning stage, no construction yet?"

"Not yet. We're still recruiting members from among the fishermen. So far we have 141 people, all from Unión Hidalgo."

"Have you begun to clear land for the project?"

"No. We just finished buying the land. There's still one more gentleman we need to pay, but we ran out of money. That's why we want to talk to the InterAmerican Development Bank."

I nodded. "Who authorized the construction plan?"

"Well, we don't have that—we haven't even talked to the IDB or any other bank yet!"

As our conversation wound down, I asked him if there were any other important details about the project. He raised his hands as if in defeat. "I already told you all of them."

I asked señor Sánchez why he, personally, had put so much effort into the project, and he launched into a story: "I am the son of a fisherman, who unfortunately died when I was just four years old. The six of us were left orphans, with an unemployed mother who earned money for our food by selling fish. And so we lived in extreme poverty, in dire straits, without even enough to eat. This affected me to the very core. I dreamed of someday helping the fishermen get out of poverty. I've worked hard to help them. I led the project to buy motorboats in 1992. I thought that would bring relief, but in the end it was a failure and our credit was ruined. I kept looking for other ways to help. I got more credit from the state government and bought a truck to help with selling the catch, but the catch was poor and that didn't work, either. But now with the shrimp farm, we think that this is really going to do it.

"I suffered as the son of a fisherman and I continue suffering because I don't have much money. I'm a primary-school teacher. My wife, my five children, and I live from my salary, and sometimes I have to go fishing or collect firewood." He gestured around the room, at the mahogany furniture and large television. "This is the product of twenty-five years as a teacher."

I stood, thanked Armando Sánchez for his time, and told him I was going to visit the planned site of Camarón Real del Pacífico.

He gave me a look of surprise. "But there's nothing to see."

When I arrived at Manzo and Sofía's house, it was already 9:30 a.m., half an hour after we'd planned to leave for the tour. The fishermen taking us to the shrimp farm site hadn't arrived yet. Leonel, Manzo, Sofía, and several others sat on the narrow sidewalk in front of the house. I joined the sidewalk line.

"So perhaps the journalist Wendy could tell us a bit about her conversation with the illustrious señor Armando Sánchez," Manzo said as he tipped his hat back, not meeting my eyes. I never knew how to respond to questions like this one. I carried around a press pass but had come to the Isthmus of Tehuantepec as a grassroots organizer looking for new ideas. I wasn't exactly a journalist, but I did tend to use that word when I introduced myself because it was one that people recognized. The only other writers istmeños usually knew about were poets and novelists, and I surely wasn't either of those.

I paused for a long time, glad to be in a place where silence is considered an essential part of conversation. Then I said, "He says there's no reason for us to make this visit because there isn't anything to see."

Everyone laughed.

"They want to meet with the InterAmerican Development Bank to ask for funding."

No one laughed. Every istmeño who had heard of the InterAmerican Development Bank had strong feelings about it. Whether it was considered savior or destroyer, everyone knew the IDB held great power.

Sitting in the shade of several almond trees, we had a long time to ponder the idea of the IDB bulldozing money into Unión Hidalgo. Occasionally someone got up to stretch, buy a soda, tell a joke, or wonder aloud at how all of this had happened. No one wondered aloud why the fishermen hadn't shown up yet. At 11:30 a flat-bed truck rolled up and several men jumped from the back. We shook hands all around and then climbed aboard.

By the time we set foot in the mangrove swamp the sun fell like a machete from directly overhead. We hiked along the edge of the Guie'e Estuary. While the fishermen and palmeros seemed to float on the melting mud, Leonel, Sofía, Manzo, and I, all strangers to this land, strained against the softness. Though it was the middle of the dry season, the easiest time of year for our walk, our boot and huarache soles sank deep, crushing delicate mangrove roots.

Jesús Martínez, a young fisherman, guided our tour to another realm. A mangrove forest of black, red, and white mangrove species rose up to our right, dwarfing us with a wall of blue-green leaves. To our left, land dissolved into water. Even at midday, clouds of birds whirled overhead, black wings angling in cerulean air. Jesús showed us the coves that filled with water only during the rainy season, becoming salt flats when the waterline receded. He described how the women of Unión Hidalgo went at the beginning of every dry season, as people had done since long before the conquest, to harvest the mineral streaks left behind by the receding waters.

Forty minutes into our trek and barely a mile from where we'd left the truck, we came upon something that none of los de afuera had expected: a few charred leaves shivering at the ends of black branches. The mangroves had been burned. The contrast between the humming thicket of healthy mangroves and the stand of charcoal sticks stopped us. I didn't even notice my ankles had sunk deep into the mud. Leonel recovered first and began taking photographs. The fishermen and palmeros watched our reactions carefully and then stated what we already knew: this was the land that Camarón Real de Pacífico had supposedly purchased.

We slogged a bit further, still in the area of the burn, and crossed a path that had been cut into the mangrove forest. Perhaps eight feet across—about as wide as a canal connecting a shrimp-farm pond to the lagoon would need to be—it stretched straight toward the coast. I looked around at the rest of the group, watching mouths settle into grim lines and shoulders slacken. For a moment I forgot the heat, thinking instead of Armando Sánchez telling me, "there's nothing to see." We walked on and came to another chopped-clear path. A few more minutes, a third one. We passed five in all, each about half a kilometer apart.

Finally, we came to the incinerated remains of a small stand of palm trees. Jesús turned to us. "This is part of the land where they want to do that project. But those of us who are the original fishermen of this place, we're against it because they're going to destroy a lot of mangrove. Maybe we'll see two hundred people employed by it, but a lot more than two hundred people live in Unión Hidalgo." Like most of the people I'd talked to in Unión Hidalgo, Jesús referred to the shrimp farm as simply "it."

"The palmeros harvest many palms here, for the bark, for the sap. The peasants gather firewood. We don't want those people—who aren't peasants—to build it just for the money, or for political reasons. We oppose them destroying a community for the benefit of just a few. We invite them to take us into account, that's all. There are iguanas here, and deer, rabbits, armadillos. Now that they are destroying this land, they are destroying not just the people, but all the living beings here."

One palmero chopped down a dead palm, slicing the trunk in half with a few clean machete strokes. Charred fronds spread around him like mourning fans at an istmeño funeral. He sliced the palm's moist center, then offered each of us chunks of the cool, yellow heart, speared at the end of the long machete blade. The palm was fresh and full of flavor; the burning was recent.

Leonel, Sofía, Manzo, and I carried two digital cameras, a film camera, a tape recorder, and a video camera. Most of the fishermen and palmeros in our group carried machetes. That latter tool has stopped many industrial development projects in Mexico. Around the time that I lived in Mexico, proposed highways, dams, and airports had all been halted by mobs of well-organized peasants twirling machetes over their heads. In the case of the Unión Hidalgo shrimp farm, the machetes would help us understand the destruction but the cameras would prove to be more important weapons.

After our tour, Sofía and Manzo took the photos of burned palm trees and mangroves to Armando Sánchez. He said that the destruction had been "a mistake." They made large color prints of the photographs of the burned trees and sent them to PROFEPA, along with yet another request that the shrimp-farm builders be required to submit an environmental impact statement. I imagined government officials staring at the images: delicate, coal-colored branches twining up toward lucent sky. Brown leaves heaped under the dead trees; scabbed earth reached toward the water. If that didn't spur them to action, what would?

A few days after those photos arrived at the PROFEPA district office, the long-awaited inspectors showed up in Unión Hidalgo. They documented the damage, listed several laws that Camarón Real de Pacífico had broken, then climbed in their trucks and drove away. As far as anyone in Unión Hidalgo could tell, they did nothing else.

Still, Sofia was glad for their presence. Just knowing that a government agency dedicated to protecting the environment *existed* was helpful, she thought. It was still something of a revolutionary idea, little known in places like Unión Hidalgo.

The whitewashed church, the most important and most impressive building in Barrio del Pescador, was too small and too hot to hold everyone, so plastic chairs and wooden benches were lined up under a large tree and a flapping red tarp out front. Shortly after 9:00 in the morning on May 27, 2001, the seats began to fill. Fisherfolk from Unión Hidalgo and other Zapotec and Huave coastal towns took their places alongside local politicians and people with master's degrees, who were visiting from big cities. I shook hands with people I knew from San Francisco del Mar, Unión Hidalgo, Juchitán, and Mexico City, then settled into a chair just as Carlos Cruz took the microphone. His clean, bright white t-shirt and serious expression indicated the event's importance. He welcomed everyone to his town's "neighborhood of fishermen" and explained, first in Spanish, then in Zapotec, that he and others had called this gathering to discuss what an industrial shrimp farm would mean for their community.

This part of the Mexican political process, of la lucha, had never appealed to me: long speeches with much repetition. The discussion lurched on and I abandoned my seat in search of a breeze. I joined Román Cruz, Leonel's uncle, at the very edge of the shaded space. I told him it was great to see him there, and he shrugged and smiled. "How could I not come? It's the same thing we're facing."

Jesús Martínez, who had led the tour the day we found the burned mangroves, came over and I introduced him to Román. At the microphone, Carlos Manzo was listing the many laws that Camarón Real de Pacífico had broken. Román explained to Jesús that they were fighting a shrimp farm in San Francisco del Mar as well. Jesús nodded politely; he already knew that.

I asked Román what was happening with Chico Toledo's shrimp farm plan.

"It's not advancing, because we say no. The rustic enclosure doesn't really hurt us. Why not? Because we don't add nutrients. We don't add anything. However, a shrimp farm *will* hurt us. Where are we going to put all the wastes?"

Jesús kept nodding; Román kept talking. "We've been able to stop it, so far, because we have communal control of the land. We're not afraid of anyone. Not the military, not anyone."

Jesús stayed quiet. I couldn't tell whether he agreed or disagreed with Román.

"You know, there are only about twenty people in that cooperative," Román said, referring to Chico Toledo's group. "But one of them is the mayor, from the PRI."

Jesús finally spoke. "Yes, it's the same here." Nearly the same. In Unión Hidalgo, Armando Sánchez wasn't yet the mayor, but he hoped to be. The current mayor of the town had approved the illegal land sales. Because there was no communal lands commissioner, there had been no one to stop him.

An hour into the meeting, a dozen women arrived from a Zapotec fishing village on the other side of Juchitán, Alvaro Obregón. All wore huipiles, long skirts cut from floral fabric, long braids, and the same serious expressions. They moved as if a single body, settling into two empty benches right in front. One of them stood to speak for the group as soon as Carlos Cruz opened the floor for comments. She thanked the meeting organizers: "How good that you are waking all of us up."

When the meeting divided up into working groups, Román, Jesús, and I rejoined it. Several of los de afuera, including a Greenpeace staffer from Mexico City, were in my group. He wore shorts—something istmeño adults hardly ever did—and the first pair of Birkenstocks I'd seen on the isthmus. He stood to speak, telling the group that the Mexican government planned to build more than 700,000 acres of shrimp farms ponds in the country. "One of the priority locations is Oaxaca. They want to fill these lagoons and the Mar Muerto with shrimp farms." People shook their heads and murmured their disgust. He continued, explaining that the lifespan of a shrimp farm is about a decade. After that, "they abandon the land."

An elderly man corrected him. "*Contaminated* land."

"Without mangrove," said another.

"Without fish," added a third.

The Greenpeace licenciado finished the list: "And salinated. We all know that the worst thing you can do to land is throw salt on it."

The elderly man interrupted, telling us about earlier attempts to privatize Unión Hidalgo's land. He turned to the man from Greenpeace: "What you say is true."

Sofía stood to speak. "Many of us did a tour. We personally went and visited the most beautiful places. Frankly, I fell in love with the land, the beautiful wildlife, the huge mangrove trees. And then we saw with our own eyes how it had been burned, and huge paths cut through the mangrove. And Armando Sánchez says, 'Oh, sorry, that was a mistake because those paths aren't on the land where we're going to do the project.' *What* do we have to do to make sure the government doesn't ignore us?"

The woman from Alvaro Obregón who had spoken first stood to answer Sofía, to say what they would do if the shrimp farm were built. "If the government doesn't respect the people, we'll just show up there and destroy it." She made a wide gesture, as if swinging a machete. "That's how people are around here."

# 10

## Celebrate Saint Francis of the Sea

Four months passed before I saw Román Cruz again. I visited San Francisco del Mar on Election Day, October 7, 2001, and found him in the town square in the middle of a long line of voters that trickled from the central kiosk. "¡Qué milagro!" he said as he took my hand. On the isthmus, people rarely said "¡Bienvenidos!" more often saying, "You have arrived!" or "What a miracle!" I admired Román's white shirt and silver belt buckle, both spotless and shining. He laughed and gestured toward his weathered huaraches: he was still a fisherman. Many of the people waiting in line and crowded around the kiosk wore their best clothes: pressed long-sleeved shirts, ankle-length skirts, embroidered huipils. Others who didn't have Sundays off came in their work clothes: cut-offs for fishermen, ragged long pants for farmers, aprons for housewives and market vendors.

As the San Franciscans stood in line waiting to vote that day, one of the big issues was the shrimp-farm threat, the chahuixtle that had been feared in the village for more than three years. My conversation with Román quickly turned to the shrimp farm plans. Chico Toledo's group had built the enclosed pond, Román told me, but it still functioned essentially

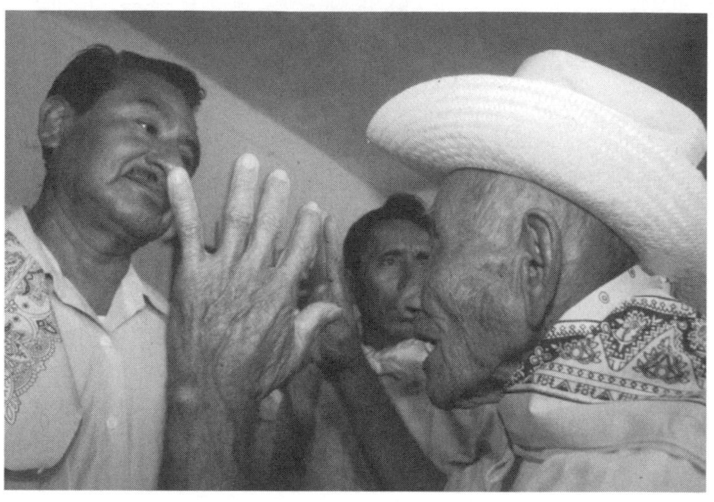

**11.** On San Francisco del Mar's Inauguration Day, January 1, 2002, a town elder urges Facundo Martínez to force the outgoing administration to hand over the municipal palace.

PHOTO BY THE AUTHOR.

as a rustic enclosure; no nutrients or other chemicals were being added. Like the anti-shrimp-farm crowd in Unión Hidalgo, the people in San Francisco del Mar had insisted on an official environmental impact study. That wasn't the sort of thing that small-town istmeños could easily accomplish, so the project had stalled at the small-pond stage.

In Unión Hidalgo, I explained to Román, the shrimp farm had been the major issue of the mayoral campaign. He hadn't heard much since the Barrio del Pescador meeting he had attended in May. I told him that the anti-shrimp-farm activists had gone door-to-door in their town, talking to people about the potential problems with the shrimp farm. Meanwhile, Armando Sánchez had secured the PRI mayoral candidacy. People saw him driving around town in a shiny pickup truck with an UGOCEM logo on the side. That was strange, since UGOCEM had never before had a presence in the town and Sánchez certainly couldn't afford that truck on his own. Three other candidates, including Carlos Manzo, also ran for municipal president, each representing a different party and each taking up the anti-shrimp-farm banner. The campaign slogan from the candidate of the PRD, the left-leaning Party of the Democratic Revolution, typified their stance: PRD supports the fishermen in opposition to the shrimp farm.

Román shook his head at my quick summary of events in Unión Hidalgo. We both wondered aloud what might happen with that town's elections. The winner would not only determine whether a road would be paved or a library would open or a few thousand dollars would disappear from public coffers—or all three. The new mayor might determine Unión Hidalgo's common future: Would the villagers continue to work as fishermen and palmeros, earning very little, or would just a few of them earn a lot working at a shrimp farm?

The line winding toward the kiosk inched forward as

Román and I speculated on Unión Hidalgo's future. Inside the kiosk at the polling table, each voter showed an identification card to a poll worker, who matched it to an exact copy in a large book then handed over a full-page ballot and a black crayon. Nearly all the voters marked their choice right there at the rusted card table. If you watched long enough you would know who was winning at that polling station. A plastic voting booth stood off to one side, nearly forgotten, the large slogan on its side—"Your vote is free and secret!"—addressing no one in particular. Mexicans had to be reminded that votes were private because it was a recent development. From the 1920s to the 1990s the PRI had managed Mexican elections. Just six years after a nonpartisan electoral council was set up for the 1994 elections, the PRI had been voted out of the presidency.

Román and I watched voters draw crayon Xs on their ballots. "So much for the secret vote," I said.

Román shrugged. "In a town this small, there aren't any secrets."

Party-based elections had replaced traditional assemblies only about fifteen years earlier in San Francisco del Mar, so the village had a long tradition of openly voicing political preferences. The current manifestation of this tradition made both vote-counting and vote-buying quite easy. At Román's polling station it seemed the votes were split evenly between the PRI and the PRD.

I asked Román, a hard-core PRDista, what he thought of the odds for his candidate, Facundo Martínez.

"Pues, I think we have a good chance. He worked hard."

Román finally reached the front of the line. With a spirited flourish he drew a thick X over the yellow and black PRD insignia. He headed home and I headed for another polling station, at the health clinic across from the village plaza.

In San Francisco del Mar the wind usually blows, the sun usually shines, and the PRI usually wins. But not always. Today everyone in Román and Leonel's family was hoping for a PRD upset over the PRI. Arriving at the Gómez Cruz household a few hours before I spoke to Román, I had caught everyone mid-frenzy, at the end of an intense month of campaigning. Leonel had spent the early morning hours in a nearby hamlet, where he had recently become the elementary school principal, rousting parents to the polls. Having returned home for a moment's rest, he stood on the veranda gulping water, his black hair dulled by dust, his white shirt stained with sweat where he'd been carrying his toddler son, Mahatma, against his hip. Leonel's sister lugged a ten-gallon pot of sweet and tangy *agua de jamaica* onto the front stoop: cool drinks for the pollwatchers, those making it harder for the PRI to buy votes. Their younger brother was out in the family-owned taxicab, ferrying voters to polling stations. Their father made predictions and took phone calls, doling out instructions and guessing the whereabouts of his children. The entire family had plunged into the mayoral campaign for its final month but Leonel had been working on it since early March. In the triangulation of small-town genealogy, Facundo Martínez, PRD candidate, was one of Leonel's many uncles.

As I headed across the town plaza toward the health clinic I noticed that not a single *bicitaxi* waited there. The three-wheel rickshaws usually gathered in that spot, waiting to take customers to a far-off house or to the bus stop or to the fishing grounds. The young bicitaxistas would sit on cracked plastic seats, turning up the volume on the radios tied to their bicycle frames, teasing one another. This morning a lone bicitaxista whizzed toward me, his face glistening with effort, his tires grinding gravel. No passengers sat on the wooden bench between the two front wheels; the driver was hunting for someone to bring to the polls. Within a few minutes several other rickshaws passed by, all carrying voters to polling stations. Each bicitaxi indicated its driver's political affiliation: a bumper sticker, yellow or green paint, or three handpainted letters: P-R-I or P-R-D. Though Mexico was for the most part a three-party country, San Francisco del Mar was a two-party town. Only one position, municipal president, would be decided that day, but many considered it the most important race of all. Everyone figured the election would be close. Six years (two election cycles) earlier, the PRD had won the mayoral race for the first time.

A man fell into step beside me. "There is a woman here," he said, referring to the health-clinic polling station, "who is buying votes." He introduced himself to me, then turned and walked away. I immediately saw the woman he referred to: with a worn green dress and a hard face, she stood a few steps away from the polling table. Arms crossed over her belly, her hands in fists, she worked small slips of paper from her palm out to her knuckles. People who had drawn their Xs over the red, green, and white PRI logo would pass by, flicking out a hand and looking away from her as their fingers clamped onto a paper square. Their movements seemed casual but the choreography was elegant: no eye contact, no words exchanged, not a single paper square accidentally fluttering to the ground. When I passed by the same polling station late in the afternoon, a somber-looking man, also dressed in green, had taken the woman's place. Leonel explained the system to me: the homemade coupons were later exchanged for cash, provided by the state party.

In a presidential election the reward for a single vote might run as high as five hundred pesos, but for this mayoral election it would be just one hundred, about ten dollars. Votes for state legislator fetched only about five dollars.

Perhaps it was a reflection of cacique culture—a holdover from colonial Mexico in which Native leaders were paid by the Spanish crown to keep their people quiet—that being village mayor carried a higher cash value than being state legislator. Or perhaps it was an indication of the structure of the Mexican political system, which granted greater power to presidents, governors, and mayors than to the state and federal legislatures.

I left the health clinic polling station and circled the plaza, looking for the man who had spoken to me. I found him quickly and asked if he might tell me more about what he had seen. As soon as he began to speak, a white truck pulled up beside us. The curling script on the cab door read Municipio de San Francisco del Mar. Three men wearing large cowboy hats climbed out as he took a deep breath and began to speak. "I just want to make sure the elections are transparent." He paused for a moment, his back stiffening. The three hats spread apart, each far enough away to seem uninterested but close enough to overhear our words.

"You were saying about the elections, señor?" I prompted.

"Ah, yes. I was saying that everything is tranquilo."

I caught a ride with Leonel to Santa Cruz, the hamlet where he worked and a place I'd never visited before. As I stepped from the car someone called, "Señorita Wendy!"

It was Chico Toledo. He didn't live here but was volunteering as a pollwatcher "for the party," as he put it. In southern Mexico "the party" was still the PRI—any other had to be indicated by name. Don Chico wasn't a particularly fervent PRIista; he had in fact supported the PRD until his brother had sought office as a PRI candidate. As istmeños liked to remind me, elections were less about political parties and more about small groups, sometimes families, struggling to wrest a bit of power from their adversaries or from other families.

Every political party that could muster it had a monitor, like don Chico, at each polling station, looking for what were politely called "irregularities." Here in sleepy Santa Cruz, Chico Toledo didn't have much to do, so he and I sat down on a log to chat. Another pollwatcher stood a short distance from the tables, marking each person's vote with a small slash in his spiral notebook. At the moment the tally was forty-nine votes for the PRI, sixty-six for the PRD, and five for the PAN—the National Action Party, President Vicente Fox's party. Don Chico didn't seem to mind that his brother's party (and, for the moment, his) was losing.

"Don Chico, how are things going with your shrimp farm?"

"Well, we didn't get enough rain this year, so the shrimp didn't grow to market size. Truth is, we had to abandon the farm. We didn't have the resources to maintain it." In spite of the lack of an environmental impact statement, the village assembly had given the Boca Barra Cooperative permission for a bigger project the following year: 700 acres. They would try again, even as Chico Toledo dreamed of an even larger project. Government officials who had visited San Francisco del Mar said that would require at least three million dollars—which seemed to him an unattainable sum. "There aren't companies that want to invest here. I just want to make sure my children have jobs." His words sounded so familiar; I'd heard them most recently, almost verbatim, from Armando Sánchez.

While Chico Toledo watched the voters in Santa Cruz, the man that most of them voted for was far from the polls. Facundo Martínez spent the entire day at home, leaving only to place his own vote in the ballot box. Campaigning is illegal during the final days before a Mexican election, so he wasn't taking any chances. He sat with several other men at a table behind his house, shirt unbuttoned. As I walked into his yard, he jumped up, shirttails flapping over his pale, round belly, and welcomed me extravagantly. He grasped my hand in a firm handshake; his skin was smooth and soft, no calluses. It was the handshake of someone who had worked a professional job.

"Mi casa es su casa, always. It is so good of you to come, to witness for yourself the antics of the PRI, the lengths they will go to so they won't lose." He sat at the table and joked about the competition, his voice a deadpan drawl. "It's very interesting, the PRI is like the cat with its paws in the air." The simile means something that is out of whack, all mixed up, but here it carried a double meaning: Facundo mimicked a dead cat's futile clutch.

But this cat was still kicking. By midafternoon, as it became clear the PRI might lose, party members stepped up their efforts to get voters to the polls. Facundo pointed this out to me as a "PRI electoral ploy," but of course it was perfectly legal. And his party had been ferrying PRD voters to the polls all day.

I had first met Facundo Martínez in May 2000, long before there was talk of his mayoral candidacy. We had both attended a three-day meeting about the potential impacts of the Trans-Isthmus Megaproject. For nearly two days he'd sat quietly, hands folded on the table in front of him, while fired-up activists and long-winded academics spoke for hour after hour. I'd wondered whether he was listening, his face mostly impassive as people raged on about present and possible future insults to local livelihoods, forests, air, and water.

When Facundo finally spoke it was to tell a story of

government workers who had shown up in San Francisco del Mar several years earlier to dig a canal between two coastal lagoons—the local fishing grounds. Many in the town believed the canal project was the first step in the construction of an industrial shrimp farm. Though the canal was unrelated to any shrimp farm development, their fears weren't far off. No one in San Francisco del Mar had known about it, but in 1994 the Mexican government received a forty-million-dollar loan from the World Bank to develop industrial shrimp farming, including five million for projects in Oaxaca. A booklet published for potential investors by the Oaxaca state government in 1993 listed two different sites within the municipality of San Francisco del Mar as "available" for intensive aquaculture.

To stop the canal project, San Francisco fishermen burned the government trucks and dredging equipment and ran the workers out of town. Facundo told his story slowly, keeping his audience waiting for each word. He concluded with the moral: "The Huave aren't against progress, but when the government is thinking of some Megaproject, some Project X, they have to take the community into account." Cheers and applause erupted, seeming to take him by surprise. Facundo wasn't much of an activist; he'd been needled into attending the meeting by Leonel. At that time Facundo had been cautious of the idea of an industrial shrimp farm, but not opposed to it. Since then Leonel had been working on him. Now when I asked Facundo what he thought of the Boca Barra Cooperative's project, he dismissed it with a shrug. "It doesn't fit with the needs of the people," he said. That was the only criterion; nothing more needed to be said.

Facundo's house smelled of freshly poured cement. He had moved back to his hometown the previous year, post-retirement, after spending most of his working life in Mexico

City. Don Facundo had returned to his village just in time to secure the mayoral candidacy. His federal pension made him one of the wealthiest people in town. As in the United States, this is a top qualification for candidates. He had left San Francisco del Mar when it was a much smaller village with few cement homes. In the concrete metropolis he had met and married Julia, a city girl, and raised two sons and two daughters with her. Their oldest child was thirty-six and the youngest twenty; all four lived at home. Julia and Facundo were still waiting for their first grandchild.

Village life in the subtropics didn't really agree with doña Julia. That election-day afternoon she planted herself next to an oscillating fan, her pale face reddened, damp, and plastered with wilted tendrils of light brown hair. I had met her the previous year when she had visited the isthmus with Facundo for a couple of days. Doña Julia had spent our day together moving reluctantly from one scrap of shade to another, borrowing my sunscreen, hyperventilating, fanning herself, suffering silently. Today she seemed slightly less stricken by the heat. Perhaps she'd acclimated, or perhaps she was carried along by electoral adrenaline.

Cousins, nephews, nieces, neighbors, and friends jammed Facundo's half-built home. All were there to savor the hopeful final hours of not knowing, and also for safety's sake. Elections were serious business in the Isthmus of Tehuantepec, and serious business sometimes involved guns.

I joined the men's table, cluttered with beer bottles, to hear the elections talk. Leonel paced the bare courtyard, greeting relatives and walking off nervous energy. The only thing he found more intolerable than just sitting around was sitting around and watching people drink. The social gathering at Facundo's exhausted his patience within half an hour, so he and I headed to the PRD headquarters.

A crowd had gathered in front of the squat building to wait for the results, complain about the PRI, and speculate about what their opponents might do if they lost. The women stood at the center of the circle of conversation; men crouched at the margins. One woman spoke, her hands and voice fluttering like dry leaves. The group shuffled me, the foreigner, over to talk to her. Guadalupe had decided about a week earlier to vote for Facundo Martínez but when her PRIista brother found out, he beat her. A few weeks earlier he had given her some money. She had considered it help among close family members; he had assumed it was insurance that she would vote for his party. One of Guadalupe's fingers bulged huge and purple. She rubbed the deep bruises on her face again and again, as if she could wipe away the evidence of her brother's anger.

As the sun curved toward late afternoon, the conversation in front of the campaign office bent more sharply toward worry. What would the PRIistas do if their candidate lost? As the PRDistas huddled in the shade in front of the sunshine-yellow office, the PRI supporters gathered just a half-block away, in the plaza: the town center still belonged to the town's ruling party.

News rolled in from the outlying polling stations: Santa Cruz, San Francisco Pueblo Viejo, and others. Everyone who wanted to vote in those hamlets had already done so, and the polls had closed—no reason to wait for the official 5:00 closing time. In Pueblo Viejo the PRD had won by fifty-two votes. In Santa Cruz, by eighteen. All the PRD had to do was split Pueblo Nuevo, the municipal seat, right down the middle.

At precisely 5:00 in the afternoon the last voter walked away from the polling station in front of the health clinic. The vote-counters lifted the polling table right over the chain-link fence into the dirt courtyard and locked the gate. As seven volunteers huddled around the table, dozens of their neighbors watched from beyond the fence, lacing their fingers though the mesh, calling out instructions. One of the ballot-counters was Leonel's younger brother, Vicente, who had spent the day taxiing people to the polls. Catching my eye in the crowd, he unlocked the gate. He waved away the people who pushed forward with one hand and pulled me inside with the other. I was so far outside this process, I stepped easily inside of it.

Vicente and three other volunteers drew long, black lines through every blank ballot, while the three party representatives and I watched. Once every unused ballot had been spoiled, they turned to a plastic box with clear sides that showed the folded ballots within. They unfolded each one and placed it in the appropriate pile, then Vicente began counting. For the PRI: 225 votes. He turned to the PRD pile and grimaced; it was obviously smaller. Total PRD votes: 158. He recounted, then counted a third time, coming up with the same numbers. The rings of onlookers thickened.

When they had finished, Vicente was sent out to write the totals for this polling station on a large chart hanging from the fence alongside the other polling stations' results. Seventy-three percent of San Francisco del Mar's 3,682 registered voters had cast ballots. The news came just a half-hour after the polls had closed: Facundo Martínez had done better at the other polling sites in the municipal center than at the health clinic, winning the election by 236 votes. He won with a 20 percent advantage over the PRI candidate, Juan Cruz. For a small moment the crowd in front of the PRD headquarters stayed silent. *Twenty percent?* They had expected to squeak to victory, not breeze into it. Leonel's eyes filled with excitement and he glanced around at women clasping their hands together and men mumbling their amazement.

"We won! We *won!*" Leonel yelled. "What is everyone just standing around for? Look happy!" He windmilled his arms, bidding people onto their feet. The old women jumped up, grinning and shaking their fists, soft bellies spilling from below their short huipils. As the shock ebbed away, the celebration echoed across the town center. Bicitaxi and truck horns blared; men bellowed and women screamed. The PRI supporters walked away from the plaza, silent.

Across the lagoon from San Francisco del Mar in Unión Hidalgo, the elections had not even been held. They were postponed for two weeks after some PRIistas were caught trying to steal blank ballots before election day. When the elections finally happened, Armando Sánchez won with 46 percent of the ballots cast. The anti-shrimp-farm voters had a majority, but it was spread among three candidates. Carlos Manzo came in last place, receiving only 5 percent of the votes. Later I would hear murmurs of dissatisfaction with Manzo's decision to run. In Unión Hidalgo, the ballot box failed as an anti-shrimp-farm tool as spectacularly as it had succeeded in San Francisco del Mar. The conflict over the shrimp farm continued to rankle Manzo's hometown, while in Leonel's village it settled back to low-grade worry.

On the morning of New Year's Day 2002, inauguration day, I sat in the concrete courtyard behind Leonel's house holding a large bowl of *champurrado* in my hands. I sipped the chocolate-corn gruel; the addition of Old World sugar had made this preconquest drink absolutely perfect. It was still early, but I'd already made the three-hour drive from Matías Romero and Leonel was already deep into worrying about what might happen later that day. Facundo Martínez's formal entrance into the municipal building was scheduled for today. In his final speech, the outgoing municipal president, PRIista

César Ventura Nieto (whose last names translate roughly as "grandson of fortune"), had mentioned something about not handing over the town hall keys to the new administration because of some unspecified bureaucratic infraction by the local PRD. Leonel paced back and forth as he told me the story, irritated by my surprise.

"Didn't you see the graffiti at the highway turnoff?"

No. Perhaps my mind had still been fuzzy from the long predawn drive; I'd hardly looked at the abandoned cement building that marked the dirt road to San Francisco del Mar.

"They are accusing Facundo of being a murderer! They're inventing all kinds of stalling tactics."

An accusation of attempted murder could be far more than a stalling tactic. My mind skipped forward to all sorts of possibilities: Facundo being barred from office, Facundo arrested, the police showing up, or guns appearing from their many hiding places. "Does this mean Facundo won't be entering the palacio municipal today?"

Leonel stopped short and glared at me. "No! Everything is all ready! They already killed the cows!"

In San Francisco del Mar cows are a sort of savings account on the hoof, sold to pay for a medical emergency, or an education, or a wedding. Of the hundred or so meals I'd enjoyed in Huave communities, only once had I eaten beef.

I left my empty champurrado bowl on the washboard stack and we left for Facundo's house. On Facundo and Julia's back porch a long row of women laughed and chatted. Each new arrival greeted the whole line with hugs; small hands patted fat upper arms, fixed pins in hair, twisted hair into braids. One woman circled the crowded dirt yard, tying a yellow bandanna around each man's neck and tucking one into the waistband of each woman's skirt. The crowd was hesitant, even slightly hushed, though their actions were animated.

The smell of fresh cement had faded from the walls of Facundo's home but the feeling of expectation matched that of election day, almost three months earlier. Facundo's expression was calm but his eyes telegraphed worry. He and Julia both looked older than they had just three months earlier. Julia leaned toward my ear and told me that the two of them had spent the previous month traveling from hotel to friend's house to hotel, threats of violence following them. Their children, *gracias a dios,* had all stayed in Mexico City until today. The four of them now milled the backyard, awkward in istmeño formal dress, smiling stiffly. Julia kept talking, low enough that only I could hear her. "People here who have known me for a long time ask, 'How can you have left your home to come to a community that has so many problems?'" She paused.

So, why did you? I asked her.

"My commitment to my husband. I haven't known a day apart from him."

Facundo, his smile and yellow shirt both crisp, nodded and shook hands and made small talk as the crowd in his home grew. Shortly after 10:30 the group poured from the house onto the unpaved road in front, just a few blocks from the central plaza and municipal building. They walked almost as a single body, the kunch kunch kunch of sand underfoot a determined rhythm.

¡Viva el presidente municipal! someone yelled.

¡Viva! The group shouted back.

¡Viva Facundo Martínez!

¡Viva!

¡Viva el Partido Revolucionario Democrático!

¡Viva!

¡Viva el pueblo!

¡Viva!

Their voices sounded slightly tinny, as if stretched tightly over anxious thoughts. Someone changed the call and response to a more relevant chant: "¡Facundo, amigo, el pueblo está contigo!" ("Facundo, our friend, the people are with you!")

*Shoosh.* The smoky plumes of bottle rockets arched above the procession. *Bang.* People walked rapidly, many of them glancing first to one side, then to the other, as they passed each building. Facundo's mask had fallen away; there was no hiding the tension.

Arriving at the municipal building, the group crowded into the block of shade under the awning. The cadence of the march dissolved into conversation, a few nervous coughs, and demands that the outgoing mayor come and open the building. They settled into their waiting.

A man walked up with a message from César Ventura Nieto: The outgoing mayor had decided not to hand over the keys; he was staying home today. The messenger smirked and walked away.

Facundo's face stayed blank. Someone yelled, "There are witnesses!"

A few people began the chants again, with less vigor than before, then their words faded. A bugle, drum, and trombone flashed in the sunlight, rolling out marching tunes, struggling to fill the hot air with something besides sweat and boredom. Morning turned to midday as the incoming and outgoing mayors tested one another's resolve. I joined the small knot of people surrounding Facundo. Another man arrived at the municipal palace and walked toward the crowd. Facundo's face softened a bit.

"A PRIista?" I asked.

"Yes," the man next to me said. "But he's also from the Council of Elders."

I drew in my breath. Here, San Francisco del Mar's four-decade-old system of party-based elections crashed up against the ancient system of traditional governance. Which would prevail?

Facundo answered the question I hadn't voiced: "I don't believe he's coming here as a party member. With this huge community demonstration, he has to respond to what's happening." Don Facundo continued, talking more to himself than anyone else. "If there's some sort of conflict, if something bad happens to me, I'm not to blame. The people are going to demand that he follow the law."

The Council of Elders member now stood before Facundo. "The president has received no official decree to deliver the municipal office to you." He added some pleasantries to his message, then turned and slowly walked back toward Ventura Nieto's home.

I asked Facundo whether he needed an official decree.

"No. The National Elections Commission issues them only if the elections results are contested. I won by a huge margin." He went on talking about Ventura Nieto, seeming to relax slightly, though still speaking as if he and I hadn't shared beers and salted tortillas at rough-hewn tables, as if he had just won a national election and I were from the *New York Times*. "I consider him a man of very limited political and intellectual capacity. The people here are conducting themselves virtuously. Up to now we have waited patiently. We'll wait here as long as we can. Until tomorrow if necessary."

An elderly man broke away from the waiting crowd and approached the mayor-elect. He raised his hands toward Facundo's placid face in a pleading gesture. His voice wavered ever so slightly: "The attorney general's office must demand that man get those keys out of his pot! He thinks he can just keep them there in his little bowl? They *must* open up here! The people at the attorney general's office had better get to work!"

Facundo's eyes darkened as he stared down at the man.

"Don't you just stay here," the man said, as if Facundo were a child. Facundo might be the new municipal president but he was a generation younger than the man hectoring him. "You are going to be here all day with your people and there is no point in *that*!"

"Ahorita. They're on their way," said Facundo, his hair still slicked into place, shirt only slightly wrinkled and damp. He repeated it several times in a low voice, more to himself than to the indignant man standing before him. *Ahorita*—the diminutive of "now"—was generally used to mean "in a little while," or, more often, "in a long while." Never, ever, did it mean "right now."

Another man joined the discussion. "What a lie! Saying that they're waiting for the official decree. There's no reason for the governor to get involved. *Here* is the official decree. *Here.*" He swept out his arm, indicating the crowd of several hundred villagers.

Others joined the argument, which had many sides. Wait right there at the municipal building for the keys, until the next day if needed. Go to the state attorney general's office. Go to Ventura Nieto's house—it was right around the corner—and demand the keys. Break down the door to the municipal building.

"No, no," Facundo said. His voice stayed calm, low enough that people leaned in to hear his words. "And what happens tomorrow, when they claim that checks and other things have gone missing? No, we can't open that door without the outgoing president." The kind of conflict that could be unleashed by a broken-down door sometimes cost lives in San Francisco del Mar.

Someone yelled, “Don’t be impatient, compañeros!”

With Facundo having settled the debate, the crowd turned away, settling back to smaller conversations. The sharp tension dissolved into a low drone of expectation, irritation, excitement. Everyone was there to support their new government, but they had different ideas of how to do that, and what it meant. Not everyone waiting with Facundo had voted for him. One of those standing before the disputed door was Rosalino Vargas, the founder of San Francisco del Mar’s nascent third political force, the National Action Party, and until recently a PRIista. As the PAN’s candidate for municipal president, señor Vargas had received a scant 4 percent of the votes in the October election. He had come to support the PRD because he didn’t support the outgoing president. Vargas had been municipal president a decade earlier and was critical of Ventura Nieto’s tenure. As for Facundo Martínez, Vargas was willing to give him a chance.

After losing the presidential elections in July 2000, the PRI had, to no one’s surprise, suffered a grand national exodus of members. It did not die, as many had expected, but it was still trying to reinvent itself—even as its former members reinvented themselves. The stories of the 2000 presidential elections were simultaneously funny and sad. The local PRI bosses in one northern isthmus town had gathered as usual on the evening of the elections to count the ballots. As was custom, heavy drinking accompanied the counting. The bosses drank themselves to sleep, awakening the next morning to find that the PRI’s presidential candidate had lost. They formed a local PAN committee on the spot, abandoning without a moment’s hesitation the only party they had ever voted for.

In front of the San Francisco del Mar municipal building, heat and hunger stretched out like a thick itchy blanket over the waiting crowd. Just as it began to suffocate, a youngish man with a fast walk and a thick gold chain around his neck approached the municipal building. Señor Ventura Nieto had arrived with the keys. A dump truck and two bulldozers paraded down the street—evidence of the state and federal dollars he'd attracted to San Francisco del Mar, his legacy to a town that had more rickshaws than taxicabs.

He bade a stiff greeting to Facundo, then requested the crowd be told to move away from the door—that is to say, out of the protective shade and into the sun.

Facundo wavered, then seemed to remember himself. "No. Why should I do that?" he asked without emotion. The ex-president then asked for the microphone. The sun glinted off his gold chain. "We have to work together with the new administration," he told the crowd. "We have to construct a society that is more just, a society that is more dignified. We must give young people opportunity but also recognize our elders. Compañeros, words are insufficient to express the gratitude that we feel." He went on and on, swiveling on the heel of his well-polished shoe.

People began to talk among themselves, their faces hardening into indifference. As the buzz of disinterest rose around him, the outgoing president ended his speech abruptly with, "¡Viva México!"—something everyone could agree on.

Finally, Facundo Martínez held the keys and the short-term future of his community in his hands. Shortly after Ventura Nieto handed these things over to Facundo, the inaugural fiesta began, with bottles of beer and large plates of barbequed beef for everyone.

Two months after Facundo Martínez took his place behind the wide desk in the palacio municipal, I visited to ask him about plans for his tenure. Elsewhere on the Isthmus of Tehuantepec, worry about the new highway had deepened into fury during those two months. The campaign against the highway grew even as the project gained traction. Construction crews broke ground on the path between Oaxaca City and the isthmus. More and more villages along the planned trans-isthmus route contacted UCIZONI, asking for help, asking how they could stop the project.

I asked Facundo about planned projects for his village. No, he wasn't going to build a shrimp farm, he assured me. He was going to build roads: a bridge across the lagoon inlet to Pueblo Viejo, a paved road connecting the town center to the Pan-American highway, a bridge over the Ostuta River to another Huave hamlet, a paved road from the village center to the fishing grounds. And they would do it with funding they would somehow find on their own. The state government would have funded at least half those projects, don Facundo thought, but only if the village agreed to other industrial projects that the fishermen believed threatened the lagoon's fisheries. That did not worry him, he told me. He would find a way to realize his paved-road dreams.

Echoing many people in many places, Facundo Martínez said he wanted these roads because "other communities have advanced while ours continues to be marginalized." That familiar desire had familiar consequences. After just a few months living on the Isthmus of Tehuantepec, I learned a simple calculation. Before visiting a village for the first time, I could roughly predict the percentage of children who could speak their indigenous language and the percentage of adults with healthy teeth: the more difficult it was to reach the town, the higher both percentages would be. Roads brought Coca-Cola, and everything that implied.

Not long after my conversation with Facundo, I saw a computer rendering of road construction and forest loss in northern Guatemala, one of the hemisphere's last great stretches of forest—not far from the Isthmus of Tehuantepec—between 1970 and 2000. Watching the time-lapse imagery was like watching a tree grow: the roads stretched out like branches, then patches of bare land opened all around them like unfurling leaves. Each of the virtual tree's new leaves represented another swath of eliminated forest. A World Bank study quantified the loss: each new mile of road built in a tropical forest meant 650 to 1,100 acres deforested. As I watched the pixilated tree flourish, something Chico Toledo had said during our first conversation at his fishing hut came back to me: "Yes, man came to earth to destroy."

# 11

## Gourd Full of Gold

Road-building dreams stretched from the Mexico City offices of Ochoa y Asociados to Facundo Martínez's municipal building and beyond, into the rainforest. The Chimalapas Mountains, visible from nearly every isthmus vantage point, curve on the horizon north of the Huave lagoons. "Todo viene de allá," the Huave fishermen would say as they sat on soft mounds of black netting in their fiberglass boats, gesturing with well-muscled arms toward the green hills. "It all comes from there." The fresh water that makes their lagoons perfect shrimp habitat pours from the Chimalapas highlands, as does nearly all the fresh water used by every istmeño.

The promise of land and timber has attracted outsiders to the Chimalapas, the heart of the Isthmus of Tehuantepec, ever since the Spanish began cutting the forest's ancient trees for ship masts more than three hundred years ago. Spanish shipbuilders complained that istmeños they hired to do that tree-cutting were unwilling to work and prone to striking for higher pay. In the 1400s the Aztecs conquered several villages in the Chimalapas foothills that lay on the trade route between central Mexico and Guatemala. The longtime inhabitants of the Chimalapas, the Zoques—sister culture

**12.** One of Juana García's nephews, Primitivo, pretends to go fishing in the creek near his home in the Chimalapas village of San Francisco la Paz (2002). PHOTO BY THE AUTHOR.

to the Mixes—fled into their mountains. They agreed to pay tribute to the Aztecs in exchange for being left alone. After the conquest, the Zoques paid tribute to the Spanish. The name Chimalapas means "gourd full of gold" in the Zoque language. In 1687 the Zoque people paid exactly that: twenty-five thousand gold pesos to buy their forest back from the Spanish invaders who had claimed it. In the early twentieth century, North Americans snatched up land titles for swaths of forest handed out by Mexican president Porfirio Díaz. Chicago Title and Trust, New York Lumber Company, and J. Henry & Sons all lost their ill-gotten tracts of land after the Mexican Revolution. In 1967 the federal government officially handed over 1.5 million acres to the Zoques. The forest on about one-third of that land has been felled, replaced with cornfields, cattle pastures, marijuana plantations, roads, and landing strips for drug traffickers' airplanes. Nevertheless, the Chimalapas rainforest is the largest still standing in North America.

The Zoque people now compose only one-third of the total Chimalapas population of thirteen thousand. The original residents have made space for immigrants, refusing only to welcome the *talamontes,* the "forest cutters." The talamontes aren't necessarily loggers, but anyone turning trees into money: drug traffickers cutting landing strips, cattle ranchers creating pastureland, overzealous peasants looking for easy income.

The Chimalapas forest stands so thick and so vast that locals claim no one has ever crossed it. This has been the forest's salvation. In 1884 the engineer charged with building a railroad across the Isthmus of Tehuantepec wrote, "The solitude of these mountains and the isolation of the population centers there, because no road reaches them, are very contrary conditions for a fast and easy colonization, so the initial challenges of setting up colonies will be greater than expected."

Roads reach more deeply into the Chimalapas every year, but still nowhere near its core. Rivers tumble down from the Chimalapas highlands on the north side, through the Uxpanapa region. Until the 1970s that region was covered by another half-million acres of forest that straddled the border between Oaxaca and Veracruz. That northern skirt of forest was razed by government plan. The rivers still flow through it, due north, toward the Gulf of Mexico. Those waterways run blue highways between the forest's mahogany and ceiba trees, allowing villagers to press farther into the Chimalapas than the roads do.

On one bend of one of those rivers, also called Uxpanapa, sits a village of five hundred souls called San Francisco la Paz. There are three ways to reach San la Paz, as the villagers called it, from the end of the nearest road: a five-hour hike and a swim across the Uxpanapa River, a four-hour horseback ride, or a two-hour ride in a motorized canoe. The first option requires good health and endurance; the second, an exceptionally sure-footed horse; and the third, several hundred pesos—more than most village residents earn in a month. In the dry season the river runs too low for the canoes. In the wet season the hike includes wading through knee-deep mud and crossing a roiling river.

Hardly anyone in San Francisco la Paz is Zoque. Nearly half are indigenous Chinantecs; a few are Zapotecs and Nahuas; and most of the rest are mestizos—the people, as the Chinantecs say, "who don't have another way of speaking." The first San la Paz settlers arrived in the 1960s after the area had been unpopulated for centuries.

As the Chimalapas community became heterogeneous, a new identity sprang up and people began to call themselves

Chimas. Indigenous Mexicans tend to identify themselves by the language they speak—or would speak if their language weren't dying out. Mestizos, those "who don't have another way of speaking," identify themselves by their hometown or home state. It's not so common in Mexico for a heterogeneous, multiethnic group to define itself as a collective, around the geographical terrain they call home.

Just as the Chimalapas forest sits at the geographic center of the isthmus, it also sits at the center of nearly every debate about the region's future. Even those pushing the Megaproject and the Plan Puebla Panama would mention the Chimalapas as the only possible loss worth noting. When I interviewed one of Veracruz's most powerful politicians, Fidel Herrera, he assured me that the Megaproject plans "didn't pose any threat to the indigenous cultures," but he couldn't say the same for the future of the Chimalapas. He admitted that the rainforest might not survive all the changes. In the end (or perhaps only short term) people are more adaptable than rainforests.

As the two years that I lived on the isthmus drew down to just a few months, I felt compelled to visit the Chimalapas rainforest one more time. Construction of one portion of the superhighway, connecting the isthmus to the state capital, was well underway. If that construction continued and the new trans-isthmus highway were built, the rainforest would face yet another threat to its survival even though the superhighway would not cross it.

On my first trip to San la Paz, I had traveled with a Zoque friend from another part of the Chimalapas and we had stayed at the home of Juana García. I called Juana to tell her I wanted to come visit a second time. Did she know of anyone headed that way who might share the trip with me? Talking on the only phone in the village, a government-provided satellite line, Juana told me that Bishop Arturo Lona Reyes would be visiting her village in mid-February. "He's coming to celebrate El día de San Valentín with us." I was surprised for just a moment, having been raised to link February 14 with drugstore greeting cards and boxes of chocolates, not a third-century Catholic martyr. "Call the priest and see if you could come with them," Juana advised me, referring to the parish priest who was organizing the bishop's visit. Juana was the sort of person who wouldn't think twice about hitching a ride with a bishop. Inspired by her courage, I tracked down the priest. He thought over my request for a couple of days and then told me, yes, I could go along.

When Bishop Lona Reyes and I arrived at the parish priest's house on midday February 11, he loaded both of us and our backpacks into a rattling pickup truck. The bishop wore a denim jacket, cowboy boots, and a simple wooden cross on a knotted string. He looked far younger than his seventy-six years, his curly hair receding only slightly from his forehead. We drove for five hours, while the bishop told us funny stories about other village visits, until the road dead-ended at the Uxpanapa River. Dusk fell as the parish priest bid us good-bye and the bishop and I stepped into a dugout canoe outfitted with a small motor. Two men from San la Paz directed the canoe southward, carrying the two of us upriver into the mountains. Since long before the Aztecs named these boats *canoas*, Chimalapas residents have carved and traveled in the slim, elegant crafts. The Zoques are mountain people renowned for their nautical skills. Our canoe tunneled through an invisible world, the motor chainsawing through a moonless, starless night. Two hours after leaving the end of the very last road, the blunt bow nudged the riverbank near San Francisco la Paz. We had arrived.

Bishop Lona Reyes and I pulled off our shoes and waded

in the direction of impact. Warm hands grasped our arms and backs; a cloud of voices speaking both Chinantec and Spanish led us up the bank and away from the river. I dug a tiny flashlight from my bag as the circle of villagers closed around the elderly man who accompanied me. In the weak battery-powered light, the bishop struggled up the incline, planting his boots wide apart and pumping his arms to keep his balance. I struggled up the riverbank behind him, the mud pulling me forward, gravity tugging me backward. Thin legs, plastic sandals, grasping hands, and giggles accompanied the two of us through the watery darkness.

The land flattened and we reached a narrow footpath, a beige strip cutting across blackish terrain. I hung back so my flashlight could illuminate all our footfalls, though the bishop and I were the only ones who needed the light. The trail unrolled before us and ended ten minutes later at a house built of rough-hewn planks and lit by a single candle. I set our bags in the corner on a jumble of saddles and machetes, as our hosts pulled us into their circle, taking our hands, pushing out chairs for us, handing us plastic cups of lukewarm coffee. Everyone turned to the bishop, thanking him, thanking him again, then three and four times, for coming to visit their village again after eight years.

The villagers called him "don Arturo" or "señor Obispo." When he had last visited San la Paz, Arturo Lona Reyes had been bishop of the Tehuantepec archdiocese. The Vatican had insisted he retire when he turned seventy-five. He had left his post in late 2001, carrying a tradition with him: he was Mexico's last liberation theology bishop, replaced by a conservative preferred by the Vatican. The people of San la Paz had no idea that don Arturo was no longer officially señor Obispo. The new bishop was not the sort to visit villages like San la Paz, so there was no way for them to know of the change.

In Juana García's kitchen, which is one half of her two-room house, the bishop and I drank coffee and ate a late dinner of chicken soup: a rubbery, turkey-sized drumstick in a yellow, oily broth. Our hosts laid out plans for the bishop's two-day visit as the candle tossed shadows onto the wood-plank walls and uneven dirt floor. The electricity had been out for two days. Fragile power lines carried a jitter of electricity up the mountainside from the end of the last road. Wind often knocked down the lines, and, when it did, the villagers had to raise the money to repair them. Juana stood between the cooking fire and the table, keeping the coffee cups full and the conversation flowing—appearing to be a hostess but actually an organizer.

Juana's older brother, Constantino, stood in the middle of the circle of people; he and Juana smiled the same smile. They were both tall by local standards, though Constantino was leaner. Winking flames from the fire and two candles exaggerated their expressions, throwing the brother and sister into high relief, while the others in the room—including Constantino's wife, Aurelia, and Juana's husband, Telo—faded into shadows. Constantino told the bishop about another parish priest who sometimes visited San Francisco la Paz to baptize children. "They call him Father Rooster. He talks in Latin," Constantino said. He closed his eyes and raised one hand, mimicking the parish priest, rocking back on his heels. "Ble-o lo-o heh-lo-oo," he droned. Don Arturo laughed and Constantino opened his eyes. "We don't understand any of it."

Don Arturo nodded. "They say it's cultural preservation, but if something's no longer useful, why conserve it? That's what we're trying to do in the Renewed Church: keep what's useful and get rid of everything else."

Bishop Lona Reyes was well known on the Isthmus of

Tehuantepec as a pragmatist, as someone who got things done. After he visited a town or village, empty health clinics, half-built roads, and long-ignored schools would suddenly be remembered by the state government. His retirement, still an unintentional secret in San la Paz, had only increased his advocacy work: he didn't have to worry about the Vatican's disapproval and he had more time to devote to his efforts.

The bishop scooped unshelled peanuts from his jacket pockets and handed them to the children gathered around him. Juana occasionally interrupted the conversation, making sure her older brother didn't forget any of the things the village needed. A wish list took shape: corrugated metal for new house roofs, a better health clinic, a proper community building, and, most important, a road from their village into town.

The first time I'd visited San la Paz, six months earlier, I had arrived at Juana's house late on an August morning after several missed connections had stretched the trip from Matías Romero (by bus, then pickup truck, then horse) to twenty-five hours. Juana was my hostess because she was an organizer, one of those people who built bridges between her village and the world beyond it, between what should be preserved about her village's way of life and what could be improved upon. When I showed up in her kitchen, Juana pretended not to notice my sweat-stained face and mud-stained shirt, welcoming me enthusiastically and then politely inviting me to join her on the daily trip to the river. Without wells or plumbing, everyone in San la Paz took everything to the river for washing, then hauled back buckets of drinking water. In August it was a short walk but during the dry season the nearby tributary disappeared and everything had to be carried half a mile. Juana gathered three freshly killed chickens, a bucket full of dirty dishes, and her three sons: Paco, who was six, Wilfredo, four, and Juan Pablo, three.

"A young man has asked for a young woman, and tonight they seal the commitment," Juana had said, by way of explaining the luxury of a chicken dinner. The young man was one of her cousins. "You can't accept a marriage proposal until the third request. That third time the man's family is supposed to give a dozen turkeys and eight loaves of bread and cartons of beer and soda. But since the girl is Highland Chinantec, they don't expect as much. We just took three turkeys and some soda and one carton of beer, and the señor was delighted." She shook her head in disbelief; the difference between the Highlanders and her people, Lowlanders, was just too much.

Only when speaking Spanish do the Chinantecs refer to themselves by the collective term *chinanteco*. The highland people call themselves *dzä jmiih* and the lowland, *tsa jujmi*; both mean "people of the language." The Lowlanders call the Highlanders *tsa ki*, "people of the mountain," while the Highlanders call the Lowlanders *dzä kïï*, "barefoot, bareheaded people."

Juana and I walked down the hill to the brook, her three sons zigzagging behind us. We joined Juana's sister Estela, sister-in-law Aurelia, and several nephews. The three women set down their loads and waded into the water, pulling off their shirts and skirts to bathe in bras and slips. I was accustomed to istmeña women who modestly waded into rivers fully clothed, long skirts ballooning around them, to wash clothes or dishes or even to go swimming. At the San la Paz brook, hair, bodies, whole chickens, dishes, and children all received the same treatment: soap, water, and a vigorous scrubbing. I washed my arms, legs, and face, then stayed on shore, just out of the splashing zone, on a flat rock that warmed my bare feet. Aurelia's teenaged son, Manuel, came by on horseback to fill water jugs and she waded out to help him. Manuel joked with the women and boys, though he was too shy to address me. Juana and Estela's father came by, too. The women continued bathing as they spoke to him, pushing their soapy hands between their legs and around their breasts. Their words lapped back and forth in Chinantec and Spanish, the old man speaking only the former and the children only the latter.

While the women washed, their young boys went to work. Estela's son fished, prowling the shallows near shore, occasionally jabbing his fat hand into the water and pulling out a ficus leaf. He collected the yellow ovals on a sharp stick, pausing now and then to show off his catch. Juana's oldest son, Paco, built a dam with his cousin's help. They constructed walls of wet sand, moved them around, tested their dam's integrity by dumping buckets of water into it, and then reengineered: pushing, patting, and pinching the river cement. Once satisfied with the construction project, their small hands pulled it apart.

These children live where they do because of a dam. The Chinantecs began to move to the Isthmus of Tehuantepec in the early 1970s, forcibly relocated by the federal government to make room for the Cerro de Oro dam in northern Oaxaca's mountains. The "Mountain of Gold" dam flooded the Chinantecs' villages and fields to provide electricity to urban Oaxacans. The government decided that rather than farm corn and hot peppers as they had for centuries, the Chinantecs should manage citrus groves, rubber plantations, and cattle ranches in their new isthmus home. In less than a decade more than half a million acres of Uxpanapa rainforest were razed, making way for these new agricultural enterprises. Biologists, anthropologists, and some local people refer to that massive forest destruction as an "ecocide" and the relocation's impact on the Chinantec people as an "ethnocide." Thirty thousand people, who spoke different dialects of Chinantec, were installed almost at random into fifteen prefab villages on the northern fringe of the Chimalapas, just north of the Oaxaca state border in Veracruz. The settlements were so generic they'd been assigned numbers rather than names. Even twenty-five years later they are called Poblado 1, Poblado 2, and on up to Poblado 15. Extended families were separated, while people from lowland and highland villages were mixed together—rather like Spanish and Italian speakers living on the same street, attending the same town meetings, and sending their children to the same schools. The deforestation made the Uxpanapa climate hotter and drier, while the soils under the felled trees were—like most rainforest soils—nutrient-poor, rocky, and acidic. No miracle happened; most of the orange groves and rubber plantations failed. Meanwhile, the seeds the Chinantecs had brought with them from their old farmlands, adapted to chilly highland Oaxaca, refused to grow. The government left the Chinantecs to their misery. Many, like Juana's parents, left the close-jammed cinderblock settlements and moved south into the Chimalapas mountains, to places like San Francisco la Paz.

Juana, Estela, and Aurelia finished their washing at the river, then gathered up their children, chickens, buckets and soap. They climbed back up the hill, still wearing only bras and slips, winding their t-shirts into donuts to cushion the 30-pound buckets of water they carried on their heads. Back in Juana's kitchen the children collapsed into hammocks for long naps and she headed for the open fire in the corner. Clouds of steam rolled from a blackened pot and curled around a rainbow of plastic cups hanging on the wall. Juana smoothed her waist-length wet hair into a topknot. She wore no jewelry, not even a wedding band, and her ears were unpierced. Her manner was unhurried but efficient; she had to finish dinner before her next task: coordinating an evening meeting.

"I put off getting married," she told me, as we watched her sleeping sons tangle themselves in fraying hammocks. She married Telo when she was twenty-four—a decade older than Aurelia had been when she married Constantino. I asked Juana whether she and Telo planned to have more children. She shook her head firmly: No, she disliked the social pressure on women to have babies young and to have a lot of them. She smiled at her three boys. "We had them fast because we were trying for a girl." In this way too, Juana and Telo were unusual: couples more often tried for boys, and too often didn't plan their families at all, ending up with however many children God intended.

Before marrying, Juana had spent two years in the port city of Coatzacoalcos, Veracruz, volunteering with the Catholic Church, and a year in Matías Romero working for an environmental organization. She had attended school only through the fourth grade—all the schooling that was available in San Francisco la Paz. She had wanted to continue to middle school but there was no money to send her to live in a town with a secondary school. There had been money for her brother Constantino, who was thirteen years older, but he had studied for only a couple of years before returning home.

I admired Juana for refusing to do what her village expected even as she carefully met community responsibilities. I admired Telo too: he had married a woman who was older and knew more of the world than he did. Their physical selves—Telo thin, wiry, and short; Juana taller, thick-waisted, and broad shouldered—mirrored their relationship: she was a more prominent participant in community life and an equal partner in family decisions. People came by the house regularly to seek Juana's opinion and request that she mediate disputes. She would lean in the doorway talking to the guest, asking thoughtful questions and doling out careful advice, while Telo sat at the small kitchen table, reading a newspaper that had passed through so many hands its ink had nearly rubbed away. His lips moved as he worked his way slowly through the pages. When the visitor left, Telo would close the newspaper and Juana would turn away from the door. He would comment on the news and she would comment on the village problem; both their observations cut directly to the heart of the issues, whatever they were.

Juana's meeting that evening, held on the covered porch in front of the one-room health clinic, was for mothers receiving public assistance to buy food, a sort of rural Mexican WIC program. She sat behind a shiny plastic table littered with government forms with several dozen women gathered around her. Juana was the only one not holding a child's hand or nursing a baby or both; Telo was taking care of their boys at home. She went through the long, confusing forms with each woman, explaining them in Chinantec, joking at the administrative errors as she waved the papers around. "Well, you thought your name was Marta, but now you're mata (killing)." After two hours a cloud of insects settled into a halo around her damp head. Men arrived to accompany their wives home from the meeting; some thought it unseemly for women to walk around the village alone. Public space was male space; and until eight years ago in San la Paz, public space had been dangerous space.

Cheerful to the very last person, Juana stood to put away the table. The creases of her sweaty t-shirt unfolded and a slogan printed across the front appeared. In elaborate script it read in English, "Of course God created man before woman. You always make a rough draft before you make the masterpiece." I asked Juana if she knew what the words said. She did not; she'd picked it at random from one of the truckloads of used clothing from the United States that are sold all over Mexico. I translated the slogan for her. One of the waiting men guffawed. Juana's round eyes widened and her face opened into a grin. "I have to put the translation on the t-shirt!" The man went silent, mid-bellow, his mouth slack with surprise.

Six months after Juana coordinated that mundane-but-important meeting, she orchestrated every hour of Bishop Arturo Lona Reyes's stay in San Francisco la Paz: daily Mass, a St. Valentine's Day fiesta, First Communion classes, meals hosted by village families, and, of course, a village assembly. Every important decision had to pass through the village's one-room assembly hall, where discussions drifted like the breeze through latticed walls.

As in most Mexican villages and towns, San la Paz's assembly hall sat right by the central plaza, along with the church, elementary school, and health clinic. Unlike most Mexican communities, this plaza was a wide green field whose fourth side was dominated by an ancient pyramid. Thickly covered with vines and bushes and obvious only by its geometric shape, the pyramid had been built by the Olmecs, southern Mexico's mother culture, thousands of years ago. After the Olmecs disappeared, it crumbled in oblivion.

The bishop and I arrived right on time at the assembly hall on the first morning of our visit. After a breakfast of chicken soup, eaten quietly in the home of a family too shy to speak to us, Bishop Lona Reyes had seemed anxious to get to the assembly hall. At 10:00, one hour after the village assembly was scheduled to begin, people began to file into the hall: women sat on the right, men on the left. Realizing

I'd sat on the wrong side, I scooted over to the right and a welcoming circle of women closed around me, patting my hands and gently tugging on my ponytail.

The bishop paced the front of the room as the hall gradually filled with the gurgles and whimpers of many babies, the soft scrape of leather sandals and rubber boots on the dirt floor, and hushed conversation. Don Arturo stared at an old administrative note written in Spanish on the chalkboard and then slowly rubbed the misspelled words out with his fingers and rewrote them.

The meeting began slowly, with the usual complaints about unfulfilled government promises and past failures. After perhaps fifteen minutes, during which only men spoke, the bishop turned to the right side of the room. "Let's have the women take the floor, so that later you won't say that we ignored you. A woman to speak? Don't you have tongues? Or don't you have permission to be here?" His questions came out fast. When the bishop finally paused, one woman said quietly, "We need the road, because it's hard to walk."

The bishop smiled. "Bueno, the women have started to talk; now we'll see if anyone can quiet them." Polite laughter riffled across the room.

Angela Méndez Escobedo, a mestiza woman and San la Paz's first resident, tried to steer the discussion away from the road. She stood, barely visible over the heads of those seated around her, a long gray braid curving down her back. Her face was firm and her arms were muscled, but her hips and legs looked soft, as if gravity had slowly worked on her body. "We need a central square in front of the school so that the children have a place to play," she said. I had considered San la Paz's green field so much more beautiful than the weed-filled cracked concrete expanses of so many Mexican villages, but for her, pavement meant progress.

A third woman pulled the subject right back to the road, insisting it was the most important thing: people needed it to get to the hospital, to take their harvest to market, to bring supplies to the village.

"Very good, would another woman like to speak?" the bishop asked.

A man stood up. "Unfortunately, I'm one of the people who's been struggling with the government for years to get this road." He went on, meandering back to the same point again and again. "What we want is our road, in concrete, now, hecho y derecho!"

The man paused after insisting they needed the road "done fast and straight," and the bishop said quickly, "Well, good, let's make sure that gets into the minutes." Don Arturo turned toward the village secretary, who sat in the room's front corner, his pen angled thoughtfully over a neat notebook page. The secretary nodded and the bishop turned back to the right side of the room.

The discussion braided through other needs and desires, then the president of the health committee stood to explain that the clinic had only some first aid supplies and the doctor visited only once every two months.

Constantino, former president of San la Paz, had been slyly moderating the meeting, even though the bishop was the one standing up front. Juana's older brother gently stopped people who tried to jump in as Chinantec comments were translated for Spanish-only speakers; his eyes traveled the room looking for people who wanted to speak. Late in the meeting he finally offered his own opinion: "If people could even just get some medicine that would help, let alone a visit from the doctor. I'm not sure if she's supposed to come every month or every other month, but it's going on four months now since she was here. Does anyone else have an opinion about this?"

The bishop stepped away from the front of the room, letting Constantino take control of the meeting. Juana stood up, her wide mouth pulled into a frown, and addressed the bishop: "What we most need is a person to attend to us, a doctor or a nurse. The last time she was here was in October. She didn't come in December because of the holidays, and then in January she claimed she had too much work left over from December. She'll give any excuse not to come. I guess we have to make sure to get sick whenever she's here!"

Like many of San la Paz's problems, lack of medical care could be partly ameliorated by a road to the village. Several times the state government had begun building a dirt road from the nearest town, Poblado 14, more than 7 miles away. Each time, the money ran out, leaving a useless quagmire. At the end of the assembly meeting the villagers arranged their requests by importance. The second priority was a new roof for the health clinic. The top priority was the road—ahead of reliable medical attention, new classrooms, potable water, local access to public assistance funds, and teachers who consistently showed up to work.

The meeting adjourned around noon, with every communal landholder signing the minutes. San la Paz's land was held in trust because it was part of the indigenous Zoque municipality that owned (at least on paper) two-thirds of the Chimalapas. Each head of household—all men, widows, and women who were still single at age eighteen—received the right to work a parcel. The *comuneros* lined up to sign or make their Xs, standing in order of their arrival to the village, with doña Angela signing first.

Though no road reached it, San Francisco la Paz might not have existed at all if it weren't for a road. Doña Angela and her husband had arrived at the spot now known as San la Paz in 1958. They came from Tapachula, Chiapas, a teeming, smoke-belching city near the border with Guatemala. Her husband had followed the roads cut through the Chimalapas for logging and oil exploration. At road's end he had pushed farther, found a spot he liked near the Uxpanapa River, then brought his wife and young sons to live there under the canopy of mahogany and cork trees. The family cleared forest to farm but the rainforest soils bore meager harvests. Still, it was better than no land at all, and they survived thanks to the fish in the river and the deer, iguana, armadillos, and pacas of the forest. One year after arriving, they secured title for their homestead from the Zoque municipal government, naming it after a ceramic figurine of Saint Francis—patron saint of animals and the environment—that they had carried with them from Chiapas.

The elderly woman sat with me for well over an hour one afternoon, recounting village history. Her voice was sure, her turns of phrase added irony, and three of her sons added dates and details she couldn't quite pull from mind. Their family eventually grew to five sons and two daughters, "seven heads," doña Angela said, as if speaking of livestock. For the first fifteen years the Escobedo Méndez family lived in San la Paz. "It was a five- or six-day walk to the closest house," she remembered. Her husband died in 1969, leaving her alone with her children. In 1974 wealthy ranchers arrived, settling on the east side of the Uxpanapa River, within sight of the Escobedo Méndez homestead. The ranchers cleared land for their cattle and regularly tossed dynamite in the river—a lazy form of fishing. In 1979 the ranchers turned their cattle loose in the family's recently planted cornfields, destroying the season's harvest. In a place like San Francisco la Paz, where food was scarce, that amounted to an act of aggression.

By the mid-1980s San la Paz had grown to eighteen families.

Most came from what the government called "reaccommodated" Chinantec villages. Others were Nahuas, Zapotecs, or mestizos who had come from farther away after learning there was available land. All were welcomed by the Escobedo Méndez family, who thought there was safety in numbers. Meanwhile, heavy rains and flooding led to poor harvests and the river dynamiting decimated the fish population. As time wore on, it became clear that San La Paz's neighbors weren't just grazing cattle and blasting fish. The airplane landing strip they constructed on the nearby mountaintop, their many guns, and their odd nighttime movements could mean just one thing: narcotics. Conflict simmered between the peasants and the *narcoganaderos*, or "narco ranchers," across the river. The ranchers occasionally shot at the villagers and burned down their houses. Many families left in the early 1990s, having decided a drug-infested rainforest was no place for peasants. Some of the families eventually returned, unable to secure land elsewhere and fearing hunger more than drug runners. New families arrived, and something of a stable campesino village developed. The San la Paz residents grew corn, beans, and chiles that people tried to sell, along with bananas, citrus, tomatoes, yucca, and a dozen other crops for local consumption.

On May 29, 1992, doña Angela's youngest son, Pablo, left home early to shop in town, an errand that would take the entire day. Several people in Poblado 14 reported that they saw him carrying his groceries late that afternoon, but he never returned home. Though only eighteen, Pablo was in charge of local land tenure at the time he disappeared. It wasn't unusual for young people to hold such important positions; they were more likely than older villagers to have the essential skills of speaking, reading, and writing Spanish. On the isthmus, where land conflicts often turned bloody, dealing with land tenure could be a dangerous responsibility. The police never formally investigated Pablo's case, in spite of years of pressure from his family. It was far from the only suspected murder connected with a land tenure dispute. But perhaps more relevant, investigating his disappearance meant challenging the narco ranchers, something few in the government were willing to do.

Two years after doña Angela's youngest son disappeared, her community finally won its battle with its erstwhile neighbors. With help from several Mexican environmental organizations, international agencies, and even a few government agencies, San la Paz pushed out the narco ranchers. The federal government hastened their departure with a compensation payment of more than four million dollars. Somehow, money could be found for these sorts of incentives but not for building village roads nor for improved medical care. In September 1994, San Francisco la Paz celebrated the departure of the narco ranchers and declared the land they regained an ecological reserve.

"We finally reached victory," doña Angela told me. "Then we could truly call ourselves San Francisco la Paz." It was an important moment, not just for the village's one hundred families but for people throughout the isthmus and across Mexico. Many people, including Bishop Arturo Lona Reyes, traveled from far-off Mexican cities, even from the United States, to celebrate with the villagers.

In the eight years between the bishop's two visits, some things had changed in San la Paz. The many Chimas, environmentalists, and human rights activists who worked together against the narco ranchers had opposed *both* of the interlopers' businesses. Drugs destroyed people and cattle destroyed rainforest. When the ranchers left, they took their cattle but left behind pasturelands of star grass, an invasive plant that chokes out native groundcover. The villagers tried planting corn in the open pastures but the star grass strangled their crops, too.

The ranchers also left behind tantalizing whiffs of the ranching lifestyle. Buying a heifer, turning it loose on that star grass, and then selling it a few years later brought a five- or six-fold return on cash investment. For poor rural people with no assets but land, it was an extremely attractive prospect. In the years after the narco ranchers left, fires became more common around the village. Several villagers told me in hushed voices that some of those fires were set by people in San la Paz opening up new pastureland. According to the local constitution, the 120-acre plots that comuneros received were to be maintained as no more than one-fifth cropland and two-fifths pasture; the rest was to be left as undisturbed forest. Anyone who opened new pasture was breaking the law.

When Juana and Telo married, both had already become comuneros and received land grants. They decided to sell Juana's user rights and work only Telo's plot. Long-term land-use rights sold for about forty-three dollars per acre of workable land. With the money they received from the sale, Juana and Telo bought several cows. In seven years of married life they had worked their way up to thirty head of cattle. "What would I do with more?" Telo told me, shrugging his shoulders. If he and Juana sold all their livestock at once they would earn about sixteen thousand dollars—a colossal sum for a family that grew and hunted its own food and lived in a house with no running water, a dirt floor, two light bulbs, and two electrical appliances (a cassette tape player and a blender). Juana and Telo were richer than most of their neighbors; only about one-third of the village's families owned cattle. Most of them, including Constantino, owned only a few animals. Still, the phenomenon represented a dramatic shift in the village: from subsistence corn farmers to small-time ranchers.

The pastures-in-the-rainforest system conflicted with the need to preserve the forest, but at the same time, San la Paz's small-time ranchers were the only real protectors of their portion of the Chimalapas. Had the villagers of San la Paz not been there to fight the narco ranchers, no one else would have done so. Thc mountain dwellers were both stress and salvation for the forest in which they lived. No one could deny that the slow economic shift from corn to cattle spelled doom for large swaths of rainforest, and yet I could not blame them. It is far easier (and less risky) to graze cattle than to plant, tend, and harvest corn year after year. Juana had worked for the environmental organization that fought the narco ranchers the hardest, and yet she and Telo owned cattle. For them, the point wasn't life in the forest, but life beyond it. They wanted their three boys to attend secondary school, which meant sending them away from San la Paz, which meant entering the cash economy.

On the last evening Bishop Lona Reyes and I spent in San la Paz, he watched television with a family—celebrating the return of electricity—and I visited the home of Constantino and his wife, Aurelia. I'd spent my first two nights on a cot in Juana's kitchen, but Aurelia insisted I spend the third night at her house. A few months earlier she and Constantino had stayed at my home in Matías Romero, while their son, Manuel, was treated at a hospital in my neighborhood. While getting take-out from the corner taquería, I had run into Constantino, his normally calm face tight with worry. I went with him to the hospital to see Aurelia and Manuel. Pale and shriveled-looking, Manuel lay in a neat hospital bed recovering from a severe kidney infection; his parents had been sleeping on the tile floor of his tiny room. It had been nothing, of course, for me to hand over the key to my house, but Aurelia was extremely eager to return the small favor.

A nail pounded into their home's front door frame held a small cross and a rusted metal sign that read, "Message to Mormons, Jehovahs, and other sects—this is a Catholic home." Aurelia had no problem with "the people who didn't have another way of speaking," but she had no patience for evangelicals. The family's two-room house, one of the few in town with a cement floor, doubled as a community store. Five years earlier Constantino had cofounded a local cooperative to support low-budget economic-development projects, ones that took both people and forest into account. About one-fifth of the village's households were members of the cooperative. Their projects included teaching people to use green manures rather than chemical fertilizers; planting "improved pasture"—a far less invasive grass—rather than the narco ranchers' star grass; and running the community store. The store had come from an earlier, unsuccessful corn-growing project. When the crop failed that year, the farmers were stuck with the unpaid government loan. Since Constantino had encouraged his neighbors to join the cooperative effort, it was left to him to figure out what to do about the failed project. He and Aurelia donated the space in their home and their time for the store, selling staples brought from town by horse or canoe. They sold them at a small mark-up and the profits paid down the old debt.

I sat in the corner of the tiny store, part of their living room, as Aurelia and Constantino stocked the dustless, well-ordered shelves. My first question to Constantino was, Why cattle ranching in a rainforest?

"Because that's what people ask for," he replied, as he and

Aurelia lined up bars of soap, bottles of cooking oil, tins of powdered milk, and bags of sugar. Also, perhaps, because that's what the government would finance. Three months earlier the federal government had made a grant of $160,000 to support cattle ranching in the Chimalapas.

Constantino had an impassive way of speaking that made it hard to determine the feelings behind his words. To discern emotion I had to look carefully at his drooping eyes. When he answered my first question his eyes beamed disappointment and resignation. He was well known both inside and outside the Chimalapas as one of the "forest defenders." Even death threats had not dissuaded him. Still, he owned three cows himself; he could do the math as well as anyone else.

I asked him about the road, the village's highest priority. What about the new immigrants it would bring? The village assembly had decided that the forest couldn't absorb a significantly larger population and had made it illegal for anyone who wasn't descended from a current comunero to become one—a typical close-the-door-behind-us immigration strategy but one that indicated they understood their land had reached its human carrying capacity. What about the timber cutters who followed every available road into the Chimalapas, illegally felling the oldest and largest trees?

Constantino nodded. "Yes, it could be that on the one hand the road will save us, and on the other hand it will destroy us." He laughed thinly. "We are thinking about the people who have met with disaster, who got sick and needed medical care but died on the way." Here Constantino had stepped squarely into the paradox of living in a fragile, isolated, endangered habitat: Should individual well-being or long-term collective health take precedence? Should the needs of the rainforest ever come before the needs of the people who chose to live within it?

The next morning, the bishop and I rose before dawn for our canoe ride back to Poblado 14. The parish priest met us at the end of the road, where he had dropped us off, and drove us back to his home. Bishop Lona Reyes stayed on for a visit to another village; I headed home to Matías Romero. A collective pickup truck took me as far as Boca del Monte. The struggle of that village with PEMEX seemed so much more straightforward: the oil company had offices they could visit, employees they could talk to, and equipment they could force off their lands. The villagers had done all those things and had made real progress. PEMEX had moved far beyond offering one-time payments for long-term damage, and had begun to offer long-term compensation—including a revolving loan fund—for the 1999 oil spill.

I waited for the bus to Matías Romero. I noticed for the first time the words carved on the back of the huge wood-and-metal archway over the turnoff from the trans-isthmus highway. The back of the sign read, *¡El que no cree que en Uxpanapa se hacen milagros, no es realista!* ("He who doesn't believe that miracles happen in Uxpanapa isn't a realist"). I thought of the half-abandoned prefab towns that dotted the razed Uxpanapa forest. The sign bore the most haunting message I would encounter in all my time on the Isthmus of Tehuantepec.

One evening three months after my visit with the Bishop Lona Reyes to San la Paz, I sat at home in Matías Romero when my front door rattled with a sharp knock. It was Telo and the president of San Francisco la Paz, both dripping wet but smiling. They were stopping by to say hello after visiting Bishop Lona Reyes, who lived in the wealthiest town on the Isthmus of Tehuantepec, a half-hour bus ride south of my house. The two men sat in my living room, shivering and cupping mugs of Nescafé with pruned hands. They had made the twelve-hour trip from San Francisco la Paz to learn what progress don Arturo had made on their top requests: money for the road and a new roof for the health clinic. When they arrived at the bishop's home, he wasn't there. They decided to wait for him through nearly two days of rainstorms—the trip back home was too expensive to abandon their mission so quickly. In the end, they told me, their visit was successful: the bishop had spoken with them for several minutes as they stood on his porch. He told them the roof materials were on the way. Seventy strips of corrugated metal would be delivered to Poblado 14. From there, the villagers would haul them on horseback ten at a time to San la Paz. The bishop also gave them far more important news: the state government had allocated funds for the road.

Stunned by their fortitude, I sat silently as Telo went on to narrate other village happenings. A wealthy man from Veracruz had bought land-use rights from two comuneros, giving him access to 240 acres of San la Paz land. It was illegal, of course, to sell user rights to people not from the village. The man planned to clear all that land to graze cattle—doubly illegal. He made it very clear he wanted more of their land and had the cash to pay for it, saying he wanted to graze one thousand head of cattle, more than the total number owned by everyone in San la Paz.

San Francisco la Paz had struggled for years to throw out the narco ranchers. Pablo Escobedo Méndez had likely been murdered because of the conflict. Constantino and many others had been arrested, shot at, beaten, or had their homes burned to cinders. Through it all they had stood their ground and tried, in their way, to protect their forest. Now the ranchers were back, with different names and different strategies, but the same result: cattle creating desert from rainforest.

"But, Telo, who would do this?" I asked, trying to keep my voice calm. "Who would sell their land, knowing that it would be turned to cattle pasture?"

Telo's answer fell on my ears like an axe. He stared into his empty coffee cup as he told me that half of the land had come from Manuel García, Constantino's son. Manuel had recently turned eighteen and become a comunero. As an only child, Manuel would someday inherit his father's land. Almost immediately the young man had sold the user rights to his own 120 acres. The rancher would pay over time, eventually handing over five thousand dollars for the land. With the first payment Manuel and his parents had bought a new refrigerator and a chainsaw.

Telo raised his eyes, meeting my shock with a stare that shifted from embarrassment, to resignation, to a sharp look that seemed to say, *you know how complicated all this is.*

Even as the residents of the Chimalapas have come to identify more with their forest home, calling themselves Chimas and learning how to mesh farming and forest management, they have also taken on the culture of other forest immigrants. More and more speak Spanish instead of Zoque, Chinantec, and Nahua. More and more leave for the United States and send back dollars, or don't, to their families. People have slid, or been pushed, ever closer to a cash economy—one in which forest has no place on the balance sheet until it is cut down.

One afternoon in San Francisco la Paz, the bishop and I had walked across the central plaza together. Although the village was only forty years old, several thousand years ago a settlement of Olmecs—mother culture of Mesoamerica's great civilizations, including the Maya, Totonac, and Zapotec—had existed precisely where the village had been founded. The

Olmecs, or "Rubber People," originated along the Gulf Coast of what is now Veracruz. Satellite maps of the Chimalapas show hints of their pre-Hispanic crop clearings, long before the Zoque people existed.

One afternoon Bishop Lona Reyes and I had taken a walk together in San la Paz. At one point he stopped to show me the ancient lay of the land. He put a hand on my shoulder and steered my gaze toward the peaks and valleys around us. He pointed out two pyramids buried deeply under bushes, small trees, and vines. I had not even noticed them before, taking them to be simple hills. In between the two was the depression of the ceremonial ball court. He commented on how strange it was that this place had been populated by the Olmecs, then abandoned for so long, then repopulated so recently by the settlers of San la Paz. That long desertion was probably the only reason the ruins had survived intact, he mused. It was probably the only reason that the forest had survived, as well.

# 12

## Redrawing the Map

A few months after the visit from Telo, with his ruinous news, my two years on the isthmus drew down to their end; it was time for me to return to the United States. I left reluctantly, thinking only of when I would be able to return. Nearly a year later, in May 2003, I received my wish: another month on the Isthmus of Tehuantepec. I packed a large suitcase full of the wishes of others, the gifts requested by istmeño friends. The collection of objects offered its own narrative about globalization, international trade, and cultural exchange. For one of the "muchachas bonitas" (referred to in the welcome sign to Unión Hidalgo), a dozen yards of filmy chiffon from Boston's Chinatown. For the young staffers at UCIZONI, memory cards for a digital camera; a Spanish edition of Naomi Klein's book, *No Logo*; a yoga mat and video; and a silk cocktail dress (that last item for one staffer's high school graduation). For Carlos Beas, a CD of Senegalese music, and for Mirna Godínez, maple syrup. (Mirna had been enchanted by that exotic treat when a friend from New England had brought it to me in Matías Romero.) Leonel Gómez asked for a computer, memory cards, and several mother boards for an internet café his youth group had started in San Francisco del Mar's PRD-controlled municipal

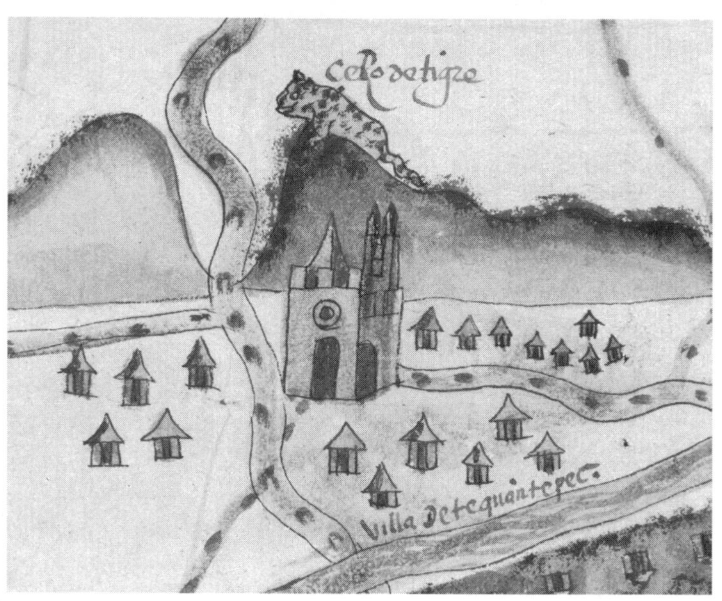


**13.** This detail, from the map of the Isthmus of Tehuantepec from the 1580 *Relación Geográfica* drawn by an unknown indigenous cartographer, is a glyph meaning "Tehuantepec," which is "Hill of the Jaguar" in Nahuatl.

COURTESY OF THE NETTIE LEE BENSON LATIN AMERICAN COLLECTION, UNIVERSITY OF TEXAS LIBRARIES, UNIVERSITY OF TEXAS AT AUSTIN.

building. For Maritza Ochoa I found a copy of Paulo Freire's *Pedagogy of the Oppressed* in Spanish.

Once in Oaxaca City, I boarded the bus to the Isthmus of Tehuantepec with keen anticipation, apologizing to the bus driver as he hefted my leaden suitcase into the luggage bay without complaint. The bus dipped and lifted on the two-lane highway through the Sierra Sur, looping around a tight curve and winging past a roadside shack. A small store's Spanglish sign offered gringo food: "Hot dogs—nachos—hamburguesas—palomitas microondas." Globalization has changed quotidian experience from the grandest to the smallest scales, replacing that most typical of Mexican snacks, *esquites* (fresh, roasted corn kernels) with microwave popcorn. Behind the shacks agave plants sprang from brown clods of soil, stretching from roadside to steepest hilltop. A few miles later the agave shrank away and the bus passed a green crease between two hills filled with nopal cacti blooming fierce fuchsia. And a few miles after that the vegetation hugged the hills and the hills hugged the earth more closely; we had arrived on the isthmus. My heart leapt.

A few miles later it sank.

The land flattened out around the bus and I saw it: terrain newly scraped and graded, the earth's thin skin peeled back to expose a delicate subcutis of red clay. The bared earth lay shaved and steamrolled, waiting for heavy machinery and construction crews. Here it was, finally: preparations for the new four-lane superhighway that would connect the Atlantic and Pacific Oceans, from the port of Salina Cruz to the railroad depot of Matías Romero to the Gulf port of Coatzacoalcos—faster than ever before. None of the istmeño friends and colleagues I had stayed in touch with had mentioned the highway construction. They preferred to give important news in person. Even Beas, who had often sent significant news both good and bad via email, had written only: "Many things have changed, as you will see."

There were other changes, too. Beas and Mirna didn't live on the Isthmus of Tehuantepec anymore. In the fall of 2002 armed men, who Beas suspected were linked to the state government, came to his front door in Matías Romero. Beas was away that night and Mirna had answered the door to insults and threats directed at Beas and their new baby boy. Mirna slammed the door, bolted it, and started packing. As soon as Beas returned the family left, abandoning the house and moving out of the state, settling in a town that was a seven-hour drive from UCIZONI's office. Beas made the commute every other week, staying in different places around Matías Romero, constantly changing his routine. No one in Matías Romero knew the name of that out-of-state town.

I leaned toward the window, stared at the red gash of earth, and began to shiver. I wore a warm sweater as protection from the relentless air-conditioning, but goose bumps rose on my arms. After six years and so much work by so many people, here was the very thing they had tried so hard to stop, or at least change to accommodate their needs. Beas's long-ago letter, written to me in July 1999, came to mind once again: "Ya nos cayó el chahuixtle." Here was the chahuixtle, the great misfortune, the thing that might, in the end, have been as inevitable as dampness-induced corn disease during the rainy season.

I slumped back in my seat and thought of what this meant for the istmeños. Perhaps it no longer made sense for some of the world's longest-time corn farmers to keep planting maize. Maybe the Zapotec and Mixe and Chintantec farmers of the isthmus should hand off that duty to the tractors and combines of midwestern *gringolandia*, put away their machetes, make way for the superhighway, and go to work in the factories that it would bring, or board its buses and ride to El Norte.

No. That was not the future that istmeños would have chosen for themselves.

The highway construction receded behind us and the bus glided into the Juchitán bus station. Most of the passengers climbed down the steps, the women's long circular skirts ballooning as chilled fabric met blistering afternoon. They moved slowly and gathered at the luggage bay, waiting for the huge bags and bundles they had brought from Oaxaca City to sell in Juchitán's vast marketplace. The sight of the *juchiteca* women easing themselves off the bus—schedules be damned—brought to mind the first time I'd seen those striking juchiteca outfits, on my first visit to the isthmus in 1997 to attend The Isthmus Is Our Own forum, the first large gathering in response to the Trans-Isthmus Megaproject. One of the juchitecas I'd met at that gathering, Marina Meneses Velázquez, had suddenly emerged from among the hundreds of people who filled the open-air amphitheater. She wore an embroidered red dress and long yellow ribbons woven through her braids. She took the stage and the microphone, staying silent, surveying the crowd with her large, expressive eyes. Then she spoke in an unhurried voice, each syllable distinct, telling the istmeños to "Volver los ojos a nuestra casa" ("Look inward; start here at home"). She explained, "The development solutions are *here*. We need to think about natural resources, not just material resources."

The problem, it seemed to me, wasn't that istmeños had failed to think about their natural resources but that *everyone* was thinking about them—imaging how dollars might be harvested from their lagoons, netted from their rivers, pumped from their oil reserves, or chopped from their forests.

Marina Meneses left the podium with a twirl of her skirt's

tropical plumage and the discussion flew in several directions. Finally a man in the audience stood up and asked, "Are we saying 'No,' or are we saying 'Yes, but with conditions'? The first thing we must do isn't to decide 'No' or 'Yes,' but to make sure that everyone in the isthmus *knows* about the Megaproject."

The person in front of the microphone, someone from Mexico City, interrupted him. "We don't have to say 'Yes' or 'No.' We have to decide what kind of development we want."

Marina leaped to her feet and shouted, "We say *No*! We say no because it's unsustainable. We say no because it doesn't consider our point of view."

My thoughts lurched from that forum and Marina's ire as the bus tilted left and dropped sharply downward from the roadway, tires sinking slightly into bald earth. Here, on the road to Matías Romero several miles north of Juchitán, the view out the window stopped my breath. A wall of perhaps one thousand cement cubes, each one taller than a person, hulked between two piles of red soil. Beyond the wall a fence of rebar stretched north toward the horizon. It was the beginning of a U.S.-style highway interchange, something wildly beyond the scale of the isthmus's built environment. The interchange-in-progress was the largest thing I'd ever seen on the isthmus: bigger, it seemed to me, than the docks of the Salina Cruz port, or even the pyramids at Guiengola. Is this what had come of so many istmeños saying *no*?

A few days later I stood with Maritza Ochoa outside don Tereso Ponce Villanueva's home in Huazantlán, while she called an Ombeayiüts greeting over the tall fence. Darkness started to gather as the shadows stretched toward sunset. The woven gate swung open and don Tereso's wife bid us to enter. Her husband had gone to cut reeds to repair their fence, she explained to Maritza, who translated into Spanish for me. That meant we should wait; unlike fishing, reed-cutting couldn't be done at night, so don Tereso would be home soon. Maritza and I sat near the golden mango tree that had shaded us the last time I'd visited this home, more than two years earlier, to attend a meeting of the San Mateo del Mar cultural group.

Maritza hadn't been here recently either; the cultural group had been pushed aside by the pressures of life, love, and work. Much had happened in Maritza's life in the year since I'd left the isthmus: a promotion, an appointment in the teachers' union, a marriage, and motherhood. Her two-month-old daughter, Mariana, lay fast asleep on her lap. While we waited for don Tereso, Maritza narrated the eleven-month gap since I had last seen her.

After four years as a preschool teacher Maritza had become the youngest administrator in her district, responsible for curriculum development in all of San Mateo del Mar's nine preschools. So far the biggest obstacle wasn't her youth or inexperience, but the group of people she called *los pesimistas*. At least a few of them managed to show up at every single meeting, shooting down everyone else's ideas for improving bilingual, intercultural education. They always saw *lo pésimo*—the worst—in everything. Maritza hunted through psychology textbooks in search of strategies to deal with los pesimistas. Meanwhile, her home life changed dramatically.

She had married her long-time sweetheart in December 2002 and given birth to a daughter a few months later. As in many istmeño communities, it wasn't the timing of the marriage but the fact that it led to children that was most important in San Mateo del Mar. For Maritza and Anastacio, the timing had seemed perfect. Her due date was the end of April, so her two-month maternity leave would end just as school vacation began in June.

But on the Ides of March, at 3:00 on the morning, Maritza's water broke. They called a doctor on Maritza's new cell phone and were told to get to a hospital right away. After a punishing hour-long ride over the dirt road to Tehuantepec, Maritza delivered her baby via an emergency Cesarean section, six weeks early.

Mariana Valdivieso Ochoa weighed only 4 pounds when she came into the world. Maritza carried her around on a pillow, afraid that her bare embrace would bruise her baby's translucent skin pulled so tightly over bird-fine bones. Maritza had refused to have any photographs taken of Mariana; she wanted no record of how very tiny she had been at life's beginning. Her daughter fed almost constantly. By the time I met her she was within the normal weight range for a two-month-old. But even at 9 pounds, Mariana seemed terribly frail.

Maritza looked at her sleeping miracle-baby and shook her head, linking the small picture of her own experience with the big picture of San Mateo del Mar's experience. Her grandmother had given birth twelve times and only two of her children had survived to adulthood. Her mother had lost her first baby, the one born before Maritza. Maritza's own Mariana had arrived six weeks early and survived. The medical progress over fifty years astounded Maritza. Still, she understood it was not really a miracle but a social and cultural shift that exacted its own price. More babies survived, yes, but San Mateo's lagoons could support fewer and fewer of them.

As the evening folded around us, the tension around Maritza's eyes disappeared and her shoulders relaxed. Just sitting and talking, with no task calling her, was a gift. Half an hour into our conversation, don Tereso climbed down from the burro cart he had borrowed from a neighbor.

"We were afraid you wouldn't be here," Maritza said to him, by way of apologizing for our surprise visit.

"I'm always here," he said, resignation in his voice. "I feel a little more tired every year." Soon he would turn sixty, he told us as he lowered himself onto a narrow chair. One of his granddaughters squatted on the ground next to him with her notebook, drawing a duck, then a teddy bear, then a kitten and telling herself stories about them. The animals' names were the lone Spanish words in a stream of Ombeayiüts: *pato*, *oso de peluche*, *gatito*.

Our conversation meandered around without don Tereso mentioning Mariana. Finally, Maritza propped up her baby girl for his inspection. "She's two months old already," she said, pride warming her voice. Don Tereso nodded silently. Maritza and I waited for more.

After a moment he said, "So, when are we going to meet again, Mari?"

A long silence hung in the air as Maritza shifted her daughter's small pillow from one side of her lap to the other. Finally she spoke. "Tomorrow I go back to work. I'm not sure how I'm going to do it."

"Ah, that's a mother's life," Don Tereso said, his tone soft and only slightly wistful.

The conversation turned to the Ombeayiüts books Maritza planned to produce in her new job as a school administrator. She told don Tereso they would be writing and illustrating storybooks for the preschools, including the one about the race between the two crabs, the *cangrejo* and the *jaiba*, that the two of them had written down and translated together two years earlier.

He turned to Maritza. "That story about the crabs, will it be just in lengua, or also in Spanish?"

"I'd like to have one book in Spanish and one in lengua. Some of my coworkers want to have just one book with Huave above and Spanish below. But that would mean a literal translation. Better to do one book in pure lengua and another book in Spanish because they don't give exactly the same message." Maritza knew there was no such thing as a perfect translation.

Don Tereso's grandson flopped into a hammock that was slung near the house, next to the porch's single lightbulb. He sang to himself as he swung, his long shadow flipping back and forth across his grandfather's face. Our conversation meandered from San Mateo's history to don Tereso's grandchildren to the years of drought and hunger he had known. He and Maritza would lapse into Ombeayiüts, go on for a bit, and then shift back into Spanish to include me in the conversation.

Don Tereso changed the subject to the cultural group and his doubts that it would continue. "We haven't been meeting," he said. "We've really abandoned the work."

"I know, I've been really preoccupied," Maritza said, apology edging her voice. "If only I could focus on just my job. If I didn't have the union responsibility, maybe we could be in better contact."

"Maybe I could come visit you, Mari."

"If it were a Sunday," Maritza said, straining to cast hope over doubt. "Because even Saturdays are full."

I looked at Mariana, still asleep on her mother's lap. Five days a week for school, one day for union and administration meetings, and now Maritza was volunteering to give up the only day she had for her husband and daughter.

We bade goodnight to don Tereso, his wife, and his

grandchildren, and drove back to San Mateo. We arrived at Maritza's house just after 9:30 in the evening. Anastacio was bent over homework for his accounting certificate class. Maritza settled Mariana on the chair next to her husband and he laid a gentle hand on his daughter's belly. In the kitchen, Maritza's younger sister, Zulma, sat over her own schoolwork. Her early marriage had ended; she had returned to her parents' home and enrolled in San Mateo's Marist high school.

Maritza had known Anastacio since he was a baby and she was a toddler. She liked to remind him of her two-year advantage: "I tell him, respect your elders." Perhaps that was why he'd accepted their rather radical living arrangement: he had come to live in her family's house. It had been her mother's idea. Months earlier, when Maritza had mentioned to her family that her wedding meant she would leave the family home, her mother had told her, "Ay, why go? You're going to live here." When Maritza floated the idea to her fiancé, he was shocked. "How am *I* going to stay in *your* house?" he replied.

"Well, why not?" Maritza asked him. "My mom and dad are *giving* it to us. We can't tell them 'No.' We've had this plan for a long time. They are going to build a little place in the countryside and who's going to stay in the house? No one. So, why don't we stay there?" Anastacio relented.

I grew sleepy as I listened to the murmur of the house: Zulma and Anastacio shuffling sheets of paper, Maritza's parents snoring in side-by-side hammocks, the plaintive singing of pop star Manu Chau on the radio. The pop tunes shifted between Spanish and English, sometimes within a single song. When Maritza and I shuffled into the bedroom at 11:30 p.m., Anastacio still sat hunched over his numbers. Maritza settled Mariana next to her in the hammock, mulling a request I'd tried to pose carefully so that she would feel comfortable declining it. Yes, she said finally, I could take photos of Mariana in the morning.

Eight hours later, Maritza and I sat at the breakfast table. She wrapped white bread around hunks of government-issue yellow cheese while Mariana nursed. She was a strangely quiet baby; when she wasn't eating, she was usually in a deep, silent sleep, her tiny fists balled next to her ears.

"Today's the first day of my triple workday," Maritza said between bites of her gringo tacos, her voice matter-of-fact. Mexican women use the term "triple workday" to refer to their simultaneous obligations as workers, mothers, and activists. Ever the optimist, Maritza focused on the details that made her balancing act seem plausible: her mother was home to care for Mariana and her office was only two blocks away, at the preschool where she used to teach. She could run home every couple of hours to feed Mariana.

At the moment Maritza should have been leaving for work, a teacher knocked at the front door; she needed a document from Maritza, her union representative. Maritza handed Mariana to her mother, then lugged a manual typewriter from the bedroom and set it up on the breakfast table. She typed out the document, signed it, affixed the official union seal, and handed it to the woman. I snapped pictures of Mariana as she bounced on her grandmother's lap. Maritza hugged me, kissed her mother and her daughter, posed with both of them for Mariana's first portraits, and then left, quite late, for her first triple workday.

Maritza's work was quiet, teacher by teacher, child by child, preserving Ombeayiüts by the word, phrase, and story. It attracted little attention, for which she was grateful. This is not to call it unimportant, but to note only that its importance was poorly understood by those who might be concerned about istmeño rabble-rousers. Maritza's efforts were as much part of the community response to the Trans-Isthmus Megaproject and the Plan Puebla Panama as the highway blockages and rallies.

The same day that Maritza began her triple workday, Carlos Manzo—one of the people who had led the battle against the shrimp farm in Unión Hidalgo—went to jail. The reasons for his incarceration were convoluted and only indirectly related to the battle over the shrimp farm. It came down to this: there were dramatically different visions for the future of Unión Hidalgo and some were willing to risk their lives to see those visions realized. Since the October 2001 mayoral elections in Unión Hidalgo, the battle against the shrimp farm had alternately stalled and surged.

Armando Sánchez, the shrimp-farm promoter, had won the election. He'd won not because most people in Unión Hidalgo wanted the shrimp farm but because the anti-shrimp-farm majority had been forced to choose among three candidates. After the election that majority chafed against Armando Sánchez's leadership. All through 2002, his first year as mayor, the few who wanted the shrimp farm and the many who opposed it had wrestled. In September, Mexico's Department for the Environment and Natural Resources SEMARNAT determined that more than half the land slated to be part of the shrimp farm was federal land—meaning Sanchez's company had no right to it.

That resolved nothing. The farther one got from the teal-green cement walls of Oaxaca City's SEMARNAT offices, the more hypothetical and abstract their pronouncements seemed.

By New Year's Day 2003, tensions over the shrimp farm plans in Unión Hidalgo stretched like invisible wires across streets and even within homes, tripping people up as they went about their daily lives. In rural Mexico, New Year's Day is the most important family holiday—the day that siblings and cousins and uncles and nieces return home to grandmothers' tables, working through the nuances of the year gone by while sharing mescal and tamales. It's also a community day of accounting, when new mayors are installed and old ones must open the town ledgers for public review. The combination had always seemed rather odd to me: villagers spent the day with family saluting the year gone by, or they spent the day standing in the cracked cement courtyard of the municipal palace, or they did both. In Unión Hidalgo, the New Year came and went, with Armando Sánchez offering a report that accounted for just three million pesos in public expenditures—equaling perhaps one-third of what his administration had actually received in state and federal allocations. His report noted funds spent on public works still incomplete or never even begun. Townspeople complained to the state legislature, which promised to send a commission to investigate on February 13, 2003. Hundreds of residents gathered in the town center that day to greet the commission, but the legislators never showed up. This annoyed people but did not really surprise them; the idea of the state legislature enforcing government transparency was only slightly less abstract than the idea of a federal government agency enforcing environmental protection.

Armando Sánchez didn't appear on February 13 either. By late afternoon, irritation turned into anger and the crowd marched to the town square for a protest sit-in. At some point the gathering of one or two thousand (depending on who was counting) decided to take over the municipal palace. It's a common strategy in Mexico. In its most frequent manifestation, striking workers occupy factories or offices or classrooms to prevent the managers from removing valuable equipment or bringing in replacement workers. The sit-ins halt business as usual.

When the crowd was about half a block from the municipal building the local police began to shoot. It's impossible to know why, but perhaps the police finally realized that the protestors would have much more power inside the building than outside of it. Or maybe the police were just following orders. Many claimed that Armando Sánchez had instructed the police to fire on the crowd. Some of the protestors even reported they had seen the mayor and two of his colleagues hiding inside the building and had heard them yell to the police to fire. When the townspeople heard the gunfire, they assumed the police were firing warning shots into the air. Then they saw some of their compañeros falling to the ground. After the smoke cleared from the *zipizape*—a word for disturbance or commotion much better than any English word—a twenty-nine-year-old man, Manuel Santiago Salinas, was dead, two people were seriously injured, and more than one hundred state and federal police were stationed around Unión Hidalgo's grubby municipal palace. Armando Sánchez, who may or may not have been there, had disappeared.

With their mayor gone and their state government apparently too busy to care, the community assembly decided to meet three days later. More than one thousand people attended the meetings that followed and elected a Provisional Municipal Council to represent them. They then chose residents to patrol the streets (since the municipal police were entirely occupied with the empty municipal palace) and collect the trash (since all municipal services had stopped). Within a week the local assembly had thrown out party-based elections, instituted a twenty-four-hour vigil in front of the abandoned municipal palace, and filed a formal request that the state government remove Armando Sánchez as mayor. The "Unión Hidalgo Citizens' Council," or CCU, also chose a council of elders (six men and four women) to make decisions between assemblies. Over the next month the CCU escalated its pressure on the state government to resolve the "crisis of ungovernability" in their town. They maintained their vigil in front of the municipal building; they organized a caravan of cars and trucks that traveled from Unión Hidalgo to the state capital and asked for a formal dialogue with Armando Sánchez's administration. They circulated petitions around the world.

At first, little came of their efforts. Mayor Sánchez hadn't been seen in town since February 13, but a few of his administrators continued to work in a private home. Two weeks after the shooting, an assembly of five hundred people sent a delegation to visit that house. The message: Sánchez's government no longer had operational authority. The administration had suspended all public services on February 13. If it wasn't doing the work of a municipal government, why should it call itself one? The confrontation was peaceful but later the señora of the house accused Carlos Manzo of stealing two computers.

In early May, villagers heard that Sánchez's phantom government had contracted workers to pave the road that passed through Barrio Palmero, south of town, to the planned shrimp farm site. Though local istmeño governments of all political stripes have similar road-building aspirations, the folks in Unión Hidalgo took this announcement to be part of the shrimp-farm conspiracy.

The workers arrived with their road-paving equipment on May 12 and were met by three hundred angry people, many of whom carried sticks and stones. Forty guards carrying canisters of tear gas arrived with the road-builders, but the crowd refused to step aside. The workers gave up, returning the following day to find the same standoff between police and villagers. Early that afternoon—the hottest hour on one of the hottest days of the year—someone threw a stone, tensions boiled over, and two municipal policemen were shot. In the aftermath of this zipizape, everyone blamed everyone else. One of the villagers must have shot the two men, the police said. But we had only sticks and stones, the villagers said. The following day, the authorities accused Carlos Manzo, one of the town's most prominent anti-shrimp-farm activists, of the attack. This accusation, combined with his outstanding warrant for the missing computers, led to his lock-up without bail in the Tehuantepec jail. Manzo was charged with armed assault; but no weapon was produced, nor was a ballistics test conducted to determine whether he had in fact shot a gun recently. Two other CCU members accused of collaborating with Manzo were arrested on the same day. The bail for one of the other men was set at thirty-seven thousand pesos, approximately the median annual income in the state of Oaxaca. The CCU managed to raise the colossal sum, thanks to an international network of supporters, but then the authorities changed their minds, saying the man was too dangerous to be released.

Shortly after Carlos Manzo and the other two men were incarcerated, I visited Unión Hidalgo for an afternoon. None of the people I had met on my previous visits were in town—many of the people who had started the anti-shrimp-farm campaign, including Sofía Olhovich, had gone into hiding, frightened by the arrests. I wandered the town's empty streets for a long half hour before coming upon a group of men in the town center. All CCU members, they crowded under a red plastic tarp around an improvised kitchen. The wind tossed tiny pollen grains against our faces and arms, each one landing with a painful nip; "the season of stinging pollen" had begun. The CCU had maintained a round-the-clock sit-in across the square from the municipal palace for three months. Some of the protestors had been fighting the shrimp farm for two years, but others had joined in the two months since Armando Sánchez's administration had been run out of town.

"I grew up here and I was just a regular community member until February thirteenth," one of the men told me. "I didn't like what I saw here on that day. The municipal government is supposed to serve the people, not kill them." Even when not doing the latter, it hardly did the former, the other men grumbled. Fernando Vásquez, the only man in the group willing to tell me his name, said of the local officials, "They start their terms poor, but they leave millionaires."

Around the small knot of CCU members the roads and low buildings of Unión Hidalgo stretched out, silent and wind-beaten, toward the Pan-American highway, toward the estuary and the lagoons. At the four corners of the town square, broken-down vehicles with smashed hoods and windows blocked each street. I walked away from the town center, picking my way over the cracked pavement, stiff grasses, and robust periwinkle bushes scratching at my knees. I traveled north from Unión Hidalgo back to Matías Romero, the bus groaning off the pavement to bypass the new highway interchange, looming over the low-lying land, oblivious to it.

Carlos Manzo would spend more than seven months that year in jail. I returned to the Isthmus of Tehuantepec in February 2004 for another visit, less than two months after his release. All the charges against him had been dropped; he had essentially been held in detention the entire time. I called to ask about visiting and happened to reach Sofía on the day they were celebrating Manzo's birthday. She invited me to join them for the evening.

I arrived in Unión Hidalgo late in the afternoon with a bottle of the best mescal I could find on such short notice. On the veranda behind Manzo's childhood home his family members, friends, fellow activists, and I talked and ate and composed elaborate toasts. Mexican birthday parties celebrate *un año más de vida*, or "one more year of life." For the group sitting around the table that night, we were marking a year of Manzo's life lost—he had spent most of it in prison.

By late evening we had returned to the kitchen to scrape a second meal from the cooking pots; the men had emptied every single beer bottle and several bottles of mescal. Friends and family slowly said their goodnights. Eventually only Sofía, Manzo, and I remained at the table. Manzo was much thinner than he had been when I'd last seen him, before his arrest. He had sustained several long hunger strikes during his detention. For the first time I noticed gray glinting in his hair. He asked me about the book I was writing; I explained that it was about community response to the Plan Puebla Panama—as manifested in the Isthmus of Tehuantepec.

He nodded and began to speak in the flat tone that had struck me the first day I had met him, the tone that made people listen. In spite of all the mescal and beer, he spoke with clarity, in complete paragraphs, laying out his argument.

"If you're going to write something about people's resistance on the Isthmus of Tehuantepec, unfortunately, you're going to have to concentrate on the rebellions. I say 'unfortunately' because all rebellions are temporary. They are single events, happenings that occur against a particular authority in a particular moment, lasting for only a very short time. This is what's documented: an inciting incident, when there's a death, or when people are wounded, a riot, an uprising, the rebellion of Year X.

"It's difficult to know what happened after that, how long the resistance endured past the climax of rebellion. After that hardly anyone pays attention. The media and the larger society stop paying attention just as things become most difficult for the people who are resisting."

Manzo was speaking of the endless work of people in Unión Hidalgo, in San la Paz, San Francisco del Mar, Boca del Monte, and many, many more indigenous people in many countries who are pushing back against colonialism, against cultural genocide, against corporate globalization. Even though the world stopped paying attention once the peak of the rebellion passed, the people's resistance went on and on. Manzo was right: people *did* stop paying attention. With so many crises vying for public attention, could that public ever sustain interest in struggles that went on and on and on? Yet it was precisely that on and on that was essential for success. The point *was* the endlessness.

On the last day of 2005, Carlos Beas sent me a Happy New Year' greeting. He and Mirna and their three children still lived far from the isthmus, but he continued his work with UCIZONI. His greeting included the worst news I'd received all year.

"Wal-Mart opened its doors in Juchitán with a ceremony at which the mayor and the state governor declared themselves 'aggressively opposed to the enemies of progress.' The business and governmental offensive is coming on strong; they want to impose their Plan at all costs." As usual, Beas combined his political analysis with a strong sense of the absurd. "Wal-Mart opened with a big sale on Jimador tequila and there were a lot of people there to witness the novelty of it. The store has 146 permanent employees, but the small businesses have already begun to feel the impact of the megastore."

Of all the things that I had thought might come to pass with the new superhighway, I had not imagined this one: a Wal-Mart—known by its Mexican retail name, Aurrera—on the edge of Juchitán. *Ya nos cayó el chahuixtle*, I thought. Juchitán—known for its locally controlled markets, known for its women who show up with sticks and machetes to chase unwanted visitors out of town, known for the horse-drawn carriages that line up at stoplights—was the last city in Mexico I had imagined would allow a Wal-Mart to be built. And so this was what happens when, as they said in Boca del Monte, "a rich man comes with his highway."

Shortly after receiving this news from Beas, I talked with Leonel Gómez on the phone. He was spending a lot of time in Juchitán, living in a neighborhood just across the street from the Wal-Mart. "Mahatma is always begging me to take him there," he said, with a note of defeat in his voice.

"You don't take him, do you?" I asked, trying to imagine Leonel—who had devoted so much time to defending village life—and his five-year-old son wandering the vast aisles stacked with boxed plastic imports.

"Oh sure, sometimes. Though not nearly as often as he asks."

"You shop at the *Wal-Mart*?"

"*Nooooooo*, we don't *buy* anything, Wendy," Leonel replied, laughing at my assumption. "We go because it's air-conditioned and Mahatma likes to play with the bouncing balls that they have in those huge metal cages. We go to stare at the towers of stuff. It's like what that Greek philosopher said when he was walking through the Athenian market: 'I never dreamed there could be so many things that I did not want.'"

On a blistering June day in 2008, I visited the Juchitán Wal-Mart / Aurrera with Leonel and Mahatma. We savored the air conditioning; Mahatma bounced the balls; Leonel shook his head at the vast quantities of plastic; and I mourned what the highway had brought.

That afternoon, riding the bus back to Matías Romero, dry-season heat surged through the open windows. Beyond, the hills slumped, with the lace of the cow paths especially pronounced. The surface of almost every hill on the Isthmus of Tehuantepec is woven with narrow white lines, traced by cattle ambling endlessly back and forth, chewing the sparse vegetation to brown nubbins.

That night the heat bore down intolerably. I lay awake, hoping that rain might come soon. I thought about the istmeños and their response to the global economy: they resisted what didn't work for them but adapted to what they could not change. The adaptation made the resistance possible—it sustained the villages economically as the local economy became harder to negotiate. Maybe people like Román Cruz, Juana García, and Maritza Ochoa—villagers all—are the last bastion against corporate control of the global economy, even as they integrate themselves into that economy. They have refused wholesale acceptance of the Trans-Isthmus Megaproject, the Plan Puebla Panama, and whatever might come next. They consider the situation, weigh their options, and take only what they need. Their refusal to simply accept it all is their refusal to accept that they, like many of the world's people, are superfluous in the global economy. As the human race faces a fundamental shift—from hunter-gatherers to farmers to industrial workers to whatever comes next—their lives constitute acts of resistance.

There is still no shrimp farm in Unión Hidalgo, nor in San Francisco del Mar, nor anywhere else on the Isthmus of Tehuantepec. The new superhighway is four lanes wide, not six, and only small portions of it require a toll. Many of the other projects proposed in El plan de Ochoa, such as the eucalyptus plantations, never came to pass. Even the steel mill that Felipe Ochoa had been celebrating when I met him in 1998 was canceled, the villagers having refused to let them build on the planned site.

The four-lane highway and the Wal-Mart are highly visible signposts of globalization, while the istmeños' victories are invisible, nonevents. Village resistance maintains situations that must be considered better, simply because they are no worse. And yet those unseen victories are crucial: evidence of the success of grassroots organizing, of the village economy's ability to persist in spite of globalization.

Shortly before 4:00 in the morning the dry-season drought split open with a gush of water. The heat melted; the temperature slipped below 80 for the first time in months. A cool wind washed over me, then a wave of relief. I felt as if I'd been holding my breath. Now the corn would grow; now the pasture would green; now the shrimp would return to the Pacific lagoons. At least for one more year.

## Source Notes

All direct dialogue and quotations are based on notes I took at the time of a given conversation or event, and most come from transcripts of recorded conversations. Some—for example, the La Ventosa rally described in chapter 7—come from videotapes recorded by others and loaned to me. The large majority, of course, I translated from Spanish. In some cases those words were translated into Spanish from Huave, Zapotec, or Mixe by a local translator. The people whose names appear throughout the book were far and away the most important source of information.

The newspapers *La Jornada*, *El Universal*, *Noticias: Voz e Imagen de Oaxaca*, and the *New York Times*, as well as the Mexican magazines *Acervos* (Oaxaca City), *Cuadernos del Sur* (Oaxaca City), *Desacatos: Revista de Antropología Social* (Mexico City), *Guchachi Rezá / Iguana Rajada* (Juchitán), *Guiengola* (Tehuantepec), and *Proceso* (Mexico City) were important sources.

The work of many librarians, archivists, and oral historians made it possible for me to access needed background and historical information—as well as to gather half a room full of documentation—in order to understand what I saw, heard, and experienced while living and working on the Isthmus of

Tehuantepec. The libraries (and their often heroic librarians) I relied upon include: Archivo de las Indias (Seville, Spain), Archivo General de la Nación (Mexico City); Biblioteca Andrés Henestrosa (Oaxaca City); Boston Public Library; Jane Bancroft Cook Library of the New College of Florida; Hermeroteca de Oaxaca; Library of Congress; Nettie Lee Benson Latin American Collection at the University of Texas at Austin; Seattle Public Library; Watertown (Massachusetts) Public Library; and the libraries of the Casa de Cultura in Juchitán, Centro de Investigaciónes de la Antropología Social (CIESAS) in Oaxaca, Instituto Nacional Indígena (Oaxaca City), and Instituto de Artes Gráficos de Oaxaca.

Two English-language books provided my earliest introduction to the Isthmus of Tehuantepec: *Mexico South: The Isthmus of Tehuantepec* by artist, anthropologist, and folklorist Miguel Covarrubias (Knopf, 1946); and *Zapotec Struggles: Histories, Politics, and Representation from Juchitán, Oaxaca* edited by Howard Campbell, Leigh Binford, Miguel Bartolomé, and Alicia Barabas (Smithsonian Institution, 1993). I can say without risk of hyperbole that the former book changed my life. Elena Poniatowska's writings about Mexican social movements in general, and the Isthmus of Tehuantepex in particular, have been enormously important to me. Luckily, much of her elegant, essential work is available translated into English. After my first visit to the Isthmus of Tehuantepec in 1997, Carlos Beas Torres sent me a book that inspired much of my fascination (some might say obsession) with the region. That book was *Economía Contra Sociedad: El Istmo de Tehuantepec, 1907–1986*, a volume edited by Leticia Reina Aoyama (Nueva Imagen, 1994).

In a sense this book began because of a single five-hundred-page document, *Integración de Proyectos de Impulso al Desarrollo del Istmo de Tehuantepec, Vol. 4: Proyectos de*

*Inversión* by Felipe Ochoa y Asociados, SC, for the Secretaría de Comunicaciones y Transporte (July 1996), describing the megaproyecto transístimico.

The sources listed below are only the most important ones for each chapter. Please direct questions about specific sources to me, via my website (www.wendycall.com). In spite of all the help I received, I'm sure I have made errors, which are entirely my responsibility.

**Further Reading**

For readers interested in learning more about the Isthmus of Tehuantepec, I am sorry to say that I can only make recommendations for those who read Spanish. Two good books offer an overview of the Plan Puebla Panama, its possible impacts, and alternative development options: *Mesoamérica Los Ríos Profundos: Alternativas plebeyas al Plan Puebla Panama* edited by Armando Bartra (Instituto Maya, 2001); and *El Plan Puebla Panama en el Istmo de Tehuantepec* by Guillermo Almeyra and Rebecca Alfonso Romero (Universidad de la Cuidad de México, 2004). An excellent collection on the 2006 uprising in Oaxaca—in which organizations like UCIZONI and Maritza Ochoa and Leonel Gómez's teachers' union were deeply involved—is *La Batalla por Oaxaca* (Ediciones Yope Power, 2007).

**Introduction: Drawing an Old Map**

I am grateful to many conservators, archivists, and librarians who have cared for the maps that I describe here—and many others that I studied. The staff members at the Library of Congress and the Nettie Lee Benson Latin American Collection at the University of Texas were particularly helpful and generous. I spent a delightful afternoon poring over the map from 1580 (Tehuantepec 1580 JGI 25–4) in the

Benson's lovely reading room; I thank the Benson staff for their patience. Secondary sources about the maps include the scholarship of Mary Elizabeth Hande, Maarten Jensen, and Michael Oudijik, and especially Barbara Mundy. Her book, *The Mapping of New Spain: Indigenous Cartography and the Maps of the Relacionies Geográficas* (University of Chicago Press, 1996), is a delight. Andrés Henestrosa's essays and his huge personal library—now, wonderfully, a public resource at the Casa de la Cuidad in Oaxaca City—were also essential for the entire book.

Miguel Covarrubias was not the only traveler to the isthmus to inspire (and vex) me. Charles-Étienne Brasseur de Bourbourg, a French anthropologist who was the first to translate and publish the Maya holy book, the *Popul Vuh*, wrote a fascinating travelogue titled (in the French original) *Voyage sur l'Isthme de Tehuantepec 1859–1860*. Italo Calvino published a light travel story, *Under the Jaguar Sun*, which first appeared in English in a 1983 issue of the *New Yorker*. Interestingly, only one North American published a significant travelogue of the Isthmus of Tehuantepec, called *The Mexican Southland*, in 1922, and he did so under a pseudonym. A man from Indiana pretended to have translated the work of the "celebrated Persian philosopher and traveler" (as he is identified on the title page) Kamar Al-Shimas.

### 1. Learning the Lay of the Land

The grassroots organizations Maderas del Pueblo (which, sadly, no longer exists) and UCIZONI (¡Viva la UCIZONI!) provided copies of many letters, reports, and news clippings. Key sources of historical information include the scholarship of four authors of seminal works about Oaxaca. The books most helpful to me were: *El Sol y La Cruz: Los pueblos indios de Oaxaca colonial* by María de los Angeles Romero Frizzi

(CIESAS/INI, 1996); *Configuraciones étnicas en Oaxaca: Perspectivas etnográficas para las autonomías*, edited by Alicia Barabas and Miguel Bartolomé (INI-CONACULTA-INAH, 1999); and Andrés Henestrosa's *Cartas sin sobre: Confidencias y poemas al olvido* (Porrúa, 1996).

2. Time Travel

Many late nineteenth-century and early twentieth-century articles from many magazines and journals, including *Bulletin of the American Geographical Society, Harper's, New England Magazine, National Geographic,* and *Scientific American* —especially one called "The Isthmus of Tehuantepec" by Herbert Corey, published in *National Geographic* 45, no. 5 (May 1924)—provided important historical detail. I also reviewed every article mentioning the Isthmus of Tehuantepec in the publication histories of the *New York Times*, *Wall Street Journal*, and *Washington Post*. The article used most extensively in this chapter was "The Tehuantepec Route: Detailed Narrative of a Journey Across the Tehuantepec Isthmus," published as a letter from John Hackett to the editor of the *New York Times* on March 8, 1858.

The books that proved most useful in writing this chapter included: *Diccionario Histórico del México contemporáneo 1900–1992* by J. de Jesús Nieto López (Addison Wesley Longman, 1998); *Mexico and Central America: Archeology and Culture History* by Susan Toby Evans (Thames and Hudson, 2004); *Lecturas Históricas del Estado de Oaxaca, Vol. 1, Epoca Prehispánica* compiled by Marcus Winter (INAH/Gob de Oaxaca, 1990); *Crónica del Comercio Prehispánico* by Jorge Díaz-Gutiérrez (Cámara Nacional de Comercio de la Ciudad de México, 1981); *Land Divided* by Edward B. Glick (University of Florida Press, 1959); *Trade, Tribute, and Transportation* by Ross Haussig (University of Oklahoma

Press, 1985); and the above-mentioned travelogue by Charles Brasseur, which I read in its Spanish translation: *Viaje por el Istmo de Tehuantepec: 1859–1860* (Secretaría de Educación Pública, 1981).

An interview with Judith Zeitlin, associate professor of anthropology, University of Massachusetts, as well as many of her writings, gave me a grounding in early isthmus history. Two articles provided key history of the trans-isthmus railroad: Paul Garner's "The Politics of National Development in Late Porfirian Mexico: The Reconstruction of the Tehuantepec National Railway 1896–1907" from the *Bulletin of Latin American Research* 14, no. 3 (1995) and Francie Chassen López's "El Ferrocarril Nacional de Tehuantepec" from *Acervos* 10 (Oct-Dec 1998). Dr. Chassen López's monograph, *Regiones y ferrocarriles en la Oaxaca porfiriata* (Colección Obra Negra, Oaxaca, 1990), and her book *From Liberal to Revolutionary Oaxaca: The View from the South* (Pennsylvania State University Press, 2004), were also important sources. The author, a professor of history at the University of Kentucky, was extremely generous and helpful in answering my questions and explaining historical scholarship to a non-historian.

### 3. Ocean's Mouth Empties

Useful books about the Huave communities and indigenous land tenure include: *Territorios Violados* by Ronald Nigh and Nemesio Rodriguez (CONACULTA/INI, 1995); *Mitos y Realidades de las Mujeres Huaves* by Margarita Dalton and Guadalupe Musalem Merhy (UABJO, 1992); *Etnografía Contemporánea de los Pueblos Indígenas de México: Transístmica* (INI, 1995); and *Cultura e Identidad Etnica en la Región Huave* by Jorge Hernández Díaz and Jesús Lizama (UABJO, 1996).

Information on the effects of shrimp farming and mangrove ecology comes from *The Biology of Mangroves* by Peter Hogarth (Oxford University Press, 1999); the review article "Biology of Mangroves and Mangrove Ecosystems" by K. Kathiresan and Brian Bingham, published in *Advances in Marine Biology* in 2001; and the Food and Agriculture Organization's report, "The World's Mangroves 1980–2005," Forestry Paper 153 (United Nations, 2007). The video "Shrimp Fever" was produced in 1991 by the UK's Television Trust for the Environment.

Several staff members from the Mexican government's Secretaría del Medio Ambiente, Recursos Naturales y Pesca (SEMARNAP, later SEMARNAT), including Fausto Burgoa and Salvador Anta, were particularly helpful and generous with their time, as were ecologists Stuart Thomson, formerly of Stockholm University, Brian Bingham, professor of biology at Western Washington University, and—most of all—many fishermen in all the Huave communities, who patiently answered my endless questions regarding the what, why, and how of fishing, shrimp, and mangroves.

### 4. A Village of Sand

Joel Hernández Sangermán's unpublished 1996 manuscript, *La cultura ikoots ante la conquista española*, provided excellent context about his hometown, the village of San Mateo del Mar. María del Rocío Vargas Ortega, professor at Mexico City's Universidad Pedagógica Nacional, offered important background on Mexico's rural and indigenous school system. Graduate theses from the Universidad Autónoma de México answered several questions for me, while the Ochoa-Jarauta family answered hundreds more. Linguist Yuni Kim of the University of Manchester, offered clarification and elegant ideas on intricacies of the Huave language(s). For a lovely though heartbreaking essay on language extinction, read Steve Pinker's "The Loss of our Species' Biography" from *The Third Culture* (January 10, 2000).

**5. Worshipping a Wooden Cross**

Marina García and Joel Venegas García were enormously helpful, patient, and giving during my time in Huatulco, offering everything from documentation, maps, and crucial social context to truck rides, entertaining stories, and good food. Important sources on the recent history of Huatulco, Oaxaca included the *Diario Oficial* of the Mexican Legislature; the 1984 editions of the newspapers *Las Noticias* and *El Nacional*; and the research of David Barkin and María Evelinda Santiago Jiménez. David Ortega, director of the National Park of Huatulco, and several of the park staff, as well as Carlos Pailles, offered essential background on the ecology of the region and were very generous with their time.

**6. Isthmus Defended**

I relied on the work of many scholars, anthropologists, archaeologists, and historians for the material in this chapter, most important among them: Joseph W. Whitecotton, Marcus Winter, Judith Francis Zeitlin, and Robert N. Zeitlin. The Zeitlins' ceaseless efforts to reconcile narrative and archeological accounts are particularly appreciated. For just one example, see Judith Zeitlin's *Cultural Politics in Colonial Tehuantepec: Community and State among the Isthmus Zapotec, 1500–1750* (Stanford University Press, 2005). *Marvelous Possessions: The Wonder of the New World* by Stephen Greenblatt (University of Chicago Press, 1992) introduced me to historical scholarship on the conquest. I drew most of the material on the Spanish conquest from *The Discovery and Conquest of Mexico, 1517–1521* by Bernal Díaz de Castillo, translated by A. P. Maudslay (Farrar, Straus and Cudahy, 1956)—which was written in the sixteenth century and first published in 1632—and from *Hernán Cortés: Letters from Mexico*, translated and edited by Anthony Pagden (Yale University Press, 1986). Another important account of the conquest is *Broken Spears: The Aztec Account of the Conquest of Mexico* by Miguel Leon-Portilla (Beacon Press, 1990). Matthew Restall's excellent books were a great help, as was the scholar himself, who graciously gave me helpful feedback on a portion of this chapter.

Three publications were particularly important for background on Guiengola, as well as great reads: Marcus Winter's edited volume, *Lecturas Históricas del Estado de Oaxaca: Vol I, Epoca Prehispánica* (INAH, 1990); Matthew Wallrath's "Excavations in the Tehuantepec Region, Mexico," in *Transaction of the American Philosophical Society* 57, no. 2 (1967); and *Guiengola: A Fortified Site in the Isthmus of Tehuantepec* by David A. Peterson and Thomas B.MacDougall (Vanderbilt University Publications in Anthropology #10, 1974). Two other books that I enjoyed—more valuable for their wonderful stories than their history—were *El Rey Cosijoeza y Su Familia: reseña histórica y legendaria de los últimos soberanos de zaachila* by Manuel Martínez Graciada (Secretaría de Fomento, 1888); and *Historia de Oaxaca* by José Antonio Gay (Porrúa, 2000, first published in 1881). Enrique Sodi Alvarez's *Istmo de Tehuantepec* (Puertos Libres Mexicanos, 1967) provided useful timeline information.

The work of anthropologists Benjamín Maldonado Alvarado, Alicia Barabas, and Miguel Alberto Bartolomé, all of the Centro Regional Oaxaca del INAH (Instituto Nacional de Antropología y Historia), helped my understanding of indigenous identity among istmeños, while long conversations (some extending over a decade) with many istmeños helped most of all.

### 7. We Come Here to Name Ourselves

Many years of tenacious, trenchant work by journalist Hermann Bellinghausen, covering the Zapatista movement for *La Jornada* and other Mexican publications, provided crucial background for this chapter. The newspaper accounts referred to in this chapter come from *El Financiero, La Jornada, Milenio Diario, San Diego Union-Tribune*, and *unomásuno*.

Other sources of information include *Grassroots Postmodernism: Remaking the Soil of Cultures* by Gustavo Esteva and Madhu Suri Prakash (Zed Books, 1998); an essay by Márgara Millán, "En Otras Palabras, Otros Mundos: la modernidad occidental puesta en cuestión," from the journal *Chiapas* 6 (1998); and conversations with poet and activist Jeff Conant—whose long-awaited and much-needed book, *A Poetics of Resistance: The Revolutionary Public Relations of the Zapatista Insurgency*, was published by AK Press in 2010.

### 8. Peregrination

Information on the photographer Charles B. Waite comes from *La Tarjeta Postal, Artes de México* #48, among other sources. Information about the Huave communities comes primarily from interviews, but some is taken from Italo Signorini's *Los Huaves de San Mateo del Mar* (Instituto Nacional Indígena, 1979) and Joel Hernández Sangermán's unpublished monograph, noted above.

### 9. Outpost of the Poor

I gleaned the history of Unión Hidalgo from interviews with several townspeople; many issues of *Guchachi Rezá / Iguana Rajada*, the excellent Zapotec arts, culture, and history magazine from Juchitán; scholarly and popular articles by Carlos Manzo; the anonymous publication *Monografía de Unión Hidalgo*, from the Colegio de Bachilleres del Estado de Oaxaca, Plante 15; and an essay by Marta Bañuelos in *Zapotec Struggles: Histories, Politics and Representations from Juchitán, Oaxaca* (Smithsonian Institution Press, 1993).

### 10. Celebrate Saint Francis of the Sea

Jeffrey Rubin's *Decentering the Regime: Ethnicity, Radicalism, and Democracy in Juchitán, Mexico* (Duke University Press, 1997) was an excellent resource for the history of electoral politics in the isthmus city of Juchitán—which have impacted elections like Facundo Martínez's in San Francisco del Mar. María Cristina Velásquez's *El Nombramiento: Las elecciones por usos y costumbres en Oaxaca* (Instituto Estatal Electoral, Oaxaca, 2000) was helpful for background on the dominant political system in Oaxaca, *usos y costumbres*, in which choosing municipal leaders and policy-setting is done by town assembly rather than partisan elections.

### 11. Gourd Full of Gold

Alvaro Román Ríos, who first took me to the Chimalapas, and Teodosio Angel, who was willing to talk with me endlessly about the rainforest, both taught me much about this always spectacular and sometimes tragic place. I also learned about the Chimalapas from books and publications including Ana Paula de Teresa's *Los Vaivenes de la Selva: El proceso de reconstitución del territorio Zoque de los Chimalapas* (Universidad Autónoma Metropolitana, 2000); a monograph published by the Vocalia Ejecutiva de los Chimalapas, *Tequio por Chimalapas* in 1990; and a 2003 master's thesis by Emanuel Gómez Martínez of the Universidad Autónoma Metropolitana / Xochimilco: "Chimalapas: Globalización y Autonomía Indígena en la Selva Zoque."

Specific details about the history of the conflict in the Chimalapas and about the people who call it home come from *Historia Zoque* by Miguel Bartolomé and Alicia Barabas (INAH, 1993); and the same authors' "Gente de una misma palabra (*dzä jmiih* or *tsa jujmi*); El grupo etnolingüistico chinanteco" in *Configuraciones étnicas en Oaxaca: Perspectivas etnográficas para las autonomies* 2 (INI/CONACULTA/INAH, 1999), as well as *Estudio de Ordenamiento Ecológico de la Zona de San Isidro "La Gringa,"* published by the organization Maderas del Pueblo in August 1995; and "San Isidro La Gringa, Area Piloto de Conservación Ecológica," an unpublished paper by Alvaro Román Ríos, written in 2001.

One of the most accessible (for Spanish readers at least) books about the Chimalapas, and the many dangers it faces, is the anthology *Chimalapas: La Ultima Oportunidad*, published by the World Wildlife Federation and SEMARNAP in 2001. For an excellent overview of the fate the Chimalapas has thus far escaped—unlike too many other tropical forests in the Americas—read Ricardo Carrere and Larry Lohmann's *Pulping the South: Industrial Tree Plantations and the World Paper Economy* (Zed Books, 1996).

### 12. Redrawing the Map

The reporting on rural Oaxaca of journalists Guadalupe Ríos, Rosa Rojas, Victor Ruiz Arrazola, and Ramón Vera Herrera for *La Jornada* provided important chronology for events described in this chapter that I did not witness.

# Index

*Page numbers in italics indicate photographs*